Beyond the Walls

UNIVERSITY PRESS OF FLORIDA

Florida A&M University, Tallahassee
Florida Atlantic University, Boca Raton
Florida Gulf Coast University, Ft. Myers
Florida International University, Miami
Florida State University, Tallahassee
New College of Florida, Sarasota
University of Central Florida, Orlando
University of Florida, Gainesville
University of North Florida, Jacksonville
University of South Florida, Tampa
University of West Florida, Pensacola

Beyond the Walls

New Perspectives on the Archaeology of Historical Households

EDITED BY KEVIN R. FOGLE, JAMES A. NYMAN,
AND MARY C. BEAUDRY

University Press of Florida
Gainesville · Tallahassee · Tampa · Boca Raton
Pensacola · Orlando · Miami · Jacksonville · Ft. Myers · Sarasota

This book may be available in an electronic edition.

First cloth printing, 2015
First paperback printing, 2019

24 23 22 21 20 19   6 5 4 3 2 1

Library of Congress Cataloging-in-Publication Data
Beyond the walls : new perspectives on the archaeology of historical households /
edited by Kevin R. Fogle, James A. Nyman, and Mary C. Beaudry.
pages cm
Includes bibliographical references and index.
ISBN 978-0-8130-6155-9 (cloth)
ISBN 978-0-8130-6417-8 (pbk.)
1. Households—United States—History. 2. Families—United States—History.
I. Fogle, Kevin R., editor. II. Nyman, James A., editor. III. Beaudry, Mary Carolyn,
1950– editor.
HQ536.B49 2015
306.850973—dc23
2015019368

The University Press of Florida is the scholarly publishing agency for the State
University System of Florida, comprising Florida A&M University, Florida Atlantic
University, Florida Gulf Coast University, Florida International University, Florida
State University, New College of Florida, University of Central Florida, University of
Florida, University of North Florida, University of South Florida, and University of
West Florida.

University Press of Florida
2046 NE Waldo Road
Suite 2100
Gainesville, FL 32609
http://upress.ufl.edu

Contents

Figures

Tables

Preface and Acknowledgments

Since the 1960s, interest in the archaeology of households has flourished, and the study of households has come to be recognized as an integral area of archaeological inquiry. Volumes on this topic have appeared sporadically over the past few decades, but most have focused on specific time periods or geographic regions. Meanwhile, the cross-cultural study of households has been steadily expanding as an academic area of interest. This is reflected both in university classrooms and in presentations at the international conferences of various archaeological organizations. There is growing need among students, scholars, and professional archaeologists for resources that are concerned with current and innovative approaches to this topic.

It was with this need in mind that Nyman and Fogle invited a diverse group of scholars working on an equally diverse range of archaeological households to participate in a thematic session at the annual conference of the Society for Historical Archaeology held in Leicester, England, in January 2013 (Mary Beaudry served as discussant for the session but here serves as a coeditor and contributor). The session brought together new voices as well as veterans in historical archaeology who not only represent the breadth of research topics across the Americas (both temporally and geographically) but also employ innovative approaches to household archaeology that reveal how far the study has evolved. This volume is the culmination of efforts that originated in the session.

Much of the scholarship in household archaeology has focused on the materiality of past dwellings or on the household as the locus for domestic production. These are important avenues for the study of households—and ones several of our contributors address. Contributors to the present volume have attempted to take these emphases further, looking beyond the house per se to investigate homes and the wider landscapes in which

xii · Preface and Acknowledgments

they are situated, as well as households in regional and global contexts.

they are situated, as well as households in regional and global contexts. This volume illustrates ways in which household archaeology can be used to address essential social issues in the past, including gender relations, domination and resistance, subsistence practices, and the effects of colonial expansion. The walls of households are metaphorically torn down in this book, as contributors incorporate elements such as yard spaces and middens as important and expressive elements in the formation of past dwelling places within larger historical and cultural contexts. Our contributors employ innovative methods to examine the intersection of households with communities, regions, and the cultural landscape writ large. The volume focuses on historical sites in the Americas, but the case studies attend to a variety of historical time periods, regions, and cultures. The result is a wide-ranging perspective on the diversity of ways in which archaeological remains of dwellings conceived in the broadest sense provide insight into how people in the past navigated, negotiated, and contested the circumstances of their lives.

We are grateful to the original participants in the 2013 SHA session in England, especially Frasier Neiman, Elizabeth Terese Newman, Suzanne Spencer-Wood, and Carolyn White, whose conference papers do not appear here. We also thank Ben Barna, Andrew Agha, and Nicole Isenbarger for their willingness to step in at short notice with their contributions, which we were most happy to include. We acknowledge and thank our contributors and everyone who supported us in bringing this volume to fruition, in particular Sonia Dickey, formerly at the University Press of Florida. Kevin dedicates his chapter to the memory of his mother, Jean Minton Fogle (1952–2011); James dedicates his to his parents and to Brooke, for all their love and patience; and Mary dedicates her contribution to the memory of her sister, Jeannette M. Beaudry (1957–2010).

1

....

Households beyond the House

On the Archaeology and Materiality of Historical Households

MARY C. BEAUDRY

Archaeologists working in almost every corner of the globe, on nearly all time periods and cultures, consider the archaeology of households an important topic "at the heart of archaeology" (Hendon 2004: 272) and see it as a useful method for studying manifold aspects of human behavior. It did not take long for archaeologists to respond to Wilk and Rathje's 1982 manifesto promoting household archaeology; in 1988 the Chacmool Conference held in Calgary, Canada, selected households and communities as its theme, and the conference drew an international group of archaeologists who by then were fully engaged in household archaeology (the conference proceedings were published as MacEachern et al. 1989). Since that time the literature on household archaeology has burgeoned; indeed, in recent years there has been a considerable upsurge in the publication of books and articles devoted to household archaeology, proving that it continues to be a vibrant area of archaeological research. There are numerous works devoted to household archaeology across time and space comparatively or that thematically treat issues of household activities and household production (e.g., Allison, ed. 1999; Blanton 1994; Douglass and Gonlin, ed. 2012; Hendon 1996), as well as works that focus on household archaeology of a particular region or time period, for example, ancient Israel (Yasur-Landau et al. 2011), Neolithic and Classical Greece (Ault and Nevett 1999; Souvatzi 2008), the ancient Near East (Parker and Foster 2012), highland and lowland Mesoamerica in both precontact and colonial times (e.g., Carballo 2011; Hendon 2006, 2004; Robin 2003; Santley and Hirth 1993; Schweitz 2012), South America (Bermann 1994; Jamieson 2002; Nash 2009), colonial South Africa (e.g., Hall et al. 1990; Malan

1999, 1997), colonial Australia (e.g., Prosser et al. 2012), and prehistoric and historical North America (e.g., Barile and Brandon 2004; Beaudry 2004, 2002, 1999, 1989, 1984; Groover 2005; Pluckhahn 2010; Wesson 2008; Young 2004). This means household archaeology now has a wide array of proponents who approach the archaeological study of households in a variety of ways, a development that has enriched the field. Nevertheless, there are certain recurrent themes in household archaeology regardless of researchers' theoretical and methodological approaches; some are the very themes originally proposed by Wilk and Rathje—household production and reproduction, household activities, and households and communities, for instance—and some newer themes have emerged over time. These include both macroscopic and microscopic scales of analysis of households in their landscapes, refuse disposal, and site formation processes, and of gender relations at the household level, as well as hybridity and the formation of alternative forms of households, which are all themes considered by the contributors to this volume.

Themes and Approaches in Household Archaeology

Archaeologists are naturally drawn to household archaeology because so many of the sites they excavate are places where people lived as well as where for much of the human past people carried out most of their daily activities; from the outset, researchers in household archaeology thought of the household as not related so much to family and kinship but primarily to production and to what households do, acknowledging that households can be multigenerational and have inmates who are not kin (such as slaves, servants, apprentices, boarders, and so forth). Archaeologists also acknowledged early on that understanding households involved more than understanding architecture and houses; throughout history, many households occupied domestic compounds and were to a greater or lesser degree incorporated into neighborhoods and communities. Archaeologists therefore were interested in activity areas both within dwellings and out of doors, in the open spaces of compounds, courtyards, patios, houseyards, and even urban backlots. Archaeologists of households often are interested in comparisons among households to facilitate an understanding of issues of power, differentiation, and inequality within given societies; such studies may consider economic aspects of household production and consumption, but they also take into account the symbolic aspects of prestige goods as ways of demarcating social difference.

One of the major themes that has characterized the archaeology of households has been finding ways of understanding functions and activities that households perform (for a recent discussion, see Douglass and Gonlin 2012); initially this often involved consideration of household production and consumption—what members of the household made and did as a collective and what the household as a collectivity consumed. Penelope Allison (1999: 1) pointed out over a decade ago that the traditional approach to the archaeology of households focuses on their "role as measurable socio-economic units" of a wider community; this definition of a household as the smallest, indivisible social unit means that a household could be seen to stand for society, and the household, thus defined as a "unit," is slotted into some sort of socioeconomic classification based on the perceived standing of its head. Despite acknowledging the productive nature of households, this approach tends to view the household chiefly as a locus of consumption, and household deposits have therefore been analyzed to ascertain what types of goods were purchased or made, how much was expended on acquisition, the sources of goods that a household consumed, and what these goods could tell of the overall socioeconomic status of households in a given society. What is perhaps surprising is that despite their frequent emphasis on household activities, household archaeologists have only recently adopted practice theory to frame analysis of household activities (see, e.g., Robin 2013). Robb (2007: 75) notes that while of course houses provide shelter, "they also embody cultural values, commitment to places, and plans of action."

Allison noted further that "the internal dynamics and interrelationships of a household have been viewed as trivial and insignificant" (1999: 2); she subscribes to the view that the household is not so much a unit as it is a system of membership. This acknowledges the internal diversity of households as well as the diversity of households within any given society; it also allows archaeologists to consider how households are differentially constituted in different times and places as well as to address spatial, status, gender, and age relationships within the organization and structure of the household. Indeed, for many, the shift of emphasis on household as productive unit to that of an often highly differentiated and complex system of both fixed and shifting relationships has led to a strong focus on the gendered nature of household activities—for instance, on women's work both in terms of tasks and chores and often as arbiters of taste, morality, and behavior (e.g., Barile and Brandon 2004; Hendon 2006, 2004, 1996; Lawrence 1999; Tringham 1995, 1991; Wall 1991). Understanding the gendered nature of household production and consumption extends, of course, to considerations of and even critical questioning of notions about the sexual division of labor as well as of the roles of children in household production and dynamics (see Baxter 2005; Scott 2004).

So it is only recently that archaeologists have been able to grapple with the internal dynamics of households. And one of the ways in which they have done this is by extending their studies of household activities and activity areas to the wider arena of the linkages between households and society (Robin 2003). In prehistory, activity area research has long been valued as a means of interpreting domestic compounds (see, e.g., Kent 1987); spatial analysis of household activities has been done with success on some sites of the early modern period (Beaudry 1989; Groover 2005), but archaeologists often find themselves constrained by the fact that by this period many households we study are urban households with very little space beyond the house and that often dwellings housed multiple families and hence multiple households, and also by the fact that while houses may be "prescriptive" in form, we cannot assume that everyone used the internal spaces of houses as they were supposed to. We also confront the fact that the composition of households might be unorthodox or alternative; a boardinghouse, for instance, requires special consideration in unpacking the assembled evidence to associate it with different members, or categories of members, of the corporate household (see, e.g., Beaudry and Mrozowski 1989).

As noted above, archaeologists have sought to overcome these problems by framing their analysis of household activities according to what they feel are tasks that are likely to have been performed by designated members of a household: in other words, women's, men's, children's, and perhaps servants' activities. This approach relies on assumptions about who did what, and what sorts of tools or equipment they used to do it, how and where they might have done it, and what sorts of residues (for example, bones, leather or textile trimmings, copper alloy scrap, slag, and so forth) might have been generated by what they did. Some seek to combine activity analysis with analysis of household choices (see, e.g., the essays in Barile and Brandon 2004), not just choices about consumption but also choices about alternative living arrangements; how to store and maintain supplies of foodstuffs after purchase, harvest, or collection; dealing with food spoilage; dealing with risk of and recovery from fire or other episodic household catastrophes; and so on.

A relatively new area of archaeological analysis, microarchaeology—an umbrella term for analysis of a wide array of remains preserved in "the invisible archaeological record" (Weiner 2010)—for historical archaeologists' case studies of households can be roughly equated with a microhistorical approach to the documentary record. Conducted at a scale that is infinitely smaller than that of spatial analysis and the analysis of site structure (e.g., Alexander 1999; McKee 1999), microarchaeology is an approach that attends to the minute details of site formation and analysis of site sediments; microarchaeology has become more and more key to understanding household activities and practices (e.g., LaMotta and Schiffer 1999; Weiner 2010), as it allows for recovery of otherwise invisible evidence of site formation as well as of an array of everyday activities that leave chemical and microscopic traces, including, for instance, information that has begun to revolutionize our understanding of "practices of dwelling" through careful maintenance of house floors (Wolff 2014) or "the menial art of cooking" (Graff and Rodríguez-Alegría 2012) as key household activities in past times.

Materiality and Households

A recent trend across disciplines has been the emergence of an interest in materiality, that is, consideration of the physical properties of the world around us, of the very "thingness" of things. The new material culture studies that have resulted from an interest in materiality invert the longstanding study of how people make things by asking also how "things make people"—how objects mediate social relationships. A quick sortie to locate arenas across multiple disciplines in which materiality has been adduced will turn up studies of the materiality of bodies, of funerals, of women's lives, of space, of landscape, of sound and music, of color, of textiles, of juncture, of algorithms, of reading, and so on and on. There is no doubt that disciplines as varied as art history, literary criticism, cultural geography, anthropology, sociology, music, and beyond have to a greater or lesser extent embraced the concept of materiality as a way of expanding how its practitioners think about their own subject matter. Thus, the "new material culture studies" is a rather all-encompassing project with input from many directions (see, e.g., Hicks and Beaudry 2010). There is surely room in all this for bringing the notion of materiality to bear upon the interpretation of archaeological households.

In her introduction to the edited volume *Archaeologies of Materiality* (2005), Lynn Meskell notes that the majority of archaeological approaches to artifacts had until quite recently been polarized into considerations of function at the one extreme and considerations of the symbolism of objects at the other extreme. Function might be seen to include economic aspects such as consumption and production; the symbolic import of things is generally considered to be culturally specific but nevertheless widely shared across a culture. She points out that the middle ground between these two approaches is a vast and largely unoccupied territory. In this middle ground we might find ways of examining personal sentiment and attachment to objects, significance of possessions to individuals and family outside the realm of broader cultural symbolism or import, various aspects of self-fashioning through goods; and emotions linked to disposal of objects through events often blandly referred to as "household clearances" or "rubbish disposal."

Meskell advocates an approach that considers what she calls *material habitus*, based in part on Bourdieu's practice theory (1977) but also on earlier scholarship by the likes of anthropologist Sir Edward B. Tylor, who wrote about culture in the late nineteenth century in much the same way that Bourdieu did in the 1970s. If *habitus* refers to "processes, customs, opinions, and so forth, which have been carried on by force of habit" (Tylor 1977: 16), *material habitus* refers to the lifeworld: "an enmeshing that combines persons, objects, deities, and all manner of immaterial things together in ways that cannot easily be disentangled or separated taxonomically" (Meskell 2005: 3; see also Hodder 2012). The grounded understanding of things, in other words, requires a consideration of immateriality, which includes the sentiments that surround how people engage with things as well as how people experience the physical presence of things. Important in considering archaeologies of households is the notion that to comprehend the materiality (and immateriality) of any given household, we need to study "specific cultural moments to understand particular contextual notions of the material world" (Meskell 2005: 6) in terms of cultural relationships. This is done by exploring and problematizing (as opposed to taking for granted) the "past and present lives of things, sometimes as objects, other times as active entities or didactic things, often as circulating cultural capital today" (Meskell 2005: 6); it involves "looking at the object world in archaeological and ethnohistoric contexts, by tracing the subsequent biographies of things, or examining the deployment of object worlds in historic and contemporary practice" (Meskell 2005: 7). Materiality of households, therefore, involves the object worlds that households create for themselves and the material habitus that develops based on the object world, the ways in which objects in those worlds affect household members in terms of their sense of self and their presentation of self to others within and beyond the household, and the sentiments and attachments that people form with their belongings.

Materializing Households through Textual Analysis

The outcomes of approaches that consider materiality and practices are enriched when documentary evidence is available (see, e.g., Beaudry 1988; Little 1991), and for many historical archaeologists, probate inventories are often most rewarding sources. It has long been acknowledged that despite all the problems that probate inventories present they nevertheless provide snapshot views of very large numbers of households, allowing a comprehensive perspective on household furnishings, room use, household production and consumption, and many other aspects of home life. Archaeologists and historians who read probate inventories almost instinctively "materialize" these documents; that is, they read out of the text the physicality of objects—words become things—and immediately begin to furnish in their minds a home and to vicariously experience the sensations of walking through it, the comfort or lack thereof afforded by a straight-back chair, a feather bed, or a settle, the heft of a cast-iron cook pot, the lustrous glow of polished pewter or of Chinese porcelain, the feel of the fabrics of which listed linens and clothing are made. The potent and potential materiality of these documents evokes as visceral a response in archaeologists as they experience when confronted with a well-preserved group of household goods recovered from an archaeological deposit. Probate inventories also allow archaeologists and historians to develop an understanding of household change over time in far greater detail than is afforded through excavation alone. Yet it should be noted that the probate process and the sorts of documents it generated did not extend much beyond the Euro-American world, and so archaeologists working on historical sites occupied by enslaved Africans, African Americans, Native Americans, and other marginalized groups do not have such sources; contributors to this volume have therefore used many other types of textual sources, such as U.S. Census data, plantation and other business records, and church and parish records in developing contexts for interpreting the archaeological record.

Ideally we would collect and synthesize archaeological data from multiple households and present and analyze aggregated data, but for many reasons this is not feasible. But we are not wholly unjustified in thinking that there is something to be said for the "case"—for the case study, which, as in this volume, is the most prevalent mode of conducting and interpreting the archaeology of households. Indeed, studies that aggregate data arise not out of the notion that the individual units that collectively constitute the aggregate are more likely to be idiosyncratic than representative but on the very opposite premise. And many of us find very attractive the paradigm espoused by microhistorians, who study individual, seemingly idiosyncratic "events" or cases as a way of exposing rents in the social fabric that lead the researcher to a newer understanding of social and cultural issues well beyond the odd or outlandish event (see, e.g., Brooks et al. 2008). In the present volume, contributors make important contributions to understanding households in contexts beyond the living quarters through the use of sophisticated spatial analyses, correspondence analysis, and other techniques that aggregate data for the purposes of strong and effective comparisons and interpretations. Before I introduce the individual chapters that follow, it is worth giving further consideration to ways in which physical and cultural analysis of discard behavior can bring greater resonance to our interpretations of historical households.

Material Habitus and the Emotional Taphonomy of Household Refuse

Refuse and midden analysis are key and critical in household archaeology. Sometimes such deposits are associated with "household clearances," in the sense that they are created rapidly when occupants abandon a site or after some sort of transitional event in the household, whether a disaster, a change in the household head or a new woman in charge of the domestic sphere, and so forth. The latter sort of deposits are more common in urban contexts than on plantations and farms such as those discussed in this volume, but in either instance, analysis of site formation processes is key. In studying deposits formed rapidly, we may benefit from considering the sentiment attached to disposal practices, in keeping with Sarah Tarlow's (2000) admonition that we should attempt to account for the emotional dimension of human experience. Most of the examples found in this volume analyze refuse and middens that seem to have resulted from gradual accumulation, intermittently, and over some period of time. Such deposits differ from the hasty "cleanup" deposits arising from natural disaster, fire, eviction, or other events that disrupt the equilibrium of everyday life. These sorts of events prompt acts of disposal that represent differential emotional reactions (see Tarlow 2000: 731) to loss, while deliberate disposal in pits and privies may reflect purposeful actions far less emotionally charged; the assumption tends to be that middens most surely represent voluntary disposal of items of no current economic or emotional value. Yet Monica Smith (2011: 132) reminds us that "studies of the placement of trash in both modern and ancient contexts provide insights on the way in which the leave-taking of possessions is as pointed a statement of identity as their production, circulation and possession." Some deposits represent voluntary disposal of unwanted household goods versus the unanticipated and involuntary deposition of things that people would rather have continued to own, use, and enjoy. Close attention to discard behavior provides a way to begin to understand refuse deposits in terms of how the people who created them related to the material goods that once made up their object worlds—their material habitus.

Pertinent here is Shannon Dawdy's consideration of the taphonomic effects of disaster and recovery in post-Katrina New Orleans (Dawdy 2006). She defines *taphonomy* as "the process through which the archaeological record is created. It describes those processes, intentional and unintentional, human and natural, large scale and nano scale, that go into the creation and distillation of the archaeological record. It includes the cultural logic that dictates what is to be recycled, what is to be discarded, and how" (Dawdy 2006: 728). Dawdy expands the concept of taphonomy, observing that it "describes the complexity, the mix of accident and manipulation, the silences and erasures, the constraining structures, and the sudden ruptures that all go into the creation of history and into the formation of the 'ethnographic present'" (Dawdy 2006: 728). She argues that "the active creation of a new archaeological record during recovery from disaster . . . is a primary medium through which individuals and communities reconstitute themselves" and urges archaeologists to account for less-obvious taphonomic processes, such as emotions and spiritual considerations, as well as to admit the great degree of contingency that dictates the laws of burial (Dawdy 2006: 720). In describing her experiences as a consulting archaeologist as well as a former member of the New Orleans community, Dawdy explores the emotionality attendant upon recovery from disaster and notes how people react to the need to dispose of the ruinous debris that once formed their daily object world and through which they had constituted their identities. Her experiences led her to observe that "although we may not be able to comfortably predict the precise cultural emotions associated with disasters, it seems a safe cross-cultural assumption that disasters define a period of heightened, and therefore perhaps more archaeologically visible, emotional responses worthy of interpretive attempts" (Dawdy 2006: 722).

Dawdy's work prompted me to consider the emotional taphonomy of discard when I was overseeing excavations of an eighteenth-century planter's house at Piper's Little Bay Plantation on the island of Montserrat in the West Indies. The house had been destroyed by a huge conflagration toward the end of the eighteenth century and was never reoccupied or rebuilt. But the people who had lived there and expended considerable expense on furnishing their home and clothing their persons in ways that were meant to exhibit gentility and wealth (MacLean 2013) did not just walk away from the house and its charred, mangled, and melted furnishings; rather, someone took the time to rake carefully through the fire debris to salvage whatever they could (Luiz 2013, 2012)—though many compelling items remained for archaeologists to discover through their own careful screening of the fire deposits some two hundred years after the fire. The postfire deposits (Doroszenko 2001–2) at Little Bay Plantation speak to us of "differential emotional reactions" to loss, though we will never know whether a member of the planter household searched through the debris for treasured personal possessions or whether a member of the enslaved labor force was assigned the task of raking through it to recover items that could be reused or materials that, even if melted or fire-damaged, would have retained some sort of monetary value. At other sites where we find deliberate rubbish disposal in pits and privies or in accumulated yard middens, it seems unlikely that disposal was emotionally charged or that attempts at recovery and salvage would have been made. Hence, the material habitus around acts of disposal and reclamation varies according to situation, as does our ability to glean insight into the emotional taphonomy of discard.

Attempting to comprehend and interpret the motivations behind involuntary versus voluntary disposal is far from a simple matter; it is an exercise that requires a good deal of cultural generalizing, but we might be able to begin to eke out some sort of understanding by comparing the contents of deposits to determine what sorts of things are considered dispensable and hence regularly and willingly discarded, as opposed to those sorts of things that people are far less willing to part with unless forced to do so. That is one potential avenue of research, though developing a means of comprehending just what sort of "house clearance" event or process we are seeing in each deposit should perhaps take priority. Whether this can be achieved without detailed documentary evidence of episodes of household upheaval is unclear. But we need to recognize that household clearance deposits are often not the results of benign events; deposits formed by cleanup of a household after disasters such as earthquake, fire, flood, and other catastrophes represent in capsule form emotional and practical responses to disaster as well as choices made to effect recovery, and as such they can provide us with different insights into families and households than deposits representing voluntary disposal. The latter represent an entirely different order of choice and decision making. Smith (2011: 136) notes that "trash has great longevity compared to the event that generated the discards."

It is worth speculating about how we make use of artifacts disposed of as trash to talk about identity and presentation of self; while people could easily have been attempting to construct identities through acquiring and using objects, items deliberately and voluntarily thrown away because they were worn out or unfashionable perhaps tell us more about *refashioning* selves and households. Smith, however, points to instances in which deliberate disposal can serve as a form of cultural "cachet," as evidence of consumption and of the affirmation of the presence of humans. She observes that trash can have great longevity and hence social meaning in and of itself, pointing to the "spectacular" example of shell middens throughout the world. These "represent a deliberately piled-up collection of discards that incrementally signal the group's size and longevity of place" (Smith 2011: 136). Actual disposal practices do, of course, provide us with information of household identity in terms of maintenance and cooperation among coresident groups and near neighbors.

Tearing Down Walls

The overriding premise behind this volume is that household archaeology is a diverse and eclectic practice to which researchers bring multiple perspectives; here the mandate was to "tear down the walls" in the sense of not just expanding the purview of household archaeology beyond dwellings and compounds (see, e.g., Robin 2002) but also to consider how individual case studies of domestic life fit into larger social processes at work on local, regional, and global scales. The key themes addressed in this volume, therefore, include ways of developing an archaeology of historical households that does not privilege the microscale *or* the macroscale (see Fletcher 1992) or limit itself to the study of houses and houseyards but explores the linkages between households and broader society. The contributors expand the concept of the household to bring different scales of analysis to bear on a diverse range of domestic sites. They seek to make household archaeology as central to historical archaeology as it is to other areas of archaeological research by pushing the boundaries of household archaeology beyond the physical walls of the house and by situating households within landscapes, larger communities, and regional and global networks. In this volume the authors focus not on dwellings per se but on *dwelling* as an agentive, everyday practice.

The chief source of information brought to bear on the households considered here is domestic refuse from inside houses as well as from middens, pit features, and in some cases broadcast sheet refuse (see Beck and Hill 2004); the focus is not so much on houses and architecture as it is on activities, consumption and economic engagement, discard, and what cultural refuse tells us of identity construction, strategies of survival, maintenance of family and communal traditions and foodways, and dwelling as place-making.

Matthew Reeves, for example, examines Montpelier, Virginia, slave households as defined by their houses, houseyards, and material culture using scalar analysis as a way of contextualizing his interpretations. He looks at markets at a regional scale and compares the regional market network in which his site was enmeshed with results of other studies of

Jamaican markets (see, e.g., Hauser 2008). Found in both locales are dipt and hand-painted ceramics, but the proportions of dipt wares to other sorts of pottery are higher in Jamaica than in Virginia; this can be interpreted chiefly as resulting from the differing nature of market connections in the two contexts. Emphasizing the widest scale of analysis lends insight into the potential interplay between modes of acquisition and of decision making. Issues such as who makes decisions—masters or enslaved householders—and what the purchases they made reflect in terms of market forces, cost, and personal preferences can perhaps be clarified by close comparisons of contexts that are similar at the regional context but differ at the more global scale.

In her study of foodways among the native peoples of the North Carolina Piedmont, Ashley Peles uses aggregated faunal and floral data from numerous sites in the region to explore the diet and foodways of communities and households within the region over a period of time that spanned from late prehistory to well into the historical period. She is able to detect significant changes in practices around foodways in response to the upheavals brought about by contact and conflict with Europeans; these changes on the one hand involved the processes of involution in the sense of intensification of feasting and ritual in response to disease and increased mortality, and on the other, revitalization, in the sense of resisting seemingly inevitable change by conscious readoption of earlier dietary practices. While these processes are discernable at the level of the household, the aggregated data show that they were clearly community-wide responses and that different communities tended to develop slight differences in the nature of their responses to the harsh effects resulting from the arrival of Europeans in the Piedmont.

James A. Nyman and Brooke Kenline employ the concept of *landschaft*, drawn from the field of human geography and meaning, essentially, "the construction of personal, political and place identity" (Olwig 1996: 631), to investigate the ways in which a succession of households living at George Washington's Ferry Farm near Fredericksburg, Virginia (Levy 2013) reflected their sense of their own identities and of their place within the landscape. Households elected either to dispose of their rubbish in ways that hid it from view or left it in plain sight, yet each also selected a distinct area for refuse disposal rather than discard items randomly as broadcast refuse. Analysis of the distribution and visibility of the resulting middens allows Nyman and Kenline to demonstrate ways in which discard has meaning (see Hodder 1987). The households that occupied Ferry Farm over time disposed of rubbish in ways that clearly reflect and symbolize the manner in which each chose to construct its identity in the landscape.

Benjamin Barna considers the formation of alternative households on company-owned sheep and cattle ranches in nineteenth-century Hawai'i, households that differed from normative households both in the sense that they were single-sex, all-male households and because they were culturally hybrid. In Hawai'i, ranch hands tended to be Japanese and Chinese immigrants who lived in a world of movement and mobility and whose improvised households provided mechanisms for socialization into the wider community. Barna offers two case studies of differently managed ranches and is able to link the management philosophy and style of the ranch owner—how they organized labor and whether they encouraged immigrant incorporation into the community—to differences in the material records of household formation.

Kevin R. Fogle's use of the notion of "discourse materialized" is a fascinating application of a cultural geographical concept to contextual historical archaeology. The notion of multiscalar landscapes bears an affinity with Rodman's (1992) notion of multilocality and multivocality as ways in which spaces are "empowered"—and surely the intimate landscapes of slave yards and cabins were also public and contested landscapes holding different meanings for slaves and masters (see also McKee 1992; Stewart-Abernathy 2004; Upton 1984). The ways in which their forms, maintenance, and inhabitation were perceived and the degree to which these were controlled by their enslaved inhabitants versus the master/owners involved a continuous discourse and resulted in multiple and possibly hybrid materialities (see Card 2013; but see also Silliman 2013, 2012).

Dual consumption practices among Chinese householders in Aurora, Nevada, provide another example of multiple or hybrid materiality in what Emily Dale refers to as transnational behavior (see Ross 2012, 2011). As noted by Praetzellis and Praetzellis (2001), Chinese in the American West often elected to use in combination elements of their own traditional material culture with Euro-American goods, in effect, "mangling the symbols of gentility" so prized by the Victorian middle class. Here that may not have been what was going on, but Dale's recognition of "transnational artifacts" leads us to a consideration of how the Chinese in

Aurora developed complex transnational identities through the choices they made in furnishing their homes and tables.

Nicole Isenbarger and Andrew Agha's excavations at the slave quarters at Dean Hall Plantation near Charleston, South Carolina, brought to light compelling evidence of strong community formation among the enslaved and a long-standing commitment to the preservation and retention of community- and household-level practices and traditions. The site proved remarkably rich, with refuse accumulations within the houses of the enslaved, perhaps in response to a reform-minded planter's concern that all components of the plantation present an external appearance of cleanliness and order (archaeologists have reported a similar lack of yard middens on a Brazilian plantation whose owner was a prominent reformer [Marcos André Torres de Souza, personal communication, 2013]). Of particular note at Dean Hall was the recovery of large quantities of decorated colonoware pottery, much of which was fired directly in the hearths within the homes of the enslaved, providing evidence of both persistence of an African-based craft tradition and community-wide persistence of African-derived foodways, as well as of participation in the informal slave economy.

In his concluding remarks, Charles R. Cobb discusses what he refers to as "the spooky entanglements" of historical households and discusses the two main threads he identifies throughout the volume. He notes that new perspectives on household archaeology, including the multiscalar perspectives adopted throughout the book, arise continuously: household archaeology itself is a process and a practice, always developing and growing and exploring new intellectual territory. Cobb notes the importance of household archaeology in the study of the emergence of the modern world and observes that case studies of households often constitute examinations of what Knauft (2002) terms "micromodernity."

Tearing down walls in a figurative sense expands household archaeology in ways that bring household archaeology into the current mix of contemporary method and theory in archaeology, regardless of whether the methods are employed at macro- or microscopic scale and whether the theoretical perspective brought to bear is contextual/interpretive, evolutionary, feminist, or Marxist. The essays in this volume move us well away from prescriptive considerations of household function and beyond simplistic task-orientation approaches to household activities to allow us to begin to better comprehend broader cultural and social aspects of households such as competition and cooperation, decision making, and identity construction. Matthews (2012: 560) makes an intriguing observation about household archaeology: that one can view it as liberation from the obligation to contribute to grand narratives in archaeology because in doing archaeology of households one is forced to focus on individuality and contingency. And while it is true that historical archaeologists often focus on household archaeology at the historical and archaeological microscale, it is abundantly clear that Matthews is correct—and the essays in this volume confirm—that household archaeology investigates issues that are relevant well beyond the individual case study and provides insight into wider social trends and processes.

References Cited

Alexander, Rani T.
1999 Mesoamerican House Lots and Archaeology Site Structure: Problems of Inference in Yaxcaba, Yucatan, Mexico. In *The Archaeology of Household Activities*, edited by Penelope Allison, pp. 78–100. Routledge, London.
Allison, Penelope M.
1999 Introduction. In *The Archaeology of Household Activities*, edited by Penelope Allison, pp. 1–18. Routledge, London.
Allison, Penelope M. (editor)
1999 *The Archaeology of Household Activities*. Routledge, London.
Ault, Bradley A., and Lisa C. Nevett
1999 Digging Houses: Archaeologies of Classical and Hellenistic Greek Domestic Assemblages. In *The Archaeology of Household Activities*, edited by Penelope Allison, pp. 43–56. Routledge, London.
Barile, Kerri S., and Jamie C. Brandon (editors)
2004 *Household Chores and Household Choices: Theorizing the Domestic Sphere in Historical Archaeology*. University of Alabama Press, Tuscaloosa.
Baxter, Jane Eva
2005 *The Archaeology of Childhood: Children, Gender, and Material Culture*. AltaMira Press, Walnut Creek, California.
Beaudry, Mary C.
2004 Doing the Housework: New Approaches to the Archaeology of Households. In *Household Chores and Household Choices: Theorizing the Domestic Sphere in Historical Archaeology*, edited by Kerri S. Barile and Jamie C. Brandon, pp. 254–262. University of Alabama Press, Tuscaloosa.
2002 Household Archaeology. In *Encyclopedia of Historical Archaeology*, edited by Charles E. Orser Jr., pp. 273–276. Routledge, London.

1999 House and Household: The Archaeology of Domestic Life in Early America. In *Old and New Worlds*, edited by Geoff Egan and R. L. Michael, pp. 117–126. Oxbow Books, Oxford, U.K.

1989 Household Structure and the Archaeological Record: Examples from New World Historical Sites. In *Households and Communities: Proceedings of the 21st Annual Chacmool Conference*, edited by Scott MacEachern, David J. W. Archer, and Richard D. Garvin, pp. 84–92. Chacmool Archaeological Society, University of Calgary, Alberta.

1984 Archaeology and the Historical Household. *Man in the Northeast* 28: 27–38.

Beaudry, Mary C. (editor)

1988 *Documentary Archaeology in the New World*. Cambridge University Press, Cambridge.

Beaudry, Mary C., and Stephen A. Mrozowski

1989 Archeology in the Backlots of Boott Units 45 and 48: Household Archeology with a Difference. In *Interdisciplinary Investigations of the Boott Mills, Lowell, Massachusetts*, vol. 3, *The Boarding House System as a Way of Life*, edited by Mary C. Beaudry and Stephen A. Mrozowski, pp. 49–82. Cultural Resources Management Series 21. National Park Service, North Atlantic Regional Office, Boston.

Beck, Margaret E., and Matthew E. Hill, Jr.

2004 Rubbish, Relatives, and Residence: The Family Use of Middens. *Journal of Archaeological Method and Theory* 11: 297–333.

Bermann, Marc

1994 *Lukurmata: Household Archaeology in Prehispanic Bolivia*. Princeton University Press, Princeton.

Blanton, Richard

1994 *Houses and Households: A Comparative Study*. Plenum, New York.

Bourdieu, Pierre

1977 *Outline of a Theory of Practice*. Translated by R. Nice. Cambridge University Press, Cambridge.

Brooks, James F., Christopher R. N. DeCorse, and John Walton (editors)

2008 *Small Worlds: Method, Meaning, and Narrative in Microhistory*. School of Advanced Research Press, Santa Fe, New Mexico.

Carballo, David M.

2011 Advances in the Household Archaeology of Highland Mesoamerica. *Journal of Archaeological Research* 19: 133–189.

Card, Jeb J. (editor)

2013 *The Archaeology of Hybrid Material Culture*. Occasional Paper 39. Center for Archaeological Investigations, Southern Illinois University, Carbondale.

Dawdy, Shannon L.

2006 The Taphonomy of Disaster and the (Re)Formation of New Orleans. *American Anthropologist* 108: 719–730.

Doroszenko, Dena

2001–2 Burning Down the House: The Archaeological Manifestation of Fire on Historic Domestic Sites. *Northeast Historical Archaeology* 30/31: 41–52.

Douglass, John G., and Nancy Gonlin

2012 The Household as Analytical Unit: Case Studies from the Americas. In *Ancient Households of the Americas: Conceptualizing What Households Do*, edited by John G. Douglass and Nancy Gonlin, pp. 1–46. University Press of Colorado, Boulder.

Douglass, John G., and Nancy Gonlin (editors)

2012 *Ancient Households of the Americas: Conceptualizing What Households Do*. University Press of Colorado, Boulder.

Fletcher, Roland

1992 Time Perspectivism, *Annales*, and the Potential of Archaeology. In *Archaeology, Annales, and Ethnohistory*, edited by A. Bernard Knapp, pp. 35–50. Cambridge University Press, Cambridge.

Graff, Sarah R., and Enrique Rodríguez-Alegría (editors)

2012 *The Menial Art of Cooking: Archaeological Studies of Cooking and Food Preparation*. University of Colorado Press, Boulder.

Groover, Mark D.

2005 The Gibbs Farmstead: Household Archaeology in an Internal Periphery. *International Journal of Historical Archaeology* 9: 229–289.

Hall, Martin, D. Halkett, Jane E. Klose, and G. Ritchie

1990 The Barrack Street Well: Images of a Cape Town Household in the Nineteenth Century. *South African Archaeological Bulletin* 45: 73–92.

Hauser, Mark W.

2008 *An Archaeology of Black Markets: Local Ceramics and Local Economies in Eighteenth-Century Jamaica*. University Press of Florida, Gainesville.

Hendon, Julia A.

2006 The Engendered Household. In *Handbook of Gender in Archaeology*, edited by Sarah Milledge Nelson, pp. 171–198. AltaMira Press, Lanham, Maryland.

2004 Living and Working at Home: The Social Archaeology of Household Production and Social Relations. In *A Companion to Social Archaeology*, edited by Lynn Meskell and Robert W. Preucel, pp. 272–286. Blackwell, Oxford, U.K.

1996 Archaeological Approaches to the Organization of Domestic Labor: Household Practice and Domestic Relations. *Annual Review of Anthropology* 25: 45–61.

Hicks, Dan, and Mary C. Beaudry (editors)

2010 *The Oxford Handbook of Material Culture Studies*. Oxford University Press, Oxford.

Hodder, Ian

2012 *Entangled: An Archaeology of Relationships between Humans and Things*. Wiley-Blackwell, Oxford, U.K.

1987 The Meaning of Discard: Ash and Domestic Space in Baringo. In *Method and Theory for Activity Area Research: An Ethnoarchaeological Approach*, edited by Susan Kent, pp. 424–448. Columbia University Press, New York.

Jamieson, Ross W.

2002 *Domestic Architecture and Power: The Historical Archaeology of Colonial Ecuador*. Kluwer, New York.

Kent, Susan (editor)

1987 *Method and Theory for Activity Area Research: An Ethnoarchaeological Approach.* Columbia University Press, New York.

Knauft, B. M.

2002 Critically Modern: An Introduction. In *Critically Modern: Alternatives, Alterities, Anthropologies*, edited by B. M. Knauft, pp. 1–54. Indiana University Press, Bloomington.

LaMotta, Vincent M., and Michael B. Schiffer

1999 Formation Processes of House Floor Assemblages. In *The Archaeology of Household Activities*, edited by Penelope M. Allison, pp. 19–29. Routledge, London.

Lawrence, Susan

1999 Towards a Feminist Archaeology of Households: Gender and Household Structure on the Australian Goldfields. In *The Archaeology of Household Activities*, edited by Penelope M. Allison, pp. 121–141. Routledge, London.

Levy, Philip

2013 *Where the Cherry Tree Grew: The Story of George Washington's Boyhood Home.* St. Martin's Press, New York.

Little, Barbara J.

1991 *Text-Aided Archaeology.* CRC Press, Boca Raton, Florida.

Luiz, Jade

2013 Fire, Clay, and Microscopes: Micromorphology at the Little Bay Plantation Site in Montserrat, W.I. Paper presented at the 46th Annual Conference of the Society for Historical Archaeology, Leicester, England, January 10, 2013.

2012 The Use of Micromorphology at the Little Bay Plantation in Montserrat, W.I. Report on file, Department of Archaeology, Boston University, Boston.

MacEachern, Scott, David J. W. Archer, and Richard D. Garvin (editors)

1989 *Households and Communities: Proceedings of the 21st Annual Chacmool Conference.* Chacmool Archaeological Society, University of Calgary, Alberta.

McKee, Brian S.

1999 Household Archaeology and Cultural Formation Processes: Examples from the Cerén Site, El Salvador. In *The Archaeology of Household Activities*, edited by Penelope M. Allison, pp. 30–42. Routledge, London.

McKee, Larry

1992 The Ideals and Realities behind the Design and Use of 19th Century Virginia Slave Cabins. In *The Art and Mystery of Historical Archaeology: Essays in Honor of James Deetz*, edited by Anne Elizabeth Yentsch and Mary C. Beaudry, pp. 195–213. CRC Press, Boca Raton, Florida.

MacLean, Jessica Striebel

2013 A House, a Pistol, China, and a Clock: The Articulation of White Masculinity and the Cult of Sensibility in 18th-Century Montserrat, West Indies. Paper presented at the 46th Annual Conference of the Society for Historical Archaeology, Leicester, England, January 10, 2013.

Malan, Antonia

1999 Chattels or Colonists? "Freeblack" Women and Their Households. *Kronos* 25: 50–71.

1997 The Material World of Family and Household: The Van Sitterts in Eighteenth Century Capetown, 1748–1796. In *Our Gendered Past: Archaeological Studies of Gender in Southern Africa*, edited by Lyn Wadley, pp. 273–301. Witwatersrand University Press, Johannesburg.

Matthews, Roger

2012 About the Archaeological House: Themes and Directions. In *New Perspectives on Household Archaeology*, edited by Bradley J. Parker and Catherine P. Foster, pp. 559–565. Eisenbrauns, Winona Lake, Indiana.

Meskell, Lynn

2005 Introduction: Object Orientations. In *Archaeologies of Materiality*, edited by Lynn Meskell, pp. 1–17. Blackwell, Oxford.

Nash, Donna J.

2009 Household Archaeology in the Andes. *Journal of Archaeological Research* 17: 205–261.

Olwig, Kenneth R.

1996 Recovering the Substance of Landscape. *Annals of the Association of American Geographers* 86: 630–653.

Parker, Bradley J., and Catherine P. Foster (editors)

2012 *New Perspectives on Household Archaeology*. Eisenbrauns, Winona Lake, Indiana.

Pluckhahn, Thomas

2010 Household Archaeology in the Southeastern United States: History, Trends, Challenges. *Journal of Archaeological Research* 18 (4): 331–385.

Praetzellis, Adrian, and Mary Praetzellis

2001 Mangling the Symbols of Gentility in the Wild West. *American Anthropologist* 103: 645–654.

Prosser, Lauren, Susan Lawrence, Alasdair Brooks, and Jane Lennon

2012 Household Archaeology, Lifecycles and Status in a Nineteenth-Century Australian Coastal Community. *International Journal of Historical Archaeology* 16: 809–827.

Robb, John

2007 *The Early Mediterranean Village: Agency, Material Culture, and Social Change in Neolithic Italy*. Cambridge University Press, Cambridge.

Robin, Cynthia

2013 *Everyday Life Matters: Maya Farmers at Chan*. University Press of Florida, Gainesville.

2003 New Directions in Classic Maya Household Archaeology. *Journal of Archaeological Research* 11: 307–356.

2002 Outside of Houses: The Practices of Everyday Life at Chan Nòohol, Belize. *Journal of Social Archaeology* 2: 245–267.

Rodman, Margaret C.

1992 Empowering Place: Multilocality and Multivocality. *American Anthropologist* 94: 640–656.

Ross, Douglas

2012 Transnational Artifacts: Grappling with Fluid Material Origins and Identities in Archaeological Interpretations of Culture Change. *Journal of Anthropological Archaeology* 31: 38–48.

2011 Factors Influencing the Dining Habits of Japanese and Chinese Migrants at a British Columbia Salmon Cannery. *Historical Archaeology* 45 (2): 68–96.

Santley, Robert S., and Kenneth G. Hirth

1993 *Prehispanic Domestic Units in Western Mesoamerica: Studies of the Household, Compound, and Residence.* CRC Press, Boca Raton, Florida.

Schweitz, Sam

2012 *On the Periphery of the Periphery: Household Archaeology at Hacienda San Juan Bautista Tabi, Yucatan, Mexico.* Springer, New York.

Scott, Elizabeth M.

2004 Introduction: Gender Research in African American Archaeology. In *Engendering African American Archaeology: A Southern Perspective*, edited by Jillian E. Galle and Amy L. Young, pp. 1–18. University of Tennessee Press, Knoxville.

Silliman, Stephen W.

2013 What, Where, and When Is Hybridity? In *The Archaeology of Hybrid Material Culture*, edited by Jeb J. Card, pp. 486–500. Occasional Paper 39. Center for Archaeological Investigations, Southern Illinois University Press, Carbondale.

2012 Between the *Longue Durée* and the Short Purée: Postcolonial Archaeologies of Indigenous History in Colonial North America. In *Decolonizing Indigenous Histories: Exploring "Prehistoric/Colonial" Transitions in Archaeology*, edited by Maxine Oland, Siobhan M. Hart, and Liam Frink, pp. 113–132. University of Arizona Press, Tucson.

Smith, Monica L.

2011 "I Discard, Therefore I Am": Identity and Leave-Taking of Possessions. In *Identity Crisis: Archaeological Perspectives on Social Identity: Proceedings of the 42nd (2010) Annual Chacmool Conference*, edited by Lindsay Amundsen-Pickering, Nicole Engel, and Sean Pickering, pp. 132–142. Chacmool Archaeological Association, University of Calgary, Alberta.

Souvatzi, Stella G.

2008 *A Social Archaeology of Households in Neolithic Greece: An Anthropological Approach.* Cambridge University Press, Cambridge.

Stewart-Abernathy, Leslie C.

2004 Separate Kitchens and Intimate Archaeology: Constructing Urban Slavery on the Antebellum Frontier in Washington, Arkansas. In *Household Chores and Household Choices: Theorizing the Domestic Sphere in Historical Archaeology*, edited by Kerri S. Barile and Jamie C. Brandon, pp. 51–74. University of Alabama Press, Tuscaloosa.

Tarlow, Sarah

2000 Emotion in Archaeology. *Current Anthropology* 41: 713–746.

Tringham, Ruth

1995 Archaeological Houses, Households, Housework and the Home. In *The Home: Words, Interpretations, Meanings, and Environments*, edited by David N. Benjamin and David Stea, pp. 79–107. Avebury Press, Aldershot, U.K.

1991 Households with Faces: The Challenge of Gender in Prehistoric Architectural Remains. In *Engendering Archaeology: Women and Prehistory*, edited by Joan Gero and Margaret Conkey, pp. 93–131. Blackwell, Oxford, U.K.

Tylor, E. B.

1977 *Primitive Culture: Researches into the Development of Mythology, Philosophy, Religions, Language, Art and Custom*, vol. 1. Gordon Press, New York.

Upton, Dell

1984 White and Black Landscapes in Eighteenth-Century Virginia. *Places* 2 (2): 59–72.

Wall, Diana Dizerega

1991 Sacred Dinners and Secular Teas: Constructing Domesticity in Mid-19th-Century New York. *Historical Archaeology* 25: 69–71.

Weiner, Stephen

2010 *Microarchaeology: Beyond the Visible Archaeology Record*. Cambridge University Press, Cambridge.

Wesson, Cameron B.

2008 *Households and Hegemony: Early Creek Prestige Goods, Symbolic Capital, and Social Power*. University of Nebraska Press, Lincoln.

Wilk, Richard R., and William L. Rathje

1982 Household Archaeology. *American Behavioral Scientist* 25: 617–639.

Wolff, Nicholas

2014 At Home in Prehistory: Critical Approaches to the Built Environment in the South Italian Bronze Age. Unpublished PhD dissertation, Department of Archaeology, Boston University, Boston.

Yasur-Landau, Assaf, Jennie R. Ebeling, and Laura B. Mazow (editors)

2011 *Household Archaeology in Ancient Israel and Beyond*. Brill, Leiden.

Young, Amy L.

2004 Risk and Women's Roles in the Slave Family: Data from Oxmoor and Locust Grove Plantations in Kentucky. In *Engendering African-American Archaeology: A Southern Perspective*, edited by Jillian E. Galle and Amy L. Young, pp. 133–150. University of Tennessee Press, Knoxville.

2

....

Scalar Analysis of Early Nineteenth-Century Household Assemblages

Focus on Communities of the African Atlantic

MATTHEW REEVES

For archaeologists, the household is often the smallest tangible unit of analysis. In recovering the features and artifacts from a house site, we obtain a snapshot regarding the lives of multiple individuals who called the site home. The artifact assemblages and features reflect decisions made by individuals, power relations that are in the realm of the economic/political structure of a society, power imbalances set by societal norms, and larger global market forces. Using the material record as a proxy to interpret these influences and actions presents a special challenge for archaeologists. By studying the archaeological remains of households, we unwittingly characterize household patterns at a predetermined scale that is influenced by spatial units we impose as archaeologists. Many authors have lamented the fact that households defined at the individual site level do not necessarily relate to the social unit at which the household acted (King 2006: 297). In other words, to assume that a household was defined by the limits of the site we excavated is to neglect the complex range of structures that existed at the family and community level. Historical archaeologists have compensated for the distinction between physical space inhabited by a household (the site) and the social structure and function of a household (social relations) by employing ethnohistorical information and documentary evidence that provide data for household composition and structure (Bonine 2004; Galindo 2004; Groover 2001; Higman 1998; Wilkie and Farnsworth 2005).

Situating Early Nineteenth-Century Virginia Households within the African Atlantic

For those of us not fortunate enough to have a documentary record whereby household composition can be reconstructed for our sites, how is it possible to overcome the stigma of households defined as architectural and spatial units without reference to the larger historical context in which they were situated? How do we place such households into the larger context that structured their members' daily lives and resulted in the archaeological record we have recovered? In this chapter I work toward situating the household into a larger context through comparative analysis. To demonstrate the methods appropriate for such a comparative study, I offer the example of a recently completed study of early nineteenth-century enslaved households at a plantation in the Piedmont of Virginia.

From 2010 to 2013 we sampled and excavated six home sites in four distinct locations at James Madison's Montpelier plantation in Orange, Virginia; each locale had been designated for house slaves, enslaved field hands, or artisans (figure 2.1). The lack of documentary evidence for the composition of slave households and their location on the landscape has prevented us from giving a name or identity to any of the occupants of the structures we examined in these excavations. What is more, the archaeological record is the only means to define the location of these buildings on the landscape, as no other drawings, plats, or descriptions survive to provide such information (Reeves 2010; Reeves and Greer 2012). What we are able to do, however, is to draw assumptions about the labor role (domestic service, craft production, or agricultural production) played by household occupants based on the location of house sites within the larger plantation complex: the homes adjacent to the Montpelier mansion presumably were inhabited by enslaved domestics, those close to the stable and craft area by enslaved artisans, and those in the farm complex by enslaved farm hands. Ostensibly, the comparison of these household assemblages allows for a comparison of how position within the labor structure potentially influenced housing and access to goods. Using such a straightforward equation of material patterns reflecting labor role would lead to rather simplistic notions of households being defined by an owner rather than by the community or regional networks in which these enslaved individuals were enmeshed. Moving our comparative analysis

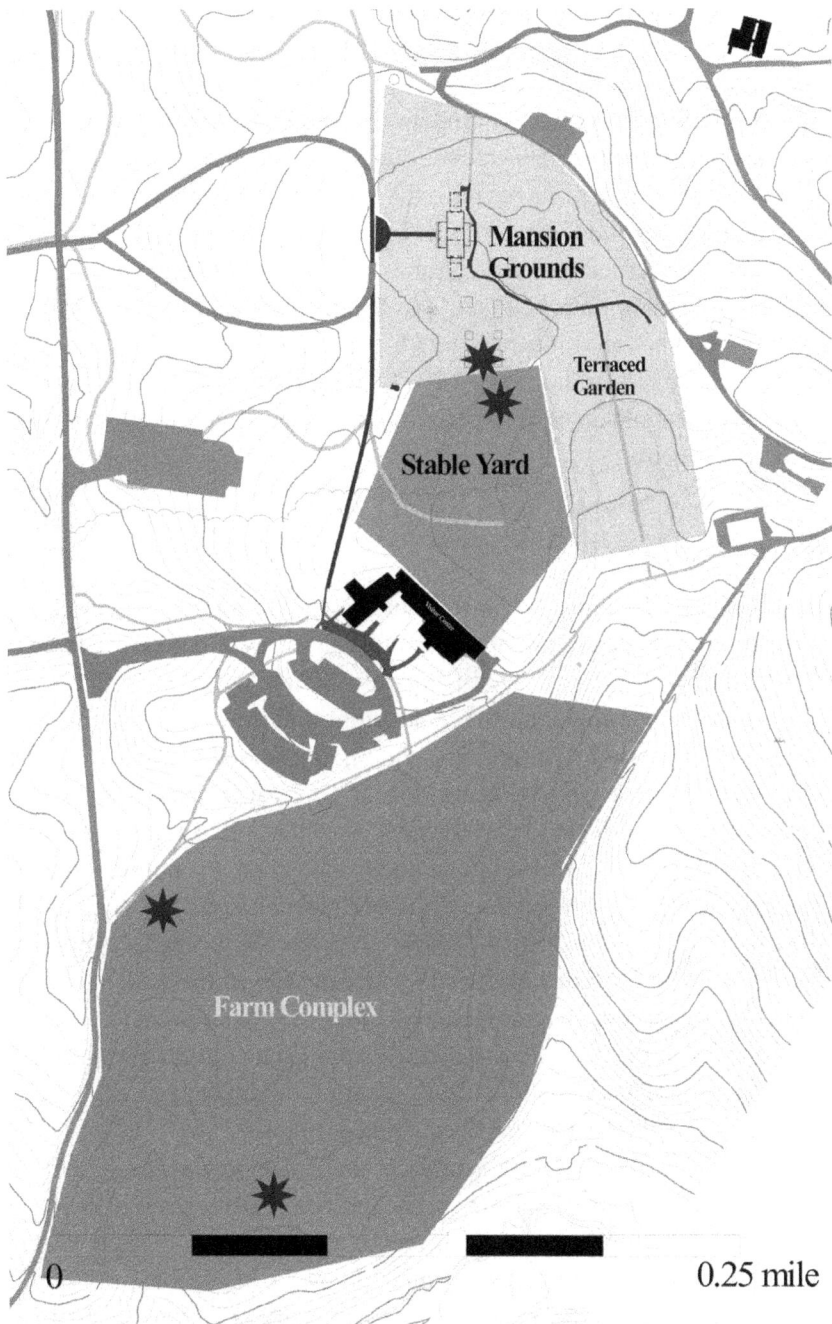

Figure 2.1. Map showing location of slave quarters (stars) excavated at Montpelier as part of 2010–13 enslaved community study. The quarters within the Mansion Grounds were occupied by house slaves, those in the Stable Yard by enslaved artisans, and those in the Farm Complex by field slaves.

beyond Montpelier by including regional and even national scales of comparison allows us to define broader patterns of influences. Here my analysis is aimed at understanding how material culture can reflect how decisions were made to delineate shifting levels of social action within and beyond the plantation. In defining the varying scales of influence, I intend to move beyond the notion that generalized life patterns are directly reflected in patterned material culture—sometimes defined as *habitus* by scholars following Bourdieu (see, e.g., Stewart-Abernathy 2004: 52)—to explore wider actions influenced by a broader narrative of events and historical contexts (Beaudry 2004: 255). To accomplish this, I employ comparative household analysis to place the sites under study within varying scales of influence.

Comparative Household Analysis

In this study, I take inspiration from other scholars looking to move beyond the simplistic assumption that households were defined solely by geographic space and assumed labor roles (Battle 2004: 40) and try to understand how individuals made decisions and were influenced at the level of the household, community, and region, as well as at the broader level of the Atlantic world (Reeves 2011, 2010). I seek to place the households under examination in a larger set of contexts that range from the local market region (defined by the trade networks that a household was in contact with) to the larger Atlantic level (trade networks that connected the communities to the British Atlantic). As such, the spaces these household assemblages occupy at the site level are seen as the nodes for the comparative process. By progressively comparing the households within our study to other excavated assemblages among plantation communities at various scales (local, regional, and Atlantic), we can gain a sense of the connections and relevance for the questions we pose.

Comparative household assemblage analysis serves as the basis for the scalar analysis used in this study. The community scale is defined through comparisons among households defined at Montpelier plantation. Regional comparisons are made between households at Montpelier and others in the Virginia Piedmont, such as at Monticello and other home sites of enslaved families in northern Virginia. While these regional comparisons doubtless combine households in different market regions (Richmond, Fredericksburg, and Alexandria), the regions shared a similar market and trade structures that allowed a wide range of goods to move quickly from the coast to the backcountry, providing the enslaved community access to global goods (Martin 2008: 9, 14, 176). For the Atlantic level of comparison, I draw upon comparative data excavated from home sites of enslaved workers in Jamaica from the same time period. Sites in Jamaica and along the Atlantic Seaboard shared some of the same trade networks with England and had direct connections through trade and the movement of goods, people, and ideas (Carrington 2000: 344). These connections extended beyond trade networks to shared cultural traditions, shared ideology concerning plantation structure, and shared economic structures. In the end, my comparisons place the households at Montpelier into a larger set of relationships that encompass the Atlantic economy of the early nineteenth century.

The idea for looking at a broader set of household comparisons came from my experience in working in Jamaica. For my dissertation fieldwork there, I examined a total of ten household assemblages from two different early nineteenth-century slave settlements (Reeves 2011, 1997). These households were raising families and trading in regional markets at the same time as the households in our current study at Montpelier were carrying out many of the same activities. Despite being over one thousand miles apart and operating in a completely different regional market system, the Jamaica sites produced much the same kinds of ceramics, glasswares, and other household goods as those found in the Chesapeake—which is no surprise, as the Jamaica households were enmeshed within the same economic trade structures as their Chesapeake brethren (Reeves 2011). In addition, plantation production was organized in the same manner, the main difference being size. Most estates in Jamaica relied on sugar production, which required large labor gangs and more-advanced industrial processing areas than existed in the Chesapeake during the same time period (Berlin 1998: 344; Higman 1988: 83). While it is no surprise that these similarities exist (all groups under study were part of the same global economy), there were key distinctions arising from differences in the regional population base and marketing of goods.

Not only were the two regions enmeshed in the same economic networks, there were direct historical links between the two regions. Throughout the eighteenth and into the early nineteenth century, the connection between the Eastern Seaboard of North America and Jamaica was quite close. This connection was not limited to trade but included the exchange of ideas and people. A rather particularistic example of this occurs in the case of James Madison. His Jamaican connection was close because his secretary of the treasury was Jamaica-born Alexander Dallas; Alexander's brother, R. C. Dallas, authored a history of Jamaican Maroons that is still cited today (Dallas 1803). Many of the treatises that were written on Jamaican slavery in the late eighteenth and early nineteenth centuries were circulated along the Eastern Seaboard. When he was secretary of state, Madison wrote a summary treatise based on Edward Long's 1774 three-volume history of Jamaica (Madison 1805). Long's history of Jamaica is a proslavery manuscript that devotes several chapters to making a case for what he perceived as the "debased" culture of slaves in Jamaica and the civilizing effect of slavery (Long 1774). Madison was not alone in his interest in things Jamaican. Ideas regarding views on enslaved Africans, management of slaves, and economic production were shared and exchanged between the regions. Comparisons between the two areas (Chesapeake and Jamaica) reflect a tangible connection that existed between the two regions, which were interwoven with trade, finances, people, and ideas. In addition, there were common cultural elements among enslaved populations in the Virginia Chesapeake and in Jamaica; Igbo influence was predominant in both regions (Chambers 2005; Mullin 2005: 28). This shared ethnic base developed in part because planters in Virginia and Jamaica shared some of the same models for plantation slavery as well as the same trade networks for importation of slaves (Dunn 1972; Eltis and Richardson 2010: 212, 234). With this said, any comparisons made between the two regions need to reflect the proper historical context with citations for specific trade histories, ethnic and regional differences, and scale of economic slavery.

To help establish the proper context for such comparisons, the underpinning for my study comes from a contextual approach via scalar analysis. The goal for this comparative approach is to begin to explain patterns seen in the archaeological record from the most appropriate context. After presenting the following example, I provide the analytical underpinning for my use of scalar analysis.

Ceramics as a Window into the African Atlantic Marketplace

A practical example of scalar analysis can be seen from a broad examination of British goods that were being sold throughout the British Atlantic, most especially in the decorative types of white refined earthenwares produced in England and exported to the Chesapeake and Jamaica. Anyone doing research at late eighteenth- and early nineteenth-century sites in the Chesapeake will be familiar with the predominance of hand-painted cups and bowls at slave quarters. While these were regarded as tea wares by their producers, there was likely a range of uses to which these bowls, saucers, and cups were put by various households (Miller and Earls 2008). In comparison with hand-painted tea wares, the frequency of dip-decorated bowls at Chesapeake sites is quite low. In contrast to this pattern, excavated assemblages from home sites of enslaved households in Jamaica have a much higher number of dipt bowls of various sizes (Reeves 2011). The question arises as to whether this difference reflects regional patterns of consumer choice at market or larger regional patterns of difference between Jamaica and the Chesapeake. A comparison of a wide range of sites from the Digital Archaeological Archive of Comparative Slavery (DAACS) database reveals some interesting patterns.

Data from several sites across Jamaica and the Chesapeake reveal that trade at the global Atlantic scale was the strongest influence on what sorts of decorated ceramics are predominant in household assemblages. Among five house areas on the northern coast of Jamaica and ten house areas in the center part of the island, there is a higher amount of dip-decorated pearlwares and whitewares as compared to hand-painted vessels (less than 40 percent were hand-painted tea wares). In comparison, among enslaved households at both Monticello and Montpelier in the Chesapeake, hand-painted tea wares occur with much higher frequency than dipt wares (more than 70 percent were hand-painted tea wares) (figure 2.2). What is worth noting about these comparisons is that among both Jamaican and Chesapeake households, the predominant proportions of hand-painted tea wares to dipt wares holds fast despite the fact that the various communities had their trade coming from different regional markets. For Monticello, most goods shipped from Richmond; for Montpelier, goods came from Fredericksburg; communities near Manassas traded via Alexandria (Reeves 2010; Wiencek 2012). In a similar fashion, the enslaved communities on the northern coast of Jamaica used Montego Bay as their trade base, and the communities of Juan de Bolas and Thetford used Old Harbor on the southern coast. What is clear among these sets of comparisons is that the trade patterns were the same between local market regions but quite different on a national level.

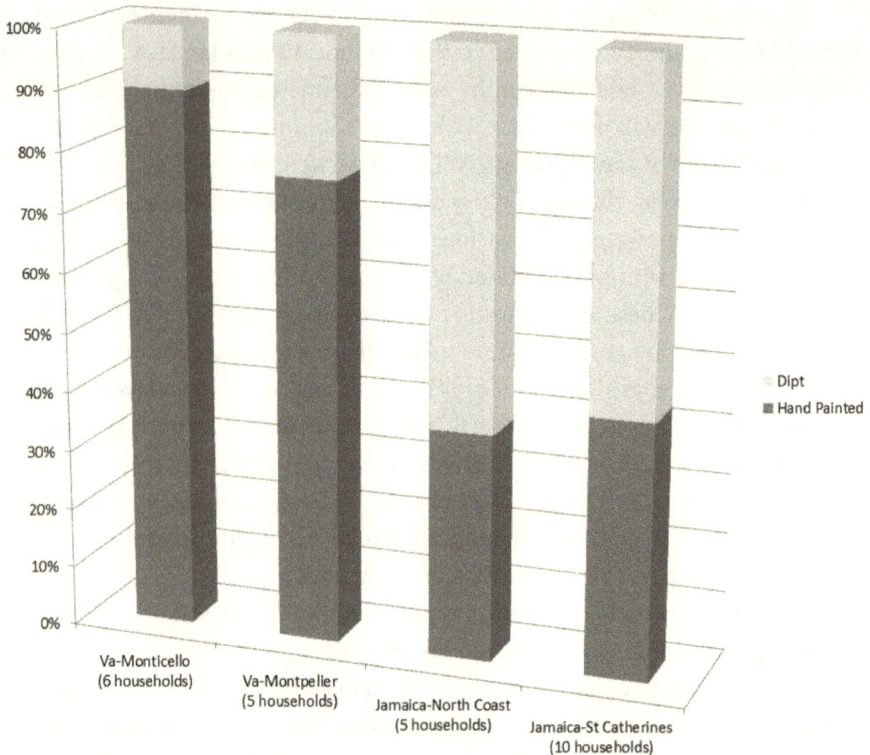

Figure 2.2. Graph showing agglomerated household comparisons of dipt versus hand-painted wares. The household percentages to the left are from sites in Virginia while those to the right are from households in Jamaica. Percentages are based on sherd count.

A possible explanation for this difference in consumer choice might rest in the market structure in Jamaica versus the Chesapeake. Jamaican markets were dominated by Jewish merchants who sold their wares on Sundays at the local slave-run produce markets (Long 1774: 573). These merchants catered almost exclusively to enslaved Jamaicans and likely selected their goods with the aim of satisfying the consumer preferences of the enslaved inhabitants of the island (Reeves 2011, 1997). Whether Jamaican merchants chose dipt wares because of their lower cost in comparison to hand-painted tea wares is difficult to state (Miller 1991). While the color palette of dipt and polychrome hand-painted wares is essentially the same (earth tones from the 1790s to the early 1820s), the decorative scheme is very different. Another major difference rests in the vessel forms available in dipt and hand-painted wares. Dipt wares tend to be part of the tavern-ware family of forms, and bowls (both large and small) and mugs dominate assemblages of both Chesapeake and Jamaican households. In contrast, hand-painted wares are predominantly tea wares, with bowls, cups, and saucers once again being the common form found within enslaved households (Trickett 2013a). What is notable about Chesapeake merchants is that they catered to a much broader range of customers than was true for Jamaican merchants. Chesapeake merchants, the majority of whose customers were free whites, nevertheless frequently sold items to slaves (Martin 2008: 8). With whites being the dominant customer base in terms of both population and purchasing power, the question arises, did this influence what ceramic wares the merchants would purchase for resale to their customers? There does seem to be a pattern (with hand-painted wares predominating), but the explanation possibly rests not with the decorative type but with the vessel form. Hand-painted wares are exclusively tea wares and were for the most part used by the white planter families for the light supper at the end of the day (Carson 1990: 78). For ceramics, the question to ask seems to be whether the robust presence of hand-painted wares in assemblages from enslaved households in the Chesapeake indicates greater assimilation to Anglo-American dining traditions—or did these households use tea wares for alternative purposes in their daily food consumption patterns? The presence of both cups and saucer forms among hand-painted wares at enslaved home sites at Montpelier suggests such assimilation, as does the wear analysis. Of the three household assemblages examined at Montpelier, each contains at least two matching teacups and saucers, suggesting that these pieces were bought as a set to be used together. In addition, little in the way of deep scratching exists on these sets, hinting at their use for beverage rather than food consumption (Trickett 2013a, 2013b). This pattern of purchasing teacups and saucers is supported from store ledgers in central Virginia that record the sale of such items to enslaved individuals (Martin 2008: 185).

Through a household-based comparison on several levels of analysis, we can begin to ask a different set of questions than if we restricted our analysis to assemblages from the same community or localized region. As such, these broader contexts afford the potential to dissect the closed notions of habitus (behavior given meaning by its association with specific sets of material culture) that often surround the study of material culture (Stewart-Abernathy 2004: 53). To equate a specific meaning to a particular piece of material culture limits our ability to understand broader sets of meanings. If we assume that material goods are conditioned by what Mary Beaudry refers to as "action sets," or the specific circumstances surrounding observed material patterns (Beaudry 2004: 255), this broader analysis provides a richer interpretation of their meaning. For this examination of households, analysis at various levels or scales of action provides a useful means of determining meaning and influence. In the case of decorated hollowwares, while the predominance of tea wares among Chesapeake households is likely a result of market forces, it seems to have influenced household use of these wares. Such use of a specific ware type was also doubtless influenced by the close interaction between white and black in the Virginia Piedmont. Such an intense degree of interaction was not as prevalent on the larger slaveholding estates of Jamaica. Use-wear analysis of tea wares found within enslaved household contexts in Jamaica revealed scratches in the bottom of cups, suggesting their use as garnish dishes for meats (Reeves 1997), a practice very different from that found in Virginia. Vessel-use patterns of this sort suggest influences stemming from labor organization, which is determined on a national level and likely reflects social and economic structures that strongly influenced how ceramics were used.

This same scalar analysis can be applied within the community to expose wider influences that often go unseen. Staying with ceramics, one decorative type that is very distinctive at Montpelier is an English-produced transfer print called Bamboo and Peony (figure 2.3). This transfer-printed pattern appears on vessels from numerous early nineteenth-century contexts across Montpelier, ranging from large quantities recovered from a midden associated with the Madisons' dining activities to all of the slave quarters sampled on the property dating to the second and third decades of the nineteenth century. The quantities of this ceramic type recovered from the Madisons' house midden suggest that this large and elaborate set of dinnerware was in frequent use at the Madisons' dinner table, but chipped and broken vessels from this set seem to have been removed from the main house and were used, hidden, or discarded in the slave quarters. The presence of Bamboo and Peony vessels or sherds in every slave household assemblage sampled at Montpelier reflects its daily use and serves as an excellent marker of links between the main house and the community.

The special nature of this set arises from the fact that it was not available through local merchants; documentary sources reveal that it was

Figure 2.3. Davenport Bamboo and Peony plate recovered from the Stable Quarter site at Montpelier. This ceramic has been recovered from every enslaved household context dating to the early nineteenth century.

purchased for the Madisons through an agent who dealt directly with the John Davenport pottery company in Longport, England (Rich and Reeves 2009). On one level, given this dinnerware set's association with the Madison household—we know they purchased it—its use and disposal could be interpreted as having been solely within the purview of the Madison household and its plantation-wide distribution as also controlled by the Madisons. This perspective could lead to the suggestion that its appearance in the quarters came about because the Madisons passed on their cast-off chipped and broken vessels to members of the enslaved community or ordered the disposal of items that may have been "salvaged" for reuse in the quarters. With multiple households and individuals finding intersection through these ceramics, the flow of control becomes complicated. It seems evident that decisions were made at various levels within the households and the wider plantation community, but the question remains as to whether the presence of elements of the extensive Bamboo and Peony dinner set in the quarters reflects decisions made by the original owners or came about through actions of individual enslaved domestics. One potential clue comes from vessel form. Most place settings (plates) were found in the trash deposit associated with the dining activities of the Madisons; plate fragments occur infrequently within the deposits from the slave quarters. In the South Yard and Stable Quarter, there was a disproportionate amount of serving pieces. Bamboo and Peony vessel sherds recovered from the field quarters are exclusively from serving pieces and were highly fragmented and scattered over a wide area. The possibility exists that damaged or broken pieces were brought from the main house to the quarters by enslaved individuals in an effort to remove evidence of breakage—serving vessels being at most risk from more frequent handling during the transport of food courses to the table. As such, individual action is potentially reflected in some vessels arriving at the quarters as broken pieces. In some cases these fragments were discarded beyond the owners' view, in the yards of the house slaves, and in other cases at locales at a distance of up to half a mile away, at the homes of field slaves. Indeed, the most highly fragmented examples of serving vessels were recovered from deposits at the field quarters.

The case of the Bamboo and Peony dinnerware is particularly apt, because this set could only be obtained from direct contact through the Madisons' British merchant factor (Rich and Reeves 2009). Such transactions were completely removed from the local economy and out of the hands of enslaved individuals. With such direct one-on-one transactions available only to the elite (Martin 2008: 45), the breakage of a single dish is enmeshed with the power dynamics of exclusivity of access. Simply put, the Madisons were the only ones who could have obtained this set, and the knowledge of its expense and uniqueness would not have been lost upon the enslaved individuals handling it, as they would have been the ones who unpacked the crates when they arrived; they would have seen for themselves an elegant dinnerware set unlike anything available in local stores. Their response to accidental breakage was tacit acknowledgment of the global networks through which this set arrived at Montpelier. The housework of an individual serving food or washing dishes in the main house can be seen as crosscutting the lines of power and domination of owner and slave, merging into the realm of community networks and power negotiation. Considering possibilities both of reuse and of clandestine disposal allows insights into webs of reciprocity and acts of survival that can be reconstructed across the entire landscape of community power relations. What is clear is that individual action transcended labor roles. Whitney Battle-Baptiste (née Battle) has rightly suggested that household theory is a means to question the standard assumption of dichotomies of field versus house extending from the work regime to community (Battle 2004: 40). In this way, we are using scale to identify where effective action takes place and how material culture is deployed within the realm of class struggle (Beaudry 2004: 255).

Scalar Analysis as a Window into the Household

With these specific examples in hand, one can see that analysis of household assemblages can take place at a variety of levels—whether it be through intercommunity comparisons to assess decision making at the individual level, local differences among plantation communities, or regional differences that are influenced by larger market patterns and availability of goods. To carry out these different levels of analysis on household assemblages, I am guided by what William Marquardt refers to as "effective scale" in human actions (1993: 107). Marquardt defined effective scale as a measure, both temporal and spatial, through which observed behavior (in this case artifact patterns) can be meaningfully understood. What Marquardt and others assert is that we are more likely to be able to ascertain broader social actions that affected what materials are found in archaeological assemblages if we examine these patterns through a range of spatial and temporal scales (McGuire 1994; Marquardt 1993: 111; Reeves 2011, 1997; Wilkie and Farnsworth 1999). In this case the scales through which enslaved households' decisions were made can be seen at the level of the household within the community (enslaved domestic or field workers), the community within the region (different markets based on export ports—Fredericksburg versus Richmond), and the region through national influences (Jamaica versus the Chesapeake in relationship to how these regions were enmeshed in the global economy). Essential to interpreting effective scale is taking into consideration historical context, ethnic identity, differential power relationships, and regional differences.

Such comparisons between regionally disparate households is not new (the DAACS analysis system is predicated on such comparisons)—and articles and papers by authors such as Jillian Galle and others have demonstrated the utility of cross-regional comparison of households to tease out everything from differences in status signaling to the impact of agricultural production on consumption patterns (Galle 2011: 233–237). What I am seeking through such comparisons is to draw out influencing factors on the household, with a heavy emphasis placed on the scale or context from which the patterns can be understood. The goal is to find the effective scale at which daily activities took place—as defined from the multiple dimensions of historical context, power relations, gender influences, and ethic identities. Combining these factors through the lens of varying scale of influence (expressed through various definitions of household, community, and region) helps avert deterministic or essentializing outcomes.

Scalar analysis also has the potential to aid in the archaeological definition of household by defining it at multiple levels of influence—from the local to the global. Many scholars have noted how translating households into an archaeologically defined space can be problematic. In her study of Bahamian households, Anderson saw the plantation as a potential household unit and found the use of the notion of nested households within several contexts to be a useful guide. Such an analytical tool frees the household from being constrained to physical house area (Anderson 2004: 115, 120). Scalar analysis involves essentially the same construct, but it allows us to see households as defined by a wider range of influences both within and beyond the immediate plantation. Using different scales (regional, community, and household) to view the material record of enslaved Africans allows interpretation of various aspects of the whole realm of their living conditions and social relations. In addition, rather than seeing actions as nested within household, community, regional, and global contexts, we could view these various influences cutting across many areas of daily life and acting on housework and life at the same time. If we view access to material culture solely at the household level, we would be blind to differences operating at the community level, such as the impact that different plantation labor systems had on the community as a whole (Reeves 2011). We see the work and daily decisions that households engage in at numerous levels within the analytical framework, from the individual to the global.

These influences extend beyond simply market patterns to daily choices and cultural traditions made by different groups of individuals depending on their place in the class system. Seeking context of household decisions at a variety of scales illuminates numerous aspects of daily life—from crockery in the home to how window glass is a reflection of choice in the home. My next example addresses window glass found at a variety of households. What at first blush seems to be merely an empirical entry into comparative household assemblage analysis (artifact and feature) leads to a contextual analysis providing explanations at various scales (community, regional, and global). In what follows I use scalar analysis of household assemblages to draw out a number of explanations that gain relevance from economic, ethnic, and power-based contexts.

Window Glass—Making Choice in Refined Materials Transparent

In comparing the three different settlement loci for the enslaved community at Montpelier, I expected there to be a correlation between labor role and relative access to material goods. One area where this became quite evident was in the arena of housing. While determined to some extent by the owner, there were choices that individual household groups could make regarding the construction materials used in their home. I sought to find a way to determine choices made by the owner versus choices made by enslaved households. To accomplish this, I studied the assemblages of window glass recovered from a variety of contexts at Montpelier.

By far the most extensive collection of window glass recovered among the Montpelier households came from the South Yard—or the homes of enslaved domestics. The number of fragments of window glass was double the amount that was found at the neighboring log cabin in the Stable Quarter, where enslaved artisans lived. Reasoning through the potential explanations for the relative abundance or absence of window glass at various house sites benefited from scalar analysis. A relatively simple explanation for this extreme divergence is placement on the landscape. The use of more-refined building materials for the residences of enslaved domestics likely reflects their location within the formal grounds of the mansion. Archaeological excavation of the homes here revealed the presence of masonry chimneys but produced no evidence for at-grade hearths, indicating that the structures were raised off the ground with wooden floors and hearths set into joists at floor level. The arrangement of footers suggested a timber frame, not a log-based architectural form. The structural evidence pointed to a high investment in refined materials used in the construction of these homes, along with design elements that were aligned with formal English building traditions as opposed to the local vernacular (Reeves and Greer 2012).

The design and style of these structures is remarkably similar to "ideal" worker housing prescribed in treatises published in England at this time. Such treatises emphasized the need for clean, well-managed housing to ensure the sobriety and health of workers on estates (Wood 1781; Wulf 2011). Research has shown that Madison had access to such treatises, and the fact that these structures are set within the formal grounds of the mansion suggests intentional design. As such, these homes for house slaves were in many ways designed to be viewed as part of the overall formal ordered grounds of the mansion—as an idealized village—and in all ways very different in appearance from the log homes that were common for enslaved peoples in Virginia at that time (Reeves and Greer 2012). In direct view of the terraces and rear lawn, where the Madisons entertained their guests, these cottages were intended to extend the same control the Madisons had over the landscape to the lives of enslaved individuals residing within this space. The proximity to the main house dictated the control over building materials and appearance of these structures. As a result, the presence of window glass at these structures was likely dictated by the owner.

In contrast, the neighboring structure at the Stable Quarter was a more traditional log dwelling with a stick-and-mud chimney, an at-grade hearth, and evidence for clay floors. This structure was outside of the formal grounds of the mansion and located within the stable yard and craft complex—an area between the mansion's formal grounds and the larger farm complex. Its construction using materials requiring little refinement (hewn logs and clay) was typical of enslaved homes across the Piedmont (Finch 1833). While this structure lacked the abundance of window glass found among homes in the South Yard, it did have enough (and in a concentrated area) to suggest the presence of a casement window. The question arises as to whether windows were installed by the choice of the residents or whether they were there because the South Yard's housing was close enough to the main house to be observed by its occupants and guests. Comparisons with other slave quarters across Virginia and Jamaica provide potential clues to help in answering this question.

For comparing the frequency of window glass among sites, I used a ratio of window glass to nails as the standard measure. The ratio of window glass to nails provides a consistent measure, as it tends to neutralize

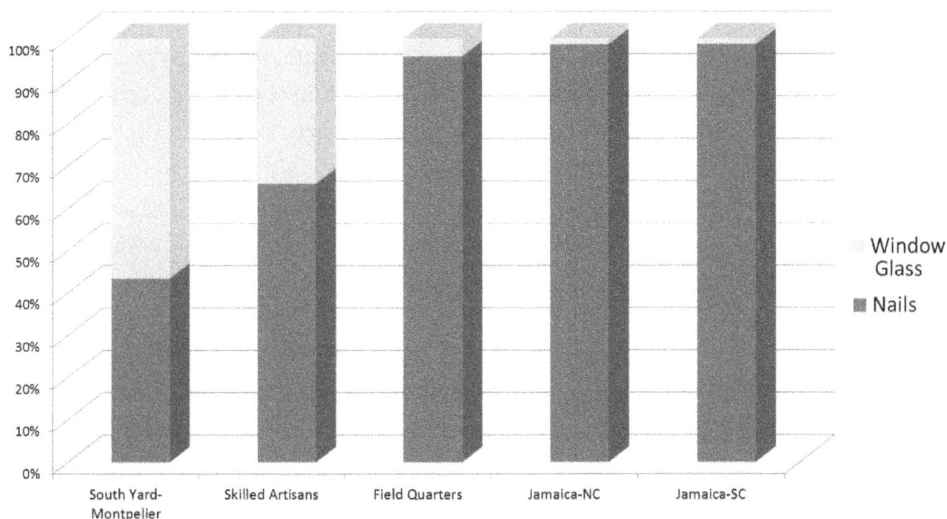

Figure 2.4. Graph showing agglomerated household comparisons of nail to window glass ratios. The household percentages on the left are from sites in Virginia while those to the right are from households in Jamaica. Percentages are based on fragment count.

postabandonment activities (such as decay of structures in situ versus removal of structures from the landscape). In looking at DAACS data with this ratio in mind, one observes that the structures along Mulberry Row at Monticello share certain attributes with the Stable Quarter: they were inhabited by enslaved artisans and were of log construction with clay floors and stick-and-mud chimneys. Given these similarities, the ratio of window glass to nails is a relevant comparison (figure 2.4). Like the Montpelier Stable Quarter, the Mulberry Row quarters have a low ratio of window glass to nails, but there is enough window glass to suggest a casement window. Within view of the main house at both plantations, these quarters were afforded window glass. The question remains: was this decision dictated by the owner rather than the household?

Farther from the main house and at another scale on the community level, the homes for enslaved field workers exhibit distinct patterns. In these cases, homes were located more than a half mile from the main house, and here the ratio for window glass to nails is even lower at both Monticello and Montpelier. The archaeological evidence at both of these plantations points to structures built with a minimum of refined materials. Preliminary analysis of window glass and nails recovered at the field quarters at Montpelier (Trickett 2012) reveals a very low ratio of window glass to nails, with the average ratio being less than 10 percent window glass. The patterns seen at Monticello consistently follow suit for the same time period, with ratios almost half of what was found among skilled artisans at Monticello and Montpelier—suggesting structures with shuttered window openings with little or no window glass.

Field quarters are located far from the designed landscape of the central main house complex. Because of their location at the periphery of the designed landscape, the amount of window glass associated with these houses is a direct reflection of the general lack of refined building materials used in these structures. For such sites in the Chesapeake, distance from the main house and its viewshed is the strongest variable influencing the kind of materials that owners were willing to purchase for building supplies. Still the question remains as to whether field slaves simply lacked the resources to purchase window glass for their houses (something that must be determined through an analysis of their overall access to household and market goods) or lacked the desire to purchase window glass, or whether this decision was solely the purview of the owner.

A comparative example from Jamaica provides potential insight into how such a question can be framed. Despite being thousands of miles from the Chesapeake, Jamaica shared with the Chesapeake common traditions in house construction, based largely on an English model. The main difference occurred in the raw materials used for laborer houses— Chesapeake builders used log construction and Jamaicans for the most part used wattle and daub (Armstrong 1990). Quantified data from slave contexts excavated in central Jamaica (Reeves 2011) analyzed in conjunction with data from Jamaican sites included in the DAACS database reveal that the patterns of frequency of window glass in Jamaican slave housing are very similar to those found among field-slave sites in the Chesapeake (see figure 2.4). Because the homes of enslaved field hands were located far from the main house and hence well out of sight, plantation owners felt little need to invest in refined building materials for such housing.

What makes the example from Jamaica particularly revealing is that households sampled at one particular sugar estate, Thetford, exhibited differences among house areas, some having very high amounts of imported goods with others more reliant on locally made household goods (Reeves 2011, 1997). Within these extreme differences in household assemblages, the ratios of window glass to nails were very similar, with almost no window glass present in any of the household assemblages. Given that some of these households had the economic ability to purchase high-cost items, the choice to not invest in window glass was likely a conscious decision. The independence to choose between purchasing housing materials and purchasing household possessions suggests that the enslaved inhabitants saw housing as outside of their purview or simply beyond their control.

What this example draws us to consider is whether investment in architectural elements was a choice of an enslaved household or of the owner. This also brings us to consider whether architectural tradition was seen by African Americans as being a necessary reflection of status within the community. Certainly our studies at Montpelier have suggested that, as with household status at Thetford in Jamaica, household goods rather than architectural forms were important for status signaling. During slavery, as shown by broader comparisons for the ratios of window glass to nails at various sites, status investment through material culture was confined for the most part to portable items—a necessary survival strategy for people who were considered chattel property and for whom mobility was an ever-present issue. Being able to quickly assemble one's material possessions was a key survival strategy within the harsh environment of British Atlantic slavery, where sale or labor reorganization would mean a change of household. Enslaved individuals would have been quite aware of sashed windows both in their owners' homes and in homes in urban areas. Declining to invest personal resources in nonportable structural amenities seems to have been a common decision made by enslaved individuals.

Conclusion

Scalar analysis of households allows questions to be framed that might not be devised if larger comparisons were not sought. In making comparisons that go beyond our regional studies, I am proposing wider-ranging comparisons that are meant to broaden the context in which we address questions about household assemblages. In asking these questions, the researcher must carefully construct the broader comparisons to take into consideration the context at hand. In the example of comparing different portions of household assemblages between Jamaica and the Chesapeake, the common heritage and economic ties make for a sound basis from which to begin to seek comparisons and to ask a wider range of questions. Such broad comparisons can seek out factors that influenced the presence or absence of certain assemblage traits between the two regions.

I did not intend here for my discussion to become bogged down with the particulars of window glass or ceramics, nor is this an exhaustive study encompassing the full range of comparative analysis that could be extracted from the assemblages mentioned. Rather, I sought to show how comparative analysis on a local and broad scale has utility for drawing out information that might otherwise be overlooked using a more insular focus. The range of historical contexts that are drawn out with broader comparative analysis has the potential to give clarity to questions that might otherwise get lost in the peculiarities of data sets from one plantation or context. In the example of window glass, we can see that looking at the presence/absence of this architectural element across several historical contexts brought out a very different perspective than if we had remained at the comparative scale of Montpelier households alone or even only those in the Chesapeake region.

I would argue that scalar analysis of households allows us to further break down the walls imposed by archaeologically defined households by moving beyond the confines of the immediate community or even regional context to which we often limit our comparisons. The households we examine as historical archaeologists are set in a global context. This wider influence is evidenced by the wide array of material goods that come from across the globe. It would be a mistake to assume that because most early nineteenth-century individuals never traveled more than twenty miles from the home, these individuals were not aware that their lives were situated within a large global context. When we have information that can shed light on the relationship of an individual household to the larger whole, totally new sets of questions emerge that can help us critically evaluate the paradigms we take for granted. By seeking causal relationships that are carefully defined by historical context but are played out on multiple levels, we can begin to refine our understanding of the material phenomena that are the purview of historical archaeology.

Acknowledgments

I thank Kevin R. Fogle, James Nyman, and Mary C. Beaudry for their comments on this chapter and for inviting me to be part of this edited volume. Funding for the research at Montpelier was provided by several sources, including a Collaborative Research Grant from the National Endowment for the Humanities and the Perry Foundation. Research in Jamaica was carried out through a grant from the Fulbright Foundation. Thanks also to Mark A. Trickett, Eric Schweickart, and Erica D'Elia for commenting on earlier drafts of this chapter and to Mark Groover and Kerri Barile for their comments on the later drafts.

References Cited

Anderson, Nesta
2004 Finding the Space between Spatial Boundaries and Social Dynamics: The Archaeology of Nested Households. In *Household Chores and Household Choices: Theorizing the Domestic Sphere in Historical Archaeology*, edited by Kerri Barile and Jamie Brandon, pp. 109–120. University of Alabama Press, Tuscaloosa.

Armstrong, Douglas V.
1990 *The Old Village and the Great House: An Archaeological and Historical Examination of Drax Hall Plantation, St. Ann's Bay, Jamaica*. University of Illinois Press, Urbana-Champaign.

Battle, Whitney
2004 A Space of Our Own: Redefining the Enslaved Household at Andrew Jackson's Hermitage Plantation. In *Household Chores and Household Choices: Theorizing the Domestic Sphere in Historical Archaeology*, edited by Kerri Barile and Jamie Brandon, pp. 33–50. University of Alabama Press, Tuscaloosa.

Beaudry, Mary C.
2004 Doing the Housework: New Approaches to the Archaeology of Households. In *Household Chores and Household Choices: Theorizing the Domestic Sphere in Historical Archaeology*, edited by Kerri Barile and Jamie Brandon, pp. 254–262. University of Alabama Press, Tuscaloosa.

Berlin, Ira
1998 *Many Thousands Gone: The First Two Centuries of Slavery in North America*. Belknap Press of Harvard University Press, Cambridge, Massachusetts.

Bonine, Mindy
2004 Analysis of Household and Family at a Spanish Colonial Rancho along the Rio Grande. In *Household Chores and Household Choices: Theorizing the Domestic Sphere in Historical Archaeology*, edited by Kerri Barile and Jamie Brandon, pp. 15–32. University of Alabama Press, Tuscaloosa.

Carrington, Selwyn H. H.

2000 The United States and the British West-Indian Trade, 1783–1807. In *Caribbean Slavery in the Atlantic World: A Student Reader*, edited by Verene Shepherd and Hilary McD. Beckles, pp. 342–354. Ian Randle Publishers, Kingston, Jamaica.

Carson, Barbara G.

1990 *Ambitious Appetites: Dining, Behavior, and Patterns of Consumption in Federal Washington*. American Institute of Architects Press, Washington, D.C.

Chambers, Douglas

2005 *Murder at Montpelier: Igbo Africans in Virginia*. University Press of Mississippi, Jackson.

Dallas, R. C.

1803 *The History of the Maroons*. A. Strahan, London.

Dunn, Richard S.

1972 *Sugar and Slaves: The Rise of the Planter Class in the English West Indies, 1624–1713*. University of North Carolina Press, Chapel Hill.

Eltis, David, and David Richardson

2010 *Atlas of the Transatlantic Slave Trade*. Yale University Press, New Haven, Connecticut.

Finch, John

1833 *Travels in the United States of America and Canada*. Longman, Rees, Orme, Brown, Green, and Longman, London.

Galindo, Mary Jo

2004 The Ethnohistory and Archaeology of Nuevo Santander Rancho Households. In *Household Chores and Household Choices: Theorizing the Domestic Sphere in Historical Archaeology*, edited by Kerri Barile and Jamie Brandon, pp. 51–74. University of Alabama Press, Tuscaloosa.

Galle, Jillian

2011 Assessing the Impacts of Time, Agricultural Cycles, and Demography on the Consumer Activities of Enslaved Men and Women in Eighteenth-Century Jamaica and Virginia. In *Out of Many, One People: The Historical Archaeology of Colonial Jamaica*, edited by James A. Delle, Mark W. Hauser, and Douglas V. Armstrong, pp. 211–242. University of Alabama Press, Tuscaloosa.

Groover, Mark D.

2001 Linking Artifact Assemblages to Household Cycles: An Example from the Gibbs Site. *Historical Archaeology* 35 (4): 38–57.

Higman, Barry

1998 *Montpelier, Jamaica: A Plantation Community in Slavery and Freedom, 1739–1912*. University Press of the West Indies, Kingston, Jamaica.

1988 *Jamaica Surveyed: Plantation Maps and Plans of the Eighteenth and Nineteenth Centuries*. Institute of Jamaica Publications, Kingston.

King, Julia A.

2006 Household Archaeology, Identities and Biographies. In *The Cambridge Companion to Historical Archaeology*, edited by Dan Hicks and Mary C. Beaudry, pp. 293–313. Cambridge University Press, Cambridge.

Long, Edward
1774 *History of Jamaica*. 3 vols. T. Lowndes, London.
McGuire, Randall H.
1994 *A Marxist Archaeology*. Academic Press, Orlando, Florida.
Madison, James A.
1805 James Madison. Extracts from a History of Jamaica. 1805. James Madison Papers, Library of Congress. http://hdl.loc.gov/loc.mss/mjm.25_1330_1331.
Marquardt, William H.
1993 Dialectical Archaeology. *Archaeological Method and Theory* 6: 100–129.
Martin, Ann Smart
2008 *Buying into the World of Goods: Early Consumers in Backcountry Virginia*. Johns Hopkins University Press, Baltimore, Maryland.
Miller, George L.
1991 A Revised Set of CC Index Values for Classification and Economic Scaling of English Ceramics from 1787–1880. *Historical Archaeology* 25: 1–25.
Miller, George L., and Amy C. Earls
2008 War and Pots: The Impact of Economics and Politics on Ceramics Consumption Patterns. *Ceramics in America 2008*: 67–108. University Press of New England, Hanover, New Hampshire.
Mullin, Michael
2005 *Africa in America: Slave Acculturation and Resistance in the American South and the British Caribbean*. University of Illinois Press, Urbana-Champaign.
Reeves, Matthew B.
2011 Household Market Activities among Early Nineteenth-Century Jamaican Slaves: An Archaeological Case Study from Two Slave Settlements. In *Out of Many, One People: The Historical Archaeology of Colonial Jamaica*, edited by James A. Delle, Mark W. Hauser, and Douglas V. Armstrong, pp. 183–210. University of Alabama Press, Tuscaloosa.
2010 A Community of Households: Early 19th-Century Enslaved Landscapes at James Madison's Montpelier. *African Diaspora Archaeology Network Newsletter*, December 2010. Electronic document, http://www.diaspora.illinois.edu/news1210/news1210.html#1, accessed August 30, 2014.
1997 "By Their Own Labor": Enslaved Africans' Survival Strategies on Two Jamaican Plantations. Unpublished PhD dissertation, Department of Anthropology, Syracuse University, Syracuse, New York.
Reeves, Matthew B., and Matthew Greer
2012 Within View of the Mansion—Comparing and Contrasting Two Early Nineteenth-Century Slave Households at James Madison's Montpelier. *Journal of Mid-Atlantic Archaeology* 28: 69–80.
Rich, Melissa, and Matthew Reeves
2009 Object Report for Dolley's Midden. Archaeology Department, James Madison's Montpelier, Orange, Virginia.
Stewart-Abernathy, Leslie C.
2004 Separate Kitchens and Intimate Archaeology: Constructing Urban Slavery on the

Cotton Frontier, Washington, Arkansas. In *Household Chores and Household Choices: Theorizing the Domestic Sphere in Historical Archaeology*, edited by Kerri Barile and Jamie Brandon, pp. 51–74. University of Alabama Press, Tuscaloosa.

Trickett, Kimberly A.

2013a Out of Site, Out of Mind: An Object-Based Analysis of the Material Culture from a Log Structure for Enslaved Artisans. Archaeology Department, James Madison's Montpelier, Orange, Virginia.

2013b In Plain Sight: An Object-Based Analysis of the Material Culture from Two Duplexes for Enslaved Domestics. Archaeology Department, James Madison's Montpelier, Orange, Virginia.

Trickett, Mark A.

2012 Homes Apart: Excavation of Montpelier's Southeast and Southwest Duplex Homes for the Enslaved Domestic Servants. Archaeology Department, James Madison's Montpelier, Orange, Virginia.

Wiencek, Henry

2012 *Master of the Mountain: Thomas Jefferson and His Slaves*. Farrar, Straus, and Giroux, New York.

Wilkie, Laurie A., and Paul Farnsworth

2005 *Sampling Many Pots: An Archaeology of Memory and Tradition at a Bahamian Plantation*. University Press of Florida, Gainesville.

1999 Trade and the Construction of Bahamian Identity: A Multiscalar Exploration. *International Journal of Historical Archaeology* 3: 283–320.

Wood, John

1781 *A Series of Plans for Cottages and Habitations of the Labourer*. J. and J. Taylor, London.

Wulf, Andrea

2011 *Founding Gardeners: The Revolutionary Generation, Nature, and the Shaping of the American Nation*. Knopf, New York.

3

....

Exploring Household Foodways in the North Carolina Piedmont, 1450–1710

ASHLEY PELES

Can archaeologists do household archaeology without access to the refuse of specific households? This question may sound trite, but the nature of archaeological deposits means that many archaeologists do not have the ability to analyze sites at such a fine-grained scale. The analysis I present in this study arose from exactly this type of conundrum. My initial question was whether there was a social identity that was marked by the types of foods that were consumed by native groups in the Piedmont region of North Carolina and whether this could be used as another way of exploring Catawba coalescence in the eighteenth and nineteenth centuries. Being less worried about the ultimate results and more interested in where such a thought process could take me, I decided to do a reanalysis of a number of previously excavated and analyzed Piedmont sites dating between the mid-sixteenth and early eighteenth centuries. The depth of research and archaeology that has been completed in this area by the Research Laboratories of Archaeology at the University of North Carolina at Chapel Hill means that there is a particularly rich source of data for putting together a synchronic view of native communities (Dickens et al. 1987, 1986, 1985, 1984; Driscoll et al. 2001; Eastman 1999; Gremillion 1989; Hogue 1988; Holm 1994; VanDerwarker et al. 2007; Ward and Davis 1993, 1988; Wilson 1983). After looking through the work that has been done, I chose six sites to use for my analysis: Powerplant (31RK5), Lower Saratown (31RK1), Upper Saratown (31SK1a), Wall (31OR11), Jenrette (31OR 231a), and Fredricks (31OR231). These sites were chosen because they produced large, diverse faunal and floral assemblages.

During the sixteenth through the eighteenth centuries, Native Americans in the North Carolina Piedmont region often resided in palisaded settlements. Refuse features excavated have included sheet middens and pits. Sheet middens of course represent an aggregation of activities, but even the pits are large enough that they have been interpreted as holding refuse from multiple households (Ward and Davis 1993). As a result, an analysis of foodways cannot be done at the level of individual households. Rather than setting aside the perspective of household archaeology for these types of sites, I instead chose to look at site remains as representative of household decisions that have been aggregated at a community level. I do not assume, however, that community decisions are cooperative and without conflict. Various households do not necessarily exist in a "cooperative equilibrium"; practices at a community level invariably involve negotiations and/or assertions of power along multiple axes of identification (Hendon 1996). Archaeological assemblages are therefore the result of the complex web of decisions made by individuals and groups within communities of practice; the nature of Piedmont deposits forces us to remember that households exist within a larger set of cultural practices.

With this being said, there are three themes that inform my analysis of Piedmont communities. The first is an understanding of the challenges of household archaeology and how archaeologists can use a theoretical perspective to confront such challenges. My second objective is to continue the work of other researchers in bringing together faunal and floral analyses (e.g., Reitz and Scarry 1985). As Andrew Sherratt (1991: 221) has pointed out, we need to continually remind ourselves that "people don't eat species, they eat meals." Too often, specialist analyses are presented in isolation not only from each other but also from the rest of the site assemblage. The fact that many faunal and floral assemblages must be sent separately to different researchers makes this somewhat inevitable, as each researcher analyzes the assemblage on his or her own and submits a separate report. This does not mean that we should not continually strive to integrate these sources of information, however (see VanDerwarker 2010). Animals and plants are generally not eaten in isolation from each other, so it seems worthwhile to explore analyses that can move us closer to a meal perspective, rather than a taxa perspective. I do this by incorporating correspondence analysis, which can find relationships among large data sets that are too big to be examined without a computer program. By combining faunal and floral data sets, I look to see whether there are relationships between certain plants and animals and whether the assemblages from different sites are similar to each other.

My third aim is to encourage more use of data from sites that were excavated many years ago. Archaeologists often do broad comparisons of sites excavated from many different time periods, but this does not always imply a reexamination of the data sets themselves. This is especially true when it comes to faunal and floral assemblages. Importantly, there can be various difficulties involved with reanalyzing old data, provided assemblage information is available. Some of the challenges simply involve the investment of a modest amount of time to convert data to digital form. While tedious, this issue is easily remedied. A more difficult issue may be methods of dealing with data that are not comparable. In the data sets I examined, certain plant remains from Piedmont sites were listed only by weight, rather than counts. This problem was also encountered by VanDerwarker, Scarry, and Eastman (2007). Their solution was to produce an average fragment weight and use that to estimate the original number of plant remains. Because our data sets overlap, I was lucky enough to be able to obtain plant count estimates from one of the coauthors and had to do conversions for only one site. In other cases, some detective work may be required to locate original assemblages, and a full reanalysis may need to be done. Regardless of the time and effort that can be involved in making data sets comparable, reincorporating old material is an important step in analysis.

Challenges of Household Archaeology

As the other authors in this volume point out, doing archaeology at a household level is an extremely useful scale of analysis. Most important is a flexibility that is inherent in the term *household archaeology*, which allows archaeologists to apply this perspective to different types of sites and deposits. As with Nyman and Kenline (this volume), a household may be historically linked to a known family and their slaves. At the Keatley Creek site, a prehistoric village site in British Columbia occupied circa 2400–1200 BP, for instance, dwellings housed corporate households whose members included people linked by kinship, client families, and slaves (Hayden 1997). Another example of alternative households is the Boott Cotton Mills boardinghouses in Lowell, Massachusetts. Here, a nineteenth-century textile company housed its workers within a planned community in corporate households (Mrozowski et al. 1989). Each of these types of sites gives rise to particular opportunities and constraints in excavation and analysis. At sites like Keatley Creek and the Boott Mills boardinghouses, it can be difficult to know how kin structures and socioeconomics map onto archaeological deposits, particularly when there may not be discrete household deposits.

It is also important to remember, however, that at most sites, we tend to assume that deposits inform us about particular members of a household (men, women, children, slaves, and so forth). Whether we recognize it or not, when a household is defined as the next unit above the individual (Hendon 1996; Wilk and Rathje 1982), we make assumptions that any patterns we observe are reflective of the people who lived in the house whose remains we excavate. It is important to recognize that household refuse exists in a dialectical relationship between the people producing the refuse and the society of which they are a part. In so doing, we are able to move between different levels of analysis—households define communities as much as they are defined by communities.

One way in which archaeologists have attempted to grapple with theorizing households is to think about what it is that households actually do. As pointed out by Wilk and Rathje (1982), our ideas about households are often colored by our own experiences; members of households may not have resided under the same roof. Instead of automatically associating the household with the nuclear family (however that may be defined), Hendon (1996: 56) considers the "household as an arena of social and economic relations that interacts dynamically with the larger society." Many have seen household archaeology as an answer to investigations at wider scales (community or regional level) that seem to assume a level of homogeneity and cooperation among individuals that is not actually present. As researchers have demonstrated, there is much to be gained from a smaller-scale perspective that allows investigation of topics such as gender, labor, and power across vastly different time periods, particularly through examining synchronic variation (e.g., Groover 2000; Hendon 2010, 1996; Jackson and Scott 1995; Pluckhahn 2010). For these types of analyses, however, we rely on our ability to recognize household artifacts and discrete patterns of refuse. When it comes to faunal and floral remains (as well as other types of artifacts), patterns of discard do not always easily lend themselves to dwelling-level identification. This is also true in terms of the representative numbers of bones and seeds needed to complete a reliable analysis.

Examining sites without clearly delineated refuse requires a broader, aggregated scale of analysis, whereby a theoretical perspective informed by household archaeology can still be useful and enlightening. Households are never completely isolated and must interact with a larger society in the same way that individuals, as a part of society, can never completely disaffiliate from it even if they want to. Thinking about households as being coresidential, as well as the implications of cooperative efforts, thus broadens the possibilities for research and analysis (Hendon 1996). I find this theoretical perspective to be particularly useful in examining native households during the early colonial period in the southeastern United States.

North Carolina Piedmont Sites

Through extensive excavations on protohistoric and early historic-period Piedmont sites, Ward and Davis (1993) have shown that the history of native groups in the Piedmont is complicated and dynamic. The Late Woodland in the Piedmont appears to have been a time of shifting settlement patterns, with unprotected households giving way to communities surrounded by palisades. English settlement in Virginia and Carolina during the early seventeenth century did not strongly affect community settlement, subsistence patterns, or mortality. The acquisition of trade goods by native groups, however, appears to have brought about shifts in intragroup hierarchies, with people gaining new opportunities to earn material goods and prestige. Groups like the Sara engaged in extensive trading with middlemen, such as the Occaneechi, for access to such European goods. The Occaneechi controlled the flow of trade between the English and other tribes in the area, which generally meant restricting access to weapons. Given the importance of the deer-hide trade in the Southeast through the nineteenth century, it is likely that Piedmont peoples were trading various grades of hides and in return receiving beads, copper, and other decorative goods (Ward and Davis 2001). Trade and contact with European groups brought about shifts in some kin patterns as well. Evidence from historical documents indicates that many Piedmont groups traced kinship through the matriline and maintained democratic societies. Alternatively, groups like the Occaneechi and Saponis, both of whom maintained close contact with the English, were reported to have had two kings (Occaneechi) or to have been ruled by a monarch (Saponi) (Ward and Davis 2001).

In broad strokes, the food eaten by native communities stayed fairly consistent throughout the early historical period. Important sources of meat, marrow, and skins were deer, bear, turkey, squirrel, fish, and turtle. Outside the palisade walls, community members grew corn, beans, and squash, practiced silviculture of oaks, hickories, and peaches, and gathered various wild seeds and fruits. It was not until the 1700s that truly drastic changes came to native communities of the Piedmont. Violence that broke the hold of middlemen like the Occaneechi resulted in other Piedmont communities gaining direct access to English traders, facilitating the acquisition of guns, especially. This increased access may also have been a vector for disease, as native deaths increased and changes in mortuary patterns occurred in the Piedmont region during the eighteenth century. Survivors of warfare and disease began to coalesce into some of the tribes we know today, such as the Catawba (Davis and Ward 1991).

Data used here are drawn from numerous sources, including two dissertations (Gremillion 1989; Holm 1994), one chapter in an edited volume (VanDerwarker et al. 2007), and the book *Indian Communities on the North Carolina Piedmont, A.D. 1000 to 1700* (Ward and Davis 1993). In deciding which sites to use for this analysis, I knew it was important to have good representation and good preservation of both floral and faunal remains. This can be difficult to find in the Southeast because of the region's acidic soils, which effectively break down most biological remains. With that in mind, I chose five sites initially to include in my analysis, as well as one other site that provides a comparison: Powerplant, Lower Saratown, and Upper Saratown, all from the Dan River drainage; and Wall, Jenrette, and Fredricks, all from the Eno River drainage (figure 3.1). These sites were occupied over a range of time periods between A.D. 1000 and 1710. While I did not have a particular cutoff for the numbers that were needed, the site with the fewest faunal remains was the Powerplant site, which is also the earliest site and serves primarily as a comparison for the later sites. After Powerplant, the next smallest assemblage consisted of over eight thousand bones, at Upper Saratown (table 3.1).

For botanical data I stayed close to the original analysts' interpretations (Gremillion 1989; VanDerwarker et al. 2007); if the numbers seemed small, but especially if the analyst discussed the remains as being poorly preserved, I generally decided not to use data from the site. One exception

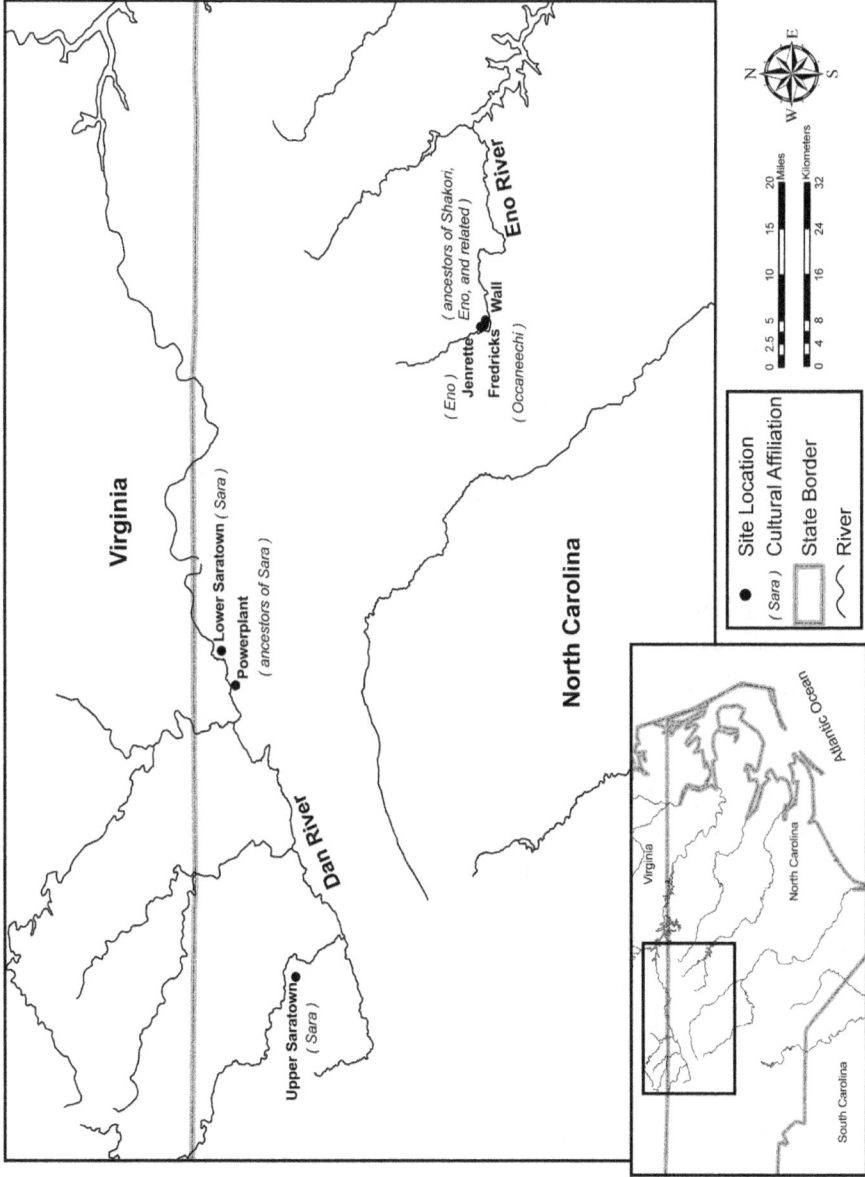

Figure 3.1. Location of archaeological sites used in analysis. Map created by Peter Molgaard.

Table 3.1. Total remains from sites used in analysis

Site name	Occupation (A.D.)	River drainage	Fauna (N)	Flora (N)
Powerplant	1000–1450	Dan River	2,176	475*
Wall	1450–1620	Eno River	29,792	1,926*
Jenrette	1600–1680	Eno River	22,818	3,891*
Lower Saratown	1620–1670	Dan River	32,976	19,565*
Upper Saratown	1650–1710	Dan River	8,353	16,635
Fredricks	1695–1705	Eno River	70,597	10,416*

* Estimated counts. See VanDerwarker et al. 2007.

to this is Lower Saratown: the botanical remains here are few in number, but the assemblage is fairly diverse. For this reason, I felt that it was an important site to include because of the time period represented and the robustness of the faunal assemblage. Obviously these sites represent two different areas of the Piedmont, but besides having some overlap, they also represent different time periods defined by differing access to European trade goods and degrees of interaction with Europeans.

Powerplant is the earliest site and dates to the Late Woodland period; it was occupied between A.D. 1000 and 1450. While the numbers of remains from this site are not large, it is one of the better-preserved sites of this time period to be excavated in the Piedmont region of North Carolina—and the species represented are still fairly diverse. Excavation took place in 1987 essentially as a salvage operation, as two-thirds of the village had already eroded out from the riverbank on which the site was located. Compared to later settlements, houses at Powerplant were smaller and more dispersed. Here, houses were located along the Dan River in a linear alignment. Excavations revealed large storage pits with secondary refuse deposits from which the faunal and floral assemblages originated. Several objects made of animal bone were recovered; this time period in the Piedmont is known for its particularly rich bone- and shell-working tradition (Ward and Davis 1993).

Chronologically, the next site is the Wall site, occupied by the Eno Indians between 1450 and 1620 and located along the Eno River in Orange County. The first excavations here occurred between 1938 and 1941; further excavation occurred from 1983 to 1984, uncovering about 25 percent of the village, including a midden up to 1.25 feet thick that was preserved along a palisade line. The site was a palisaded village where 100–150 people resided; they are thought to have been the ancestors of the Shakori, Sissippahaw, and related tribes. It is important to note here that the analyzed assemblages came from the large sheet midden. Although the context affected the preservation of the samples, there is still good representation of a variety of species. Remains from the 2001–2 field seasons, which came from a number of large pits, have yet to be analyzed (Ward and Davis 1993).

Also in the Eno River drainage is the Jenrette site, which was occupied between 1600 and 1680 and excavated from 1989 to 1990. This site was discovered during testing near the Fredricks site, with excavations aimed at exposing and retrieving feature data as well as assessing village size and internal structure. The Jenrette site is thought to have been occupied by the Eno as well and was also a palisaded village. It seems to have been the location of the earliest regular trade with Virginians; evidence of indirect contact with Europeans comes from peach pits that were recovered here. Peaches are a fruit that spread rapidly following their introduction by the Spanish. The site also produced a few trade goods. In comparison to later sites, here there are not many burials, so it is believed that the residents had not begun to be affected by European diseases. Excavated houses showed no evidence of rebuilding or superimposition, so the excavators believe that the site was occupied for only about ten years. Faunal and floral data analyzed here came from roasting and storage pit features (Ward and Davis 1993).

The next site, Lower Saratown, is located in Rockingham County along the Dan River bottomlands, and it appears to have been occupied from about 1620 to 1670. It was first excavated in 1938 by Joffre Coe and was revisited in 1988, at which time a total of fourteen units measuring 10 × 10 feet were excavated to expose pit features. The site was occupied when European trade goods first appeared in the northern Piedmont; the analysis stressed that little else besides the source of materials seems to have changed from earlier times. The site is thought to have been an intensively occupied palisaded village. The Sara probably obtained their trade goods from middlemen, as indicated by a lack of guns, hatchets, and knives at the site. As at most of the other sites, food remains were recovered from various large, shallow roasting pits that seem to have been used to prepare food for social units larger than the nuclear family, as well as from several storage pits. Some features resemble smudge pits, their contents consisting mainly of charred corncobs and corn cupules. Botanical remains from these features were removed from the current analysis so as not to bias the calculations (Ward and Davis 1993).

Lower down the Dan River is the Upper Saratown site, also occupied by the Sara and dating from roughly 1650 to 1710, although the site was probably not occupied for more than a decade or so. For the Sara, this was a period of far-reaching change. Guns and knives were finally added to the spectrum of trade goods; their presence on archaeological sites such as Upper and Lower Saratown is seen as evidence of the end of the Occaneechi role as middlemen and the beginning of direct trade with the English. Evidence abounds of devastating epidemics; the entire village seems to have been a huge burial site, with every 5-foot excavation unit exposing at least one burial. In addition to being hard hit by diseases, the Sara were also dealing with raids by the Iroquois and Westoes. The Sara continued to follow older practices that involved burying the dead within the walls of the palisade and ritually burning the house in which the deceased had lived. Mortuary and botanical analyses done by Eastman, VanDerwarker, and Scarry (Eastman 1999; VanDerwarker et al. 2007) indicated a shift in feasting practices during this time that they identified as ritual purification and renewal ceremonies held after the deaths of community members. They interpret the shift as evidence for intensification of ritual observances in response to intense distress experienced by the community. In their analyses, these researchers singled out two pit features as ritual deposits; the material from these features was excluded from the present analysis (VanDerwarker et al. 2007).

The last site I analyzed is Fredricks, located less than 450 feet away from the Wall site and excavated between 1983 and 1986. Nearly all of the entire palisaded village was excavated, with the material from forty-seven pits analyzed. This was the home of the Occaneechi after their defeat in Bacon's Rebellion in Virginia; they appear to have occupied this area only from roughly 1695 to 1705. Fredricks was a small settlement, made up of no more than seventy-five people, and was also a palisaded village. The posthole patterns revealed that most houses were circular to oval wall-trench structures, while other houses were recognized by postholes forming a circular structure. Many large storage features were associated with domestic structures; they appear to have been rapidly filled with domestic refuse. This refuse included material from hearths, as well as from cleaning activities in and around structures and perhaps from ritual feasting/refuse deposition, which is why the material in the pits cannot be positively associated with any one structure (Ward and Davis 1988). The large number of storage pits at this site is seen as evidence that people often secreted their food supplies underground while they were away from the village to secure against raiding. The large number of burials reveals that this small community had a very high mortality rate (Gremillion 1989; Holm 1994).

Foodways Analysis

To compare the floral and faunal remains from so many sites, I decided to use exploratory data analysis (EDA), which focuses on summarizing the main characteristics of data, rather than determining statistical significance. Because my data set consists of nominal category counts, I used correspondence analysis, which provides a way to analyze two-way tables by measuring the degree of correspondence between columns (cases) and rows (units). This works well for simplifying large tables that have many cases and/or units and would otherwise be too large to provide easily discernible patterns. Computer programs that run correspondence analysis take multidimensional data and look for relationships between variables that make them redundant, thereby reducing the dimensionality of real numeric data (Shennan 2004). The important starting point for correspondence analysis is to make data comparable, although programs like STATA convert data into percentages/proportions automatically. Results are reported in a table and in visual form, whereby close spatial proximity indicates a close relationship and greater distance indicates a weaker relationship (VanDerwarker 2010). In a more direct sense, the position of the points in visual form is determined by their chi-squared distance from the calculated overall expected average; the longer the distance from the origin, the more any variable deviates from the amount that is expected. Variables that fall close together are similar in their profile, and variables that behave in similar ways (that is, their relative counts are high) plot close together. When variables are at 180-degree angles to one another, it means they are inversely related (Shennan 2004).

To render the botanical and faunal data comparable, I decided to use the number of identified specimens (NISP). For the floral data this research is drawn from, plants are generally reported as number of seeds/fragments. There is no attempt made to calculate the minimum number of individuals (or plants) that it would have taken to create the assemblage, because of both the nature and the inherent difficulty of its use with botanical assemblages. This does carry certain biases with it, which are inherent in any botanical report as well. Plants that may be used as fuel in fires, such as nuts (or at least their shells) and corn, will be comparatively overrepresented because of their likelihood of being charred, whereas other plant remains will be charred only accidentally, so their importance in people's diets will be underrepresented (Reitz and Scarry 1985). This is similar to the problems of using solely NISP in relation to faunal data. Smaller animals require less butchery than do large ones, meaning it is common to recover whole to mostly whole elements of small animal skeletons, making the bones easier to identify. Bones from larger animals are more often butchered and broken down into smaller pieces for cooking; although larger bones may preserve better, they may also be more fragmented, with the result that many bones are classified generically as long bones or as unidentifiable (Reitz and Wing 2008). This points to the importance of having a robust collection as the data are combined in analyses.

Beyond the necessity for developing a comparable metric between floral and faunal data, the species that are included in analysis also play an important role in the reliability of the analytical outcome. With this in mind, I ran my data with two different data subsets. I first combined the data into larger analytical groupings, bringing more of the data available into my analysis. For plants, the groups included mast, garden plot, fruit trees, wild fruit, and wild taxa, while faunal groupings were based on habitat preferences for animals, including aquatic, woodland, and edge habitats. Deer and bear have been kept separate because of those animals' importance in the hide trade with the English; this helps to avoid possible skewing of data. Arranging the data like this has the advantage of including almost all of the faunal and floral data recovered, as well as helping to compare broader subsistence patterns of the households included. In the second analysis, analytical units consisted of the most important plants and animals by ubiquity and biomass, respectively. Plant remains therefore included acorn, hickory, walnut, maize cupules, maize kernels, peach pits, common bean, grape, maypop, and persimmon. For the animals, I compiled data on deer, turkey, bear, raccoon, squirrel, box turtle, and mud turtle. Because all of the study sites are located near major rivers, I decided to also use fish, although I recognize the bias that small differences in preservation can make with this resource. Together, these categories constitute the major food sources on which people focused, rather than the entire range of foodstuffs available for consumption.

Results of Correspondence Analysis

The results of the correspondence analysis show some expected as well as unexpected patterns in the different sites that were examined. Figure 3.2 shows the results of the subsistence plot, which gives a broad environmental view of what people were consuming. The center point on the plot represents the program's calculation of expected proportions for faunal and botanical elements; Lower Saratown is sitting almost on that spot and is the site that comes closest to the expected results for faunal and floral remains. This suggests that in terms of broad subsistence patterns, people living at Lower Saratown followed a strategy of planting, foraging, and hunting that did not strongly emphasize any one strategy over another. The earliest site included, Powerplant (A.D. 1000–1450), and one of the latest sites included, Fredricks (A.D. 1695–1705), cluster together on this plot. They are associated with wild plant taxa, woodland animals, and bear (which can be considered a woodland species). A focus on wild and woodland resources is not surprising for the Late Woodland Powerplant site, which fits in well with Dan River phase eating patterns involving a mix of hunting, gathering, and agriculture (Ward and Davis 1993). It is surprising, however, to see that the dietary patterns of the Occaneechi at Fredricks are broadly similar to those from a much earlier time period and a different river drainage. From what we know historically and archaeologically about the Occaneechi, even after their defeat they are thought to have remained heavily involved in the fur and hide trade (Ward and Davis 1993). Fredricks especially has a high proportion of bear remains, which would have been one of the species targeted for the hide trade. If Occaneechi households spent a lot of time hunting, it would make sense for their diet to be focused on woodland plant taxa and animal species that could have been caught or collected while hunting bears. Additionally, if much of the community was involved in hunting, there would have been less time for people to tend to horticultural plots, making wild plants a more reliable resource.

The Wall and Jenrette sites also cluster, but in the first quadrant of the plot diagram. The associated cluster of taxa are edge habitat animals, deer

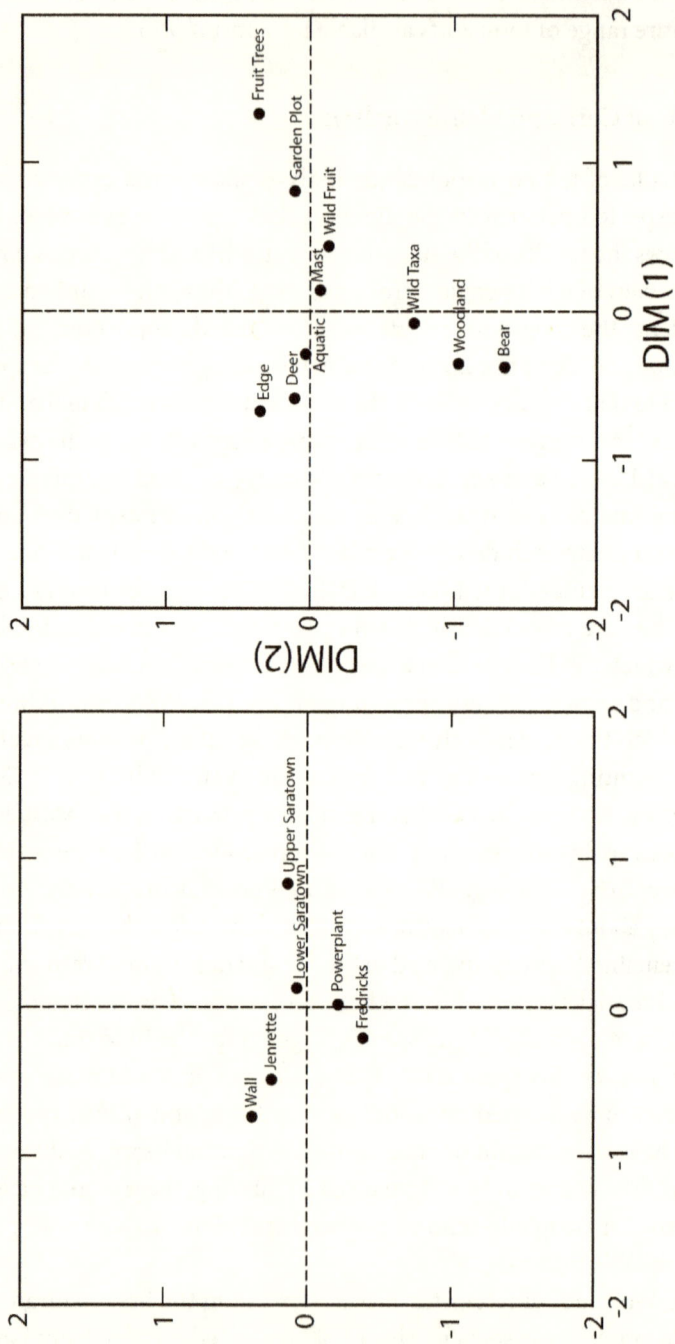

Figure 3.2. Correspondence plot of Piedmont sites and broad subsistence strategies.

(which prefer edge habitats), and aquatic species. Both Wall and Jenrette are located along the Eno River, essentially right next to each other, and are believed to have been occupied by the Eno Indians. Additionally, the two sites were occupied one after the other, with Wall (1450–1620) settled first and Jenrette (1600–1680) occupied next, with some overlap possible. Given that the people who lived here may merely have moved their homes from elsewhere, it is not surprising that households seem to have been pursuing the same broad dietary strategy, focusing heavily on edge habitat animals and deer, as well as taking advantage of the aquatic resources available to them.

The last site represented in this plot is Upper Saratown, which was occupied from 1650 to 1710 and may overlap with Lower Saratown (A.D. 1620–1670) to some degree. There are several Sara sites along the Dan River, so it is unclear whether these were the same people living at different sites, but given that they are thought to have been a part of the same larger community, we would expect them to be following broadly similar subsistence strategies. This is especially so given that the span of time represented between both sites is only about ninety years. Instead, households at Upper Saratown seem to have shifted their diet somewhat to focus on fruit trees and garden plots—essentially a horticulturalist strategy. To some degree, wild fruit and mast trees can also be included in this cluster. Wild fruit trees could have been growing in fallow fields, while mast trees would have been encouraged in a fashion similar to fruit trees.

The second set of correspondence plots is related to the dominant taxa from each site (figure 3.3), which were determined by ubiquity and biomass. Interestingly, Dimension 1 separates faunal resources from almost all flora—at the sites on the left side of the plot (Powerplant, Jenrette, Fredricks, and Wall), people focused on specific animals, while at the sites on the right side of the plot (Upper Saratown and Lower Saratown), people focused more on plants. In this case, the four sites of Powerplant, Jenrette, Fredricks, and Wall all cluster on the left side of the plot, with Fredricks plotting the closest to the expected proportions of taxa in the center. It is not surprising that the three Eno River sites are clustered; people living in almost the same spot along the same river were pursuing the same major types of animals, especially box turtle, turkey, bear, and deer. In contrast, the Dan River is represented by the Powerplant, Lower Saratown, and Upper Saratown sites, which do not cluster at all. Dominant taxa consumed by the people living at Powerplant are much more

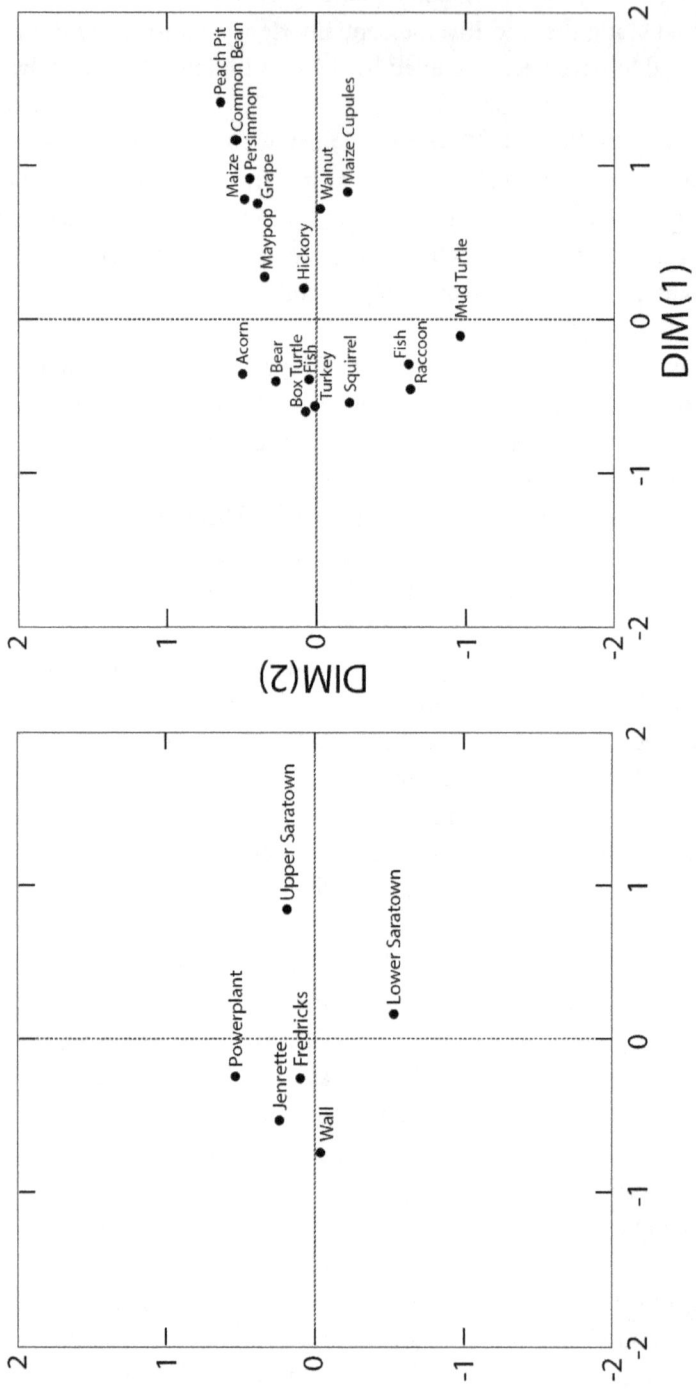

Figure 3.3. Correspondence plot of Piedmont sites and dominant taxa.

aligned with those exploited by people living along the Eno River, with the addition of a high proportion of acorn. Lower Saratown is off by itself, with some overrepresentation of plant remains (likely walnut and maize cupules), as well as mud turtle, raccoon, and fish. The increased focus on plants at Upper Saratown is well illustrated in this dominant taxa plot as well, with the inhabitants consuming much more than the expected amounts of plants for all taxa considered. Households in this palisaded village seem to have been very focused on the food available in the immediate environs of the village in garden plots and orchards, a result that mirrors the general subsistence plot in figure 3.2.

Discussion

One way that faunal and botanical assemblages have been analyzed is to look for patterns related to environmental zones (e.g., Gremillion 1989; Holm 1994), based on the assumption that people's diets will be composed of what is available where they live. While my analysis was not specifically designed to test this theory, aspects of it are applicable. Three sites examined are located along the Dan River (Powerplant, Lower Saratown, and Upper Saratown), and the other three sites are located along the Eno River (Wall, Jenrette, and Fredricks). If diet was based solely on what could be obtained in the immediate environment, we might expect sites to cluster according to river drainage and to have similar proportions of taxa. This does happen in the dominant species plot of faunal taxa for Wall, Jenrette, and Fredricks. This is not surprising, given that most animals could be hunted in similar areas around these villages and all the species represented are known to have been important to native groups. That two groups of people at three different sites were naturally following similar consumption habits may be too easily assumed, however, and it is important to remember to ask ourselves why they would have been eating the same things over vastly different time periods, with different historical events occurring during each.

In contrast, the Dan River sites do not cluster together at all, regardless of which correspondence plot is examined, which indicates that in this instance environmental zone as a determinant of diet cannot be taken as a given. People living at the Powerplant site in the Late Woodland period focused on wild and woodland resources rather than on horticulture, a pattern that shifted at Lower Saratown, where people were consuming a variety of plants and animals from all different types of habitats. Their probable descendants shifted their diet to focus on plants grown in garden plots. This was a period of intense stress for the Sara, who experienced high mortality rates from disease, increased raiding from groups like the Iroquois and Westoes, and direct trade with the English (Ward and Davis 1993). This could have meant that the members of the community focused their energies on obtaining resources close to home so that they would be close enough to retreat to the fortified village to protect themselves and their families in case of an attack. This may be why no Late Saratown features were found outside of the palisade; people living here during the Early Saratown phase (circa 1450–1620) appear to have engaged in processing activities outside of the palisaded compound (Eastman 1999).

In terms of a broader subsistence strategy, while we already know that the Dan River sites do not cluster (although here Powerplant and Lower Saratown are similar to each other), the Eno River sites reveal some interesting patterning. The Wall and Jenrette sites reflect the shared cultural affiliation of the group who inhabited them. Earlier analyses stress that the lives of the Eno at this point seem to have been little touched by Europeans; trade seems to have occurred through middlemen, which may have spared the Eno heavy mortality related to disease. The end of the Jenrette occupation occurred around the same time that Bacon's Rebellion (1676) broke the power of the Occaneechi, opening new opportunities for trading, while at the same time people living in the Piedmont were no longer protected by the Occaneechi from heavy raiding by other groups. The lack of a subsistence shift among the Eno sites may result from their geographic location and time period; a comparison to the next historical site occupied by the Eno may have presented a very different dietary picture. When the Occaneechi moved into Fredricks, while the main taxa they focused on remained the same, the broader subsistence strategy that families pursued was very different from that of the Eno Indians. The subsistence strategy indicated by the woodland animals including bear, as well as the wild plants that the Occaneechi focused on, closely resembled the subsistence strategy pursued by the families living at Powerplant two hundred years before. With their prior position as middlemen to the English traders, the Occaneechi would have been heavily involved in the hide trade for many years. Without a comparison to earlier Occaneechi sites, we cannot be certain how long-standing their dietary pattern was, but it likely remained fairly consistent throughout this period of heavy trade. By the time the Occaneechi moved to Fredricks, their dietary pattern focused on woodlands may have been well established from the point of view of the families actually practicing it.

Understanding the different focus of Occaneechi dietary patterns helps to further illuminate the lives of community and household members. At a community level, the structure of Fredricks is strikingly similar to that of Upper Saratown, which was occupied at almost the same time. Both communities lived in villages with a central plaza, and a few domestic features and houses around the plaza were associated with storage pits and shallow basins. Households were also dealing with similar circumstances of death and disease, the reaction to which seems to have been manifested in repeated feasting. While the specific construction techniques of houses are different and the types of ceramics within the features are different, the food patterns have been interpreted as largely similar. Correspondence analysis clearly illustrates that there were differences in the ways in which households responded to their historical circumstances, differences reflected in their meals. Households at Upper Saratown seem to have turned inward to respond to death and disease, avoiding processing activities outside of their palisade and focusing on foodstuffs that could have been grown/collected/hunted close to their homes. In contrast, the people living at Fredricks appear to have maintained an outward gaze, seeing survival as rooted in engagement with British traders, which meant access to large amounts of trade goods. Unfortunately, excavations did not extend far enough outside of the palisade to permit a determination of whether community members maintained activities outside of the protection of their walls. Regardless, the strong focus of the Occaneechi on woodland species and bear would have required significant time away from the village for hunting parties. A parallel piece of evidence is the fact that, even after their defeat in Bacon's Rebellion, the Occaneechi were still able to restrict trade goods available to groups like the Sara. Firearms, ammunition, metal objects, and white ball clay pipes were all more common at Fredricks than at other Late Contact period sites in the Dan River drainage. So while households continued to maintain garden plots, to collect plants, and to hunt nearby, members of the community engaged in hunting to a degree that is reflected in both the correspondence plot and the artifacts recovered from their village.

The larger pattern shown here is that while subsistence strategies in the Piedmont region of North Carolina seem very similar at a broad level, they are considerably more variable at a community level. In the first correspondence analysis (figure 3.2), focusing on broad subsistence strategies, Dimension 1 seems to separate wild from cultivated resources (fallow garden plots would have been an ideal habitat for wild fruits). Dimension 2 then further separates cultivated plants and the animals that would have been attracted to those types of edge environments from wild resources that were less managed. Wall and Jenrette cluster, which is expected given that they were occupied sequentially and by the same cultural group. Unexpectedly, Fredricks (which is located next to Jenrette) clusters with Powerplant, likely because of different strategies followed as a result of trade with the English. Further, Lower Saratown and Upper Saratown do not cluster at all, which may be explained by changes in subsistence strategies the Sara adopted in reaction to the disruptions caused by death and disease.

The second correspondence analysis (figure 3.3), which looks at dominant taxa, mirrors figure 3.2 in some ways; Dimensions 1 and 2 tend to divide wild and cultivated resources in similar ways. The groupings of some sites change slightly, however, testifying to a targeting of specific animals or plants by each community. Powerplant, Jenrette, Fredricks, and Wall all cluster in a large grouping, with Powerplant households specifically focused around acorn and Wall households targeting squirrel and turkey. Once again, Lower and Upper Saratown show very different dietary focuses, with Lower Saratown residents spending more time acquiring aquatic resources and Upper Saratown families focused on cultivated plots close to their protected village.

Conclusions

So, can household archaeology be done without access to specific households? Given the flexibility of the term *household* and the different theoretical perspectives that household archaeology encompasses, I think it clearly can. While the features from which I have drawn my data cannot be connected to individual households, and certainly not to nuclear families, a theoretical perspective focused around households provides an opportunity to look at village-wide data as resulting from the collective decisions of households within the community. While this may seem simplistic, it offers a useful way to remember that households and their members had agency within the communities they were living in, and responded to (and were affected by) historical processes in ways that could result either in maintenance of traditional foodways or in dietary shifts within broad subsistence patterns. Where shifts occurred, they seem to have resulted from a combination of both internal and external pressures. At a regional level, we know that from the Late Woodland period to the contact period, people seem to have been consuming more hickory nuts and fewer acorns and placing a greater importance on farmed and horticultural plants (Scarry 2003). While we do not know the reasons for this, after European intrusion we have documents that can point to more-specific influences of change. In the case of the Occaneechi, we have a good idea about when they began living at Fredricks, why they moved there, and what activities they were involved in. Although their subsistence pattern could be looked at as a return to more-"traditional" ways of living, it can also be understood as an adaptation that allowed families to stay involved in the trade that had enriched them in previous years. The need to secure hides to exchange for guns for self-defense during a period of dislocation and upheaval may have limited the options open to the Occaneechi. The Sara, who lived along the Dan River, shifted their subsistence strategies at the same time that we have strong historical data that their lives were changing in drastic ways. Other analyses of Upper Saratown have looked at the intense feasting that seems to have occurred there, likely in response to violence and death. Researchers have interpreted the food remains from two pits containing waste from episodes of feasting as evidence of rejection of European food (mainly peaches) and the development of a new pattern that focused on native domesticates (VanDerwarker et al. 2007). That this focus took place in a new direction, rather than a return to "traditional" ways, is reflected in the subsistence correspondence plot, which shows that Upper Saratown is different from every other site in terms of food remains.

What correspondence analysis seems to be able to show, then, are shifts in subsistence patterns that, at a broader scale, are seen as being fairly similar. In other instances, it provides a stronger case that eating patterns among these groups truly remained consistent over a wide swath of time. Perhaps most important, however, is that no particular subsistence pattern completely dropped out in any period; families continued to hunt in different ecological areas, to plant food, and to tend to trees. What could and did change in various time periods and with different groups was which strategies were more strongly emphasized. This points to the wide range of knowledge that families possessed, as well as to the adaptability that was inherent in any subsistence strategy being used. We know that different things happened from a historical perspective, inside communities and outside, regardless of whether we have documents through which to know the events or whether we can only make speculations based on the artifacts recovered. People responded to change in the best ways they knew how, which sometimes meant adopting an entirely new dietary strategy and at other times resulted in reintroducing the foodways of their ancestors. By looking more deeply into the data we already have available, we can take broad, region-level patterns and break them down into community-specific patterns, and we can gain a better idea of how similar or different these different community patterns of practice may have been.

Acknowledgments

I would like to thank James Nyman, Kevin Fogle, and Mary Beaudry for giving me the opportunity to join their session and for working tirelessly on such a thoughtful volume. I would also like to thank the Research Laboratories of Archaeology at the University of North Carolina, Chapel Hill, in particular R. P. Stephen Davis Jr. and C. Margaret Scarry. Without the raw data they so willingly supplied to me, this chapter would not have been possible. In addition, I am grateful to Peter Molgaard for taking the time to produce my site location map.

References Cited

Davis, R. P. Stephen, Jr., and H. Trawick Ward
1991 The Evolution of Siouan Communities in Piedmont North Carolina. *Southeastern Archaeology* 10 (1): 40–53.
Dickens, Roy S., Jr., H. Trawick Ward, and R. P. Stephen Davis Jr.
1985 *The Historic Occaneechi: An Archaeological Investigation of Culture Change. Preliminary Report of 1985 Investigations.* Research Report 2. Research Laboratories of Archaeology, University of North Carolina, Chapel Hill.
1984 *The Historic Occaneechi: An Archaeological Investigation of Culture Change. Preliminary Report of 1984 Investigations.* Research Report 1. Research Laboratories of Archaeology, University of North Carolina, Chapel Hill.
Dickens, Roy S., Jr., H. Trawick Ward, and R. P. Stephen Davis Jr. (editors)
1987 *The Siouan Project: Seasons I and II.* Monograph Series 1. Research Laboratories of Anthropology, University of North Carolina, Chapel Hill.

1986 *The Historic Occaneechi: An Archaeological Investigation of Culture Change. Final Report of 1985 Investigations.* Research Report 4. Research Laboratories of Archaeology, University of North Carolina, Chapel Hill.

Driscoll, Elizabeth, R. P. Stephen Davis Jr., and H. Trawick Ward

2001 Piedmont Siouans and Mortuary Archaeology on the Eno River, North Carolina. In *Archaeological Studies of Gender in the Southeastern United States*, edited by Jane M. Eastman and Christopher B. Rodning, pp. 127–151. University Press of Florida, Gainesville.

Eastman, Julia

1999 *The Sara and Dan River Peoples: Siouan Communities in North Carolina's Interior Piedmont from A.D. 1000 to A.D. 1700.* PhD dissertation, University of North Carolina at Chapel Hill. ProQuest, UMI Dissertations Publishing, 9954626.

Gremillion, Kristen Johnson

1989 *Late Prehistoric and Historic Period Paleoethnobotany of the North Carolina Piedmont.* PhD dissertation, University of North Carolina at Chapel Hill. ProQuest, UMI Dissertations Publishing, 9032969.

Groover, Mark

2000 Creolization and the Archaeology of Multiethnic Households in the American South. *Historical Archaeology* 34: 99–106.

Hayden, Brian

1997 Observations on the Prehistoric Social and Economic Structure of the North America Plateau. *World Archaeology* 29: 242–261.

Hendon, Julia

2010 *Houses in a Landscape: Memory and Everyday Life in Mesoamerica.* Duke University Press, Durham, North Carolina.

1996 Archaeological Approaches to the Organization of Domestic Labor: Household Practice and Domestic Relations. *Annual Review of Anthropology* 25: 45–61.

Hogue, Susan Homes

1988 *A Bioarchaeological Study of Mortuary Practice and Change among the Piedmont Siouan Indians.* PhD dissertation, University of North Carolina at Chapel Hill. ProQuest, UMI Dissertations Publishing, 8914429.

Holm, Mary Ann

1994 *Continuity and Change: The Zooarchaeology of Aboriginal Sites in the North Carolina Piedmont.* PhD dissertation, University of North Carolina at Chapel Hill. ProQuest, UMI Dissertations Publishing, 9430835.

Jackson, H. Edwin, and Susan Scott

1995 Mississippian Homestead and Village Subsistence Organization: Contrasts in Large-Mammal Remains from Two Sites in the Tombigbee Valley. In *Mississippian Communities and Households*, edited by J. Daniel Rogers and Bruce D. Smith, pp. 32–57. University of Alabama Press, Tuscaloosa.

Mrozowski, Stephen A., E. L. Bell, M. C. Beaudry, D. B. Landon, and G. K. Kelso

1989 Living on the Boott: Health and Well Being in a Boardinghouse Population. *World Archaeology* 21: 289–319.

Pluckhahn, Thomas
2010 Household Archaeology in the Southeastern United States: History, Trends, and Challenges. *Journal of Archaeological Research* 18: 331–385.
Reitz, Elizabeth J., and Margaret C. Scarry
1985 *Reconstructing Historic Subsistence, with an Example from Sixteenth-Century Spanish Florida.* Special Publication 3. Society for Historical Archaeology, Glassboro, New Jersey.
Reitz, Elizabeth J., and Elizabeth S. Wing
2008 *Zooarchaeology.* 2nd edition. Cambridge University Press, Cambridge.
Scarry, C. Margaret
2003 Patterns of Wild Plant Utilization in the Prehistoric Eastern Woodlands. In *People and Plants in Ancient Eastern North America*, edited by Paul E. Minnis, pp. 50–104. Smithsonian Institution Press, Washington, D.C.
Shennan, Stephen
2004 *Quantifying Archaeology.* 2nd edition. Edinburgh University Press, Edinburgh.
Sherratt, Andrew
1991 Paleoethnobotany: From Crops to Cuisine. In *Paleoecologia e arqueologia II: Trabalhos dedicados a. R. Pinto de Silva*, edited by F. Queiroga and A. P. Dinis, pp. 221–236. Centro de Estudos Arqueologicos Famalicences, Vila Nova de Famalicao, Portugal.
VanDerwarker, Amber
2010 Simple Measures for Integrating Plant and Animal Remains. In *Integrating Zooarchaeology and Paleoethnobotany: A Consideration of Issues, Methods, and Cases*, edited by Amber M. VanDerwarker and Tanya M. Peres, pp. 65–74. Springer, New York.
VanDerwarker, Amber, C. Margaret Scarry, and Jane Eastman
2007 Menus for Families and Feasts: Household and Community Consumption of Plants at Upper Saratown, North Carolina. In *We Are What We Eat: Archaeology, Food, and Identity*, edited by Kathryn Twiss, pp. 16–58. Occasional Paper 34. Center for Archaeological Investigations, Southern Illinois University, Carbondale.
Ward, H. Trawick, and R. P. Stephen Davis Jr.
2001 Tribes and Traders on the North Carolina Piedmont, A.D. 1000–1700. In *Societies in Eclipse: Archaeology of the Eastern Woodland Indians, A.D. 1400–1700*, edited by David S. Brose, C. Wesley Cowan, and Robert C. Mainfort, pp. 125–142. Smithsonian Institution Press, Washington, D.C.
1993 *Indian Communities on the North Carolina Piedmont, A.D. 1000 to 1700.* Monograph 2. Research Laboratories of Anthropology, University of North Carolina, Chapel Hill.
Ward, H. Trawick, and R. P. Stephen Davis Jr. (editors)
1988 Archaeology of the Historic Occaneechi Indians. *Southern Indian Studies* 36–37: 1–128.
Wilk, Richard R., and William L. Rathje
1982 Household Archaeology. *American Behavioral Scientist* 25: 617–639.
Wilson, Jack H., Jr.
1983 A Study of Late Prehistoric, Protohistoric, and Historic Indians of the Carolina and Virginia Piedmont: Structure, Process, and Ecology. Unpublished PhD dissertation, Department of Anthropology, University of North Carolina, Chapel Hill.

4

....

Landschaft and Place-Making at George Washington's Ferry Farm

JAMES A. NYMAN AND BROOKE KENLINE

Situated on a bluff above the Rappahannock River, the site called Ferry Farm has been a place of human habitation almost continuously for over eight thousand years. At Ferry Farm one experiences a phenomenological connection with place. It is a feeling you get when standing on the bluff edge just above the river gazing at the nearly unobstructed view of historic downtown Fredericksburg, Virginia, on the opposite bank. Few structures are around you on the bluff edge. Instead the fields above the river are open, expansive, and quiet, except for the hum of cars traveling the Kings Highway (Route 3) behind you. Ferry Farm is not as highly trafficked as other historic Virginia plantations associated with American presidents, such as Thomas Jefferson's Monticello in Charlottesville and James Madison's Montpelier outside the town of Orange. Here, a visitor is just as likely to encounter deer or even the occasional black bear as another person.

Where you stand is a place of veneration, however: there is a certain weight associated with the land upon which our nation's first president spent his childhood. The Washington family presence is palpable in this place of reverence. The feeling you achieve standing there on the bluff edge is the experience of *being* in this place, what Ingold and Thomas refer to as *dwelling* (Ingold 2005, 1993; Thomas 2008).

Julian Thomas (2008: 303) writes that places emerge out of the "*background* of the landscape" (emphasis in the original) as something we "already understand to some degree." Visitors to Ferry Farm do not imbue the land with meaning and in turn make it *place*. Instead, they experience it as place because there is already an inherent meaning in the land that intersects with memory and the process of remembering. Thomas (2008:

303) points out that we do not experience the land as if it were divorced from history or tradition—our familiarity with this place has been inherited, passed down, and revealed to us through seemingly mundane engagement such as taking a simple stroll across Ferry Farm. Walking there along the bluff edge, experiencing your bodily presence in this place, while picking up on the cues that remind you that the land you tread upon has a deep history and above all else is a monument, you have engaged with the process of dwelling, and in turn *place* is revealed to you (see Thomas 2008).

For well over two hundred years, this land has been associated with the Washington family in general, but it is more specifically associated with the boyhood of George Washington. This connection is emphasized on pamphlets, on road signs, and by the sign at the front gates of the property: "George Washington's Boyhood Home at Ferry Farm." As one Ferry Farm archaeologist mentions in a video posted to the George Washington Foundation website (2012), even when you uncover artifacts through excavation at the site, "you are always thinking George Washington." Ferry Farm today is set up primarily as a monument to our first president; reminders of this occur across the landscape both in the broader context of the Fredericksburg landscape and across the bluff top at the Ferry Farm site. Knowing that this place is a monument is very much a part of the experience of being here.

A sense of place emerges from the intersection of the experience of the land (picking up on cues) and memory (Van Dyke 2008: 278). In the case of Ferry Farm, the George Washington Foundation and the archaeologists it employs are actively engaged in the process of accessing and constructing memories about this place that inform the experience and meaning visitors take away. In turn, the meaning that is revealed to visitors through their experience of dwelling in this place structures, in part, how they behave.

As a culture we revere our founding fathers. The presidential properties Ashlawn-Highland, Ferry Farm, Montpelier, Monticello, Mount Vernon, Wakefield, and the Woodrow Wilson Birthplace cumulatively draw thousands of visitors every year. Visitors for the most part behave in a certain way as they experience history as it is presented to them and have the meaning of these places revealed to them. As visitors to this "hallowed ground" (Journey Through Hallowed Ground Partnership 2014) they are provided with neat walkways to stroll, roped-off areas to avoid, reenactors to help make "the past come alive," and special trash disposal areas and/or receptacles to keep these monuments neat and clean. Visitors to places like Ferry Farm are not likely to throw their trash just anywhere but instead make conscious or unconscious efforts to dispose of their refuse in specific places. This behavior is largely routinized among visitors when visiting such places, structured by external and internal forces that may not be entirely understood on the conscious level. Such behaviors are likely influenced by how visitors feel about the places, in the context of the larger social and cultural landscape of the present day that venerates presidential sites as hallowed ground.

Ruth Van Dyke (2008: 277) writes that "landscapes are meaningfully constituted physical and social environments. . . . As humans create, modify and move through a spatial milieu, the mediation between spatial experience and perception reflexively creates, legitimates, and reinforces social relationships and ideas" (see also Bourdieu 1977). Clearly, this is the case today among visitors to places like Ferry Farm, but can we extend this logic to the past? What about the other inhabitants who established their homes at Ferry Farm prior to and following the Washington occupation? How did the residents of these homes engage with the process of dwelling in this place within the context of the political, economic, and social climates of their eras? How can archaeologists uncover the sorts of meaning these people experienced as they actively shaped their household identities while reinforcing their connection to the larger social and cultural landscape? These are the types of questions we seek to answer as we investigate the connection between seemingly mundane routinized behaviors such as the disposal of rubbish and larger cultural processes such as the formation of household identities and to place in the past.

Landschaft, Ritualized Activities, and the Process of Place-Making

Archaeologists take it as a given that data recovered from accumulated domestic refuse, representing anything from short-term camp sites to entire communities, is of enormous scientific value. Domestic refuse— meaning the materials contained in areas where household trash accumulates and the behavioral patterns they inform us about—is significant in many ways. Recent studies using data recovered from domestic refuse deposits have addressed such topics as identity and ethnicity, labor, hierarchy, and inequality (e.g., Beaudry 2004, 1999; Beaudry and Mrozowski

1989; Heath 2010; Heath and Bennett 2000; Hendon 2006; Jamieson 2002; Lawrence 1999; Lydon 2009; Prosser et al. 2012; Rodman 1992; Wesson 2008; Wurst 1999; Young 2004). This research reveals how the seemingly mundane practices surrounding daily refuse disposal can be used to make compelling inferences about the underlying structures, practices, and cultures of past societies at multiple scales. Two of historical archaeology's most seminal works, *In Small Things Forgotten: An Archaeology of Early American Life*, by James Deetz (1996), and *Method and Theory in Historical Archaeology*, by Stanley South (1977), are perfect and somewhat disparate examples of how archaeologists use refuse discard patterning to make inferences about past human behaviors.

Deetz (1996: 172–174) draws attention to the difference between undifferentiated trash disposal practices versus compartmentalized refuse discard in circumscribed features such as trash pits. Deetz's hypothesis is founded on the premise that in New England prior to 1750 people discarded their daily rubbish as undifferentiated sheet refuse around households with seemingly little concern about the ways trash might interfere with daily life. In response to the emerging Georgian worldview in the mid-1700s, people, Deetz asserts, began to dispose of their trash in neat trash pits in response to population increases and peer pressure. South (1977: 47–48) takes a contrary position. Following a behavioral approach to the archaeological record (see Schiffer 2002), South identifies pre- and post-1750 refuse patterns at colonial Brunswick Town, North Carolina, that exhibit the kind of secondary refuse disposal practices associated with the purposeful disposal of rubbish in differentiated midden areas and even tertiary disposal following landscaping efforts. Our analysis of diachronic household refuse disposal patterning here is aligned with South's behavioral perspective.

We feel it is important to note that we have never been particularly satisfied with archaeological interpretations of disposal practices at sites as falling into the category of "sheet middens" or "sheet refuse." As Michael Schiffer's work on site formation processes points out (Schiffer 1987), the origins of much of the patterning associated with trash disposal has to do with the practical issues human agents dealt with in the past concerning the trash they produced through their daily activities. These concerns included how dangerous or noisome their trash was, or the degree to which it interfered with other activities associated with house sites. The category "sheet midden" or "undifferentiated trash disposal" seems to ignore the existence of such behavioral patterns among members of ordinary house-holds. We feel that categorizing refuse deposits as just "sheet midden" is based largely on assumptions, absent the kind of spatial analysis of artifact quantities and weights associated with more-convincing refuse disposal patterns that clearly reveal specific behavioral patterns associated with the disposal of rubbish in discrete loci and/or trash disposal associated with the maintenance of space (e.g., Bon-Harper and McReynolds 2011).

It is easy to imagine that household residents disposed of their rubbish following unconscious cultural patterns indicative of their habits and practices embedded within their cultures. We wonder, however, whether the patterns associated with refuse discard practices reflect purely practical considerations, as Schiffer claims, or are there other unconscious (or conscious) symbolic expressions embedded in the action of routinely throwing away the daily trash and/or where trash ends up after it has been discarded? We believe that there is an implicit and largely unconscious symbolic dimension inherent in refuse disposal practices during the historical period that cannot be easily divorced from the action of trash disposal as a whole.

Certainly, the practical dimensions leading to trash disposal or the desire to maintain yard space and keep activity areas clean are important considerations human agents make regularly. We assert that there is nevertheless a symbolic aspect to these patterns that reflects both a sense of how people related to the land and established and maintained their identities, and the larger social, political, and cultural processes that shaped their worldviews. We see both the practical and the symbolic dimensions associated with the discard of domestic refuse as working in concert and not as mutually exclusive. It is in this sense that the location of domestic refuse accumulation on a site reveals how the inhabitants viewed their household as a part of that landscape and gives us a sense of how identities were shaped and maintained within the larger political and social context specific to historical moments in time.

Fundamentally, we wish to show that where refuse accumulates at house sites in middens—or areas purposely maintained or kept free from refuse accumulation—is structured by how household inhabitants created and maintained their identities and a sense of place (see Edwards-Ingram 1998; Heath 2010). We believe that the inhabitants of the past, as in the present, performed these actions in reference to, and were influenced by, their specific cultural contexts and historical moments. These factors intersected and united their households within the framework of the lands, laws, customs, and communities that formed the landscape as a whole. We assert that these are integral aspects to consider when archaeologists are working toward an understanding of the meaning underlying refuse disposal patterns.

Admittedly, this is a bit of a departure from how historical archaeologists have commonly conceptualized trash discard and patterning. As noted above, archaeological analyses and inferences have commonly revolved around the practical aspects of refuse disposal and accumulation (e.g., Groover 2001; King 1988; King and Miller 1987; Stewart-Abernathy 1986; for an alternative perspective, see Beaudry, this volume). We assert that it is not enough to interpret spaces as intentionally maintained or to fail to fully pursue, at multiple levels, the context in which such deposits were made. As Barbara Heath (2010) and others (see Heath and Bennett 2000) have revealed, how space was structured has as much to do with the formation of household identities as do the bodies dwelling inside the homes and the activities performed within these spaces. For example, Sara Bon-Harper and other researchers at Thomas Jefferson's Monticello (see Bon-Harper 2010; Bon-Harper and Devlin 2012; Bon-Harper and McReynolds 2011) created a useful model for the prediction of subsurface features and the presence of maintained general activity areas based on the size and quantity of artifacts systematically recovered across a site. This model allowed the Monticello archaeologists to make inferences about how space was maintained around slave dwellings and, in part, to infer the relationships among individual households. This work highlights how important understanding the behavioral aspects of refuse discard is for historical archaeological research on households. The focus of much of this research, however, leans more toward the practical aspects of refuse discard and accumulation at the expense of its broader cultural meaning. This integral dimension to the study of patterned refuse disposal, and the significance of what these patterns meant to the inhabitants of households in the past, has become an important emphasis to some researchers, however.

Barbara Heath uses patterns associated with refuse discard and accumulation identified on domestic sites associated with enslaved Africans to talk about meaningful aspects of household composition, social relations, gender relationships, spirituality, and how economic activities associated with yard space affected the material lives of the enslaved (e.g., Heath 2010; Heath and Bennett 2000). Heath and Bennett have likewise stressed the importance of finding a way to integrate within landscape archaeology a consideration not only of how spaces were defined by past cultures but also of the culturally relevant activities performed in these spaces that serve to define group identity, class, and relationships between individuals and communities (Heath and Bennett 2000: 45). In doing so, they further a broader discussion about meaning and cultural expression in relation with house sites. This more closely represents the type of integration we seek to explore in our own work. Our goal is to find a more holistic approach to understanding the patterns associated with the disposal and accumulation of domestic refuse.

We consider the practical and symbolic aspects associated with refuse disposal and accumulation in the past to be indivisible; we see the act of throwing away the trash from day to day both as imbued with practical considerations regarding space and activity and, concomitantly, symbolic in terms of how this behavior relates to the historically and culturally significant association with constructing a household identity within the larger context of community and the land.

Middens are more than the sum of their parts. People choose where their refuse does or does not accumulate. How they choose is a part of the way they constructed their identities in place. The practice of disposing of household waste is performed in keeping with how members perceived their household, in the context of their sense of the land, customs, and the larger community that formed the larger landscape of which they were a part. Such patterning is likely also a reflection of the response to household residents dwelling in place. It also represents the types of daily routinized activities that contributed to the kind of meaning inhabitants derived from place while also allowing archaeologists the ability to discern how meaning and places changed over time as different households undertook this process. Therefore, in our analysis we follow an interpretive analytical approach to archaeology (e.g., Beaudry 1993). Through this approach we highlight the importance of incorporating belief systems, worldviews, and meaning within the cultural historical context while working toward an interpretation of the observations we make archaeologically (see Beaudry 1993: 91). Our attention to ritualized action allows us to understand how this seemingly practical activity is inseparable from the symbolic as being expressive of beliefs and worldviews, as well as how household identities were constructed, maintained, and associated with a sense of place and the land.

By ritualized activity we reference a discussion begun by Joanna Brück (1999) with regard to how within archaeology and anthropology we unwittingly follow post-Enlightenment rationalization in terms of considering ritual actions as being essentially separate from practical daily activity. Brück points out that archaeological definitions of ritual tend to focus on it as being an activity that is separate from other technological acts in terms of its association with elements of expressive or symbolic meaning only (Brück 1999: 314–315). She notes that archaeologists tend to implicitly interpret "ritual and non-ritual practices as mutually exclusive" but that a clear boundary between either is absent since defining criteria for either dimension of practice rarely fit into neat categories (Brück 1999: 316). Therefore, archaeologists implicitly identify ritual as those actions seemingly lacking practical function and therefore define ritual in opposition to practical or functional activities (Brück 1999: 317); archaeologists tend to think about ritual activity as something separated "spatially, temporally, and conceptually" from other day-to-day activities (Brück 1999: 319). This is the sort of dichotomy we wish to question with regard to the practice of refuse disposal and site maintenance in the past. We believe that thinking about the practical and symbolic aspects of trash discard and site maintenance as not mutually exclusive helps us to see how these dimensions work in concert. Doing so helps to contribute to understanding the ways household identities are formed and maintained within the confines of the cultural contexts and historical conditions that contribute to, and constrain, how households were materialized as part of a landscape. Throwing out the trash has a clear practical dimension, but the practices associated with trash disposal and accumulation can be linked to other, more meaningful, symbolic actions: for example, as Heath and Bennett note, the maintenance of yard space creates spaces for profane spiritual activities (Heath and Bennett 2000). In short, one practical action facilitates other, greater symbolic actions.

We also evoke the concept of *landschaft* to confront the dichotomization of refuse disposal as either practical or symbolic (Olwig 1996). The notion of *landschaft* permits consideration of how communities and households shape the landscape they are a part of through their ideas and cultural laws. As Kenneth Olwig (1996) points out, lands are defined by their customs and culture, not always by physical characteristics (Olwig 1996: 630–631). *Landschaft* also addresses how cultural identities are influenced by politics and economics inherent within specific cultural contexts and historical moments. *Landschaft* encompasses the feeling of different places under the umbrella of laws and customs. We believe this is important to consider when pursuing the archaeology of households because it requires archaeologists to pose the question of how social expressions, including the orientation of peoples' homes, household architecture, maintenance of space, and even trash disposal, reminded people about the laws of their "world" or the places they helped to legitimate. Such laws and customs influenced where people chose to discard their rubbish, because maintaining—or not maintaining—the areas around a home explicitly or implicitly contributed to the establishment of a sense or a feeling about place and household identity within the context of the landscape. In part, how these identities were shaped within specific circumstances can be seen through how the inhabitants of different dwellings presented their households to the outside world within the context of their sense of place and the land. We believe that tracing where accumulations of domestic refuse ended up on the landscape can give us a sense of how household inhabitants contributed to their sense of place and identity in reference to the customs and cultural laws of the land. It is, however, important to highlight that social actors do not respond passively to cultural constraints. As we show in this chapter's examples, human agents were, and continue to be, very much actively contributing to the sense of the land and the formation of their worlds through their daily habits and practices. The meaning they derive from place is both revealed and reproduced through the simplest of daily activities, including throwing out the trash. The unique historical, cultural, political, and archaeological circumstances surrounding our case study, the site of Ferry Farm, George Washington's boyhood home in Fredericksburg, Virginia, provide an example of these processes diachronically. We begin with a historical background of the Ferry Farm property and then examine the dynamic residents and households that appeared through time within this ever-shifting landscape.

Historical Background of Ferry Farm Occupations

During the historical period, the first occupant of this property was Maurice Clark, a newly released indentured servant and small planter. Clark purchased the property around 1710 and lived there with an indentured servant of his own. The two men lived under the same roof in a two-room, post-in-ground structure typical of later seventeenth- and early eighteenth-century Virginia vernacular architecture associated with middling planters (see Glassie 1976). This house was built at the top of the bluff, toward the northern extent of the Ferry Farm site, overlooking the flood plain and Rappahannock River below. Though during this period the town of Fredericksburg was not yet established (that would not come until 1728), a community did exist in the region (see Levy 2013). In the early eighteenth century, this area was considered part of the Virginia frontier, but it was of clear interest as more and more Englishmen arrived in the colony and sought land on which to grow lucrative Orinoco tobacco plants (Levy 2013: 32). Though some scattered homesteads may have been situated across the river from Ferry Farm, in the 1670s the land up and down the river consisted mainly of agricultural fields and forests and was largely "unsettled" (Levy 2013: 25).

Most of the Clark house was uncovered during archaeological excavation between 2002 and 2003 (Muraca, Nasca, and Levy 2011). These excavations showed that while the architecture of the Clark household may have been simple, hinges, pintles, clenched nails, window glass, and other architectural improvements reveal that Clark focused his limited means toward making the interior of the house comfortable for visitors. Similarly, the presence of paste jewels, cufflinks, and decorative objects made from pewter and copper attest to how he adorned his body to present himself as fashionable within his means. Clark's attention appeared to be directed toward expressing his status outwardly through bodily adornment and by making the occupants and visitors to his home comfortable.

In 1732, following Clark's death, a gentleman planter named William Strothers purchased the land. He built a one-and-a-half-story five-room clapboard dwelling in the hall-and-parlor Georgian style (Muraca, Nasca, and Levy 2011). His home, along with several storehouses and outbuildings, was located at the top of the bluff overlooking the Rappahannock, just south of the former Clark dwelling. This dwelling was likely the same that was purchased by Augustine Washington in 1738 following Strothers's death; it was identified archaeologically in 2008. This 280-acre tract likely appealed to Augustine because of its close proximity to two other parcels of land he already owned. It was also attractive because by this time Fredericksburg had been fully established and may have provided Augustine with new investment opportunities and access to the materials required to express his family's station in the top 10 percent of wealthy Virginians

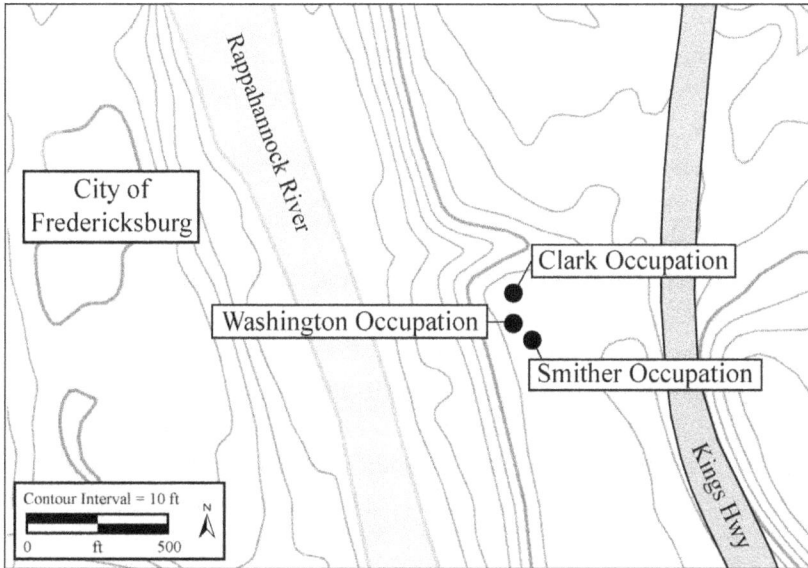

Figure 4.1. Location of Ferry Farm property and sites.

at this time (Warren 1999: 5787). A ferry crossing, after which the site is named, was also located directly below Ferry Farm. The ferry linked the Washingtons' side of the Rappahannock with Fredericksburg and was serviced by a public road that crossed the Ferry Farm property just north of the Washington household. The road connected with the Kings Highway directly east of the main house (figure 4.1). This important artery for travel and commerce connected the colonies along the Eastern Seaboard from Charleston, South Carolina, to Boston, Massachusetts. No longer part of the Virginia frontier, Fredericksburg and the Washington household were part of an increasingly urban landscape, welcoming to travelers and to trade and connected to the wider world of ideas and materials. The Washington household complex was highly visible not only to travelers along the roads but also to anyone in the burgeoning town of Fredericksburg or on ships traveling the river to and from the port. It was natural for the Washingtons to express their station on this landscape within the context of their connection to the community, their sense of identity, and their English worldview.

Augustine lived at Ferry Farm with his family and their twenty African slaves until his death in 1743. At that time his son, eleven-year-old George Washington, inherited the plantation and lived there with his mother,

Mary, and his three siblings. This was a period of financial uncertainty for the family (Galke 2009). Mary Washington managed both the household and the plantation until her sons came of age, but she chose not to remarry. Though this was not an uncommon decision for women of Mary's status and age (Vickery 2009: 218), remarrying a person of similar or greater station would have certainly eased the family's financial difficulties (Galke 2009: 31). As Laura Galke's research has revealed, Mary Washington's choice to remain a widow was strategic for a number of reasons (Galke 2009). Given English common law of the eighteenth century, married women and their legal identities were subsumed by their husbands' identities (Vickery 2009: 192–193). Personal property, land, capital, and material goods became the property of the patriarch (Galke 2009: 41). Unmarried or widowed women retained a legal status that allowed them to keep their personal wealth and to take legal actions including dictating a will and managing finances (Galke 2009: 41). Widows of Mary Washington's status, age, and means enjoyed greater freedom and social options to forge their own identities than did married women or spinsters (Galke 2009; Vickery 2009). Archaeological excavations around the Washington home at Ferry Farm indicate that Mary used this freedom to express materially her family's genteel status to visitors and to impart to her children a domestic education in genteel behaviors. In this regard, such an education was critical for training the Washington children in the standards of etiquette and socialization—vital skills for their advancement through the ranks of the gentry (Galke 2009: 33).

Archaeological evidence also indicates that Mary Washington invested in decorative elements for her household, including ceramic figurines and upholstered furniture (Galke 2009). The remains of at least seven teapots have been recovered from the Washington home (Galke 2009: 37). These include one Jackfield type, one Whieldon ware, one black basalt, one Astbury type, and three hand-painted polychrome creamware teapots. This variety appears to reflect Mary's desire to remain in step with the latest ceramic fashions from England and with the importance of the tea ceremony in the Washington home (Galke 2009: 37). Likewise, the recovery of more than 150 clay wig curlers from around the Washington home indicates not only that the Washington boys adhered to the fashion of the day but also, given the importance of wigs in signaling status and their requirement for constant maintenance, that some form of wig maintenance was being performed at the household complex (Muraca, Coombs et al. 2011). The picture emerging from the historical and archaeological records is of a female-led household in which refinement, fashionability, and mastery of the language of display and ritualized activity such as the tea ceremony all played key roles in the Washingtons' construction of their genteel identities within the broader social landscape.

By the 1770s George Washington's military career had set him on a course to participate in the American Revolution. In 1774 George Washington sold the plantation to Dr. Hugh Mercer of Fredericksburg. Mercer, however, was killed during the war before he could occupy the former Washington plantation. Between this time and 1846 when the property was again sold, Ferry Farm was intermittently leased to tenant farmers. More important, this was a period during which Ferry Farm increasingly became a site of tourist pilgrimage. The Washingtons' history and mythologies about George Washington's boyhood popularized by books such as Mason Locke Weems's *Life of Washington* (1809) contributed to making this a place of veneration. Though by the 1830s the Washington home had fallen to ruin and was slowly erased materially from the landscape, the Washington legacy was integral to how this place would be conceptualized and experienced for years to come. As the nation sped toward violent conflict over its fundamental contradictions regarding slavery, however, the Ferry Farm landscape again experienced a period of transition.

In 1846 the Bray family took possession of the former Washington property as one of several plantation holdings they owned and cultivated. Though they never lived at Ferry Farm themselves, in 1856 the Brays built a small house over a stone-lined cellar as a dwelling for one of their plantation overseers. The house and its detached kitchen stood just south of the old Washington dwelling at the top of the bluff, also overlooking the Rappahannock. By 1860 an overseer and widower, John S. Smither, lived in this home with an enslaved woman as his common-law wife, with whom he had several children. During the antebellum period, the Ferry Farm landscape was a place of contradiction reflecting the tensions emerging across the nation as the country was increasingly forced to confront the institution of slavery. Regardless, the overseer, his enslaved wife, and their children were in the process of making a household within this landscape at the dawn of the Civil War.

Union forces occupied Ferry Farm in 1862 during the two Fredericksburg campaigns. Given the site's strategic location, the Union Army dug trenches across the bluff to withstand Confederate attacks including an artillery bombardment in the winter of 1862. Ironically, this trench clipped a portion of the Washington house ruins without the soldiers noticing. The site was bombarded, fences were torn up to fortify the soldiers' trenches, and the entire landscape endured the scarring associated with the disturbances and brutalities of war. Despite this, the Northerners were well aware of the connection between the property and our first president. In their letters home they sent cherry pits and carved fragments of cherry wood to their families (Laura Galke, personal communication 2012). They also wrote about their feelings regarding the contradiction they observed around them between the place of a founding father's dwelling and the presence of slaves working the land during their occupation. Despite the horrors of war and the battlefield that Ferry Farm resembled, the place took on a particular meaning to the soldiers, whose experience of dwelling in this place, and its meaning, was marked by their intersection with the land and memory.

Some of the soldiers seem to have been under the impression that the house the Smither family lived in was the former Washington home (Laura Galke, personal communication 2012), and one can only speculate as to how the presence of a white overseer and his enslaved wife and children in this home may have affected their experience of place at Ferry Farm. Sadly, much of this dwelling was destroyed in the twentieth century when an icehouse was built over the remains of the stone cellar. A portion of the cellar and the Smithers' detached cellar survived, however, and have been excavated by Ferry Farm archaeologists. After the war, Ferry Farm was subdivided, changed hands several times, and in 1914 would be the site of the fourth household, that of the Carsons, whose house lay just east of the previous occupations. This house stood until it was destroyed by fire in 1994.

Clearly, what one can gather from this historical backdrop is that the various occupants over time experienced dwelling within the landscape differently. Their experiences were based on the broad cultural and historical circumstances of their eras. We believe that the material remains of these dynamic occupations can tell us something about how the inhabitants meaningfully constructed their identities and a sense of place within the landscape.

Archaeological Analysis of Patterned Refuse Discard at the Ferry Farm House Sites

Our approach to our analysis of the spatial distribution of trash accumulation areas considers that daily ritualized activities, that is, throwing out the trash or maintaining activity areas around households, combined with both practical and symbolic considerations, lead to middens being indexically associative of the ways household identities are formed and maintained within the confines of cultural context and historical conditions while concomitantly contributing to, and constraining, how these households were materialized within the spirit of *landschaft*.

The goal of our analysis was to identify the main domestic refuse disposal areas for the three pre-twentieth-century occupations: Clark, Washington, and Smither (see figure 4.1). As the Ferry Farm landscape is a dynamic palimpsest of human activities and the activity areas of each occupation may overlap, it was important to select artifacts that could be associated with each discrete occupation. Therefore we looked at the distribution of ceramics with tightly bounded manufacture dates contemporary with each occupation. Although heirlooming—retention of valued objects—is possible, we believe that the densest clusters of appropriately dated ceramics are indicative of the refuse disposal areas of each occupation. For the Clark occupation, Rhenish/Westerwald and North Devon wares were selected. For the Washington occupation, Astbury type, white salt-glazed stoneware, Whieldon ware, and creamware were isolated. Finally, the overseer's occupation was delineated using ironstone, yellowware, and various decorated whitewares. The distributions of these specific time-sensitive ceramics were plotted using ArcGIS and prediction surface maps were created using kriging interpolation methods. These were used to visually identify discrete clusters of the ceramic artifacts that we interpret as elements of the principal domestic refuse disposal areas for each occupation; analysis reveals distinct refuse disposal areas for each of the three occupation periods. We believe that these distributions, when considered within the cultural and historical contexts specific to each occupation, will help us to understand how household identities were being established and maintained.

For example, Maurice Clark's new status as a freeman allowed him new rights and privileges, which he used to purchase land in the Virginia frontier. Despite his modest circumstances, Clark appears to have made

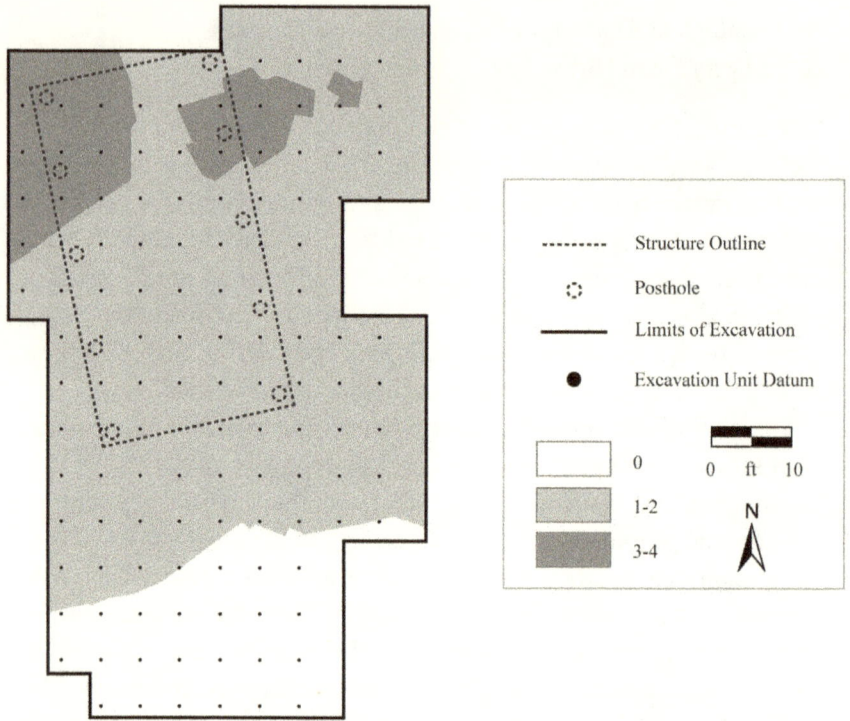

Figure 4.2. Distribution of recovered diagnostic ceramics around the Clark household.

strides toward advancing his station by presenting himself to guests entering his dwelling as more than just a middling planter. Archaeological evidence reveals that he used his limited means to express his identity through bodily adornment and by making his visitors comfortable with small architectural comforts. It is possible that Clark was attempting to advance socially not only through his planting interests but also by entertaining guests. The distribution of domestic refuse behind the northern storeroom and downslope, away from the house (figure 4.2), indicates that he was attempting to mask accumulations of refuse from visitors by discarding trash out of visitors' view. Though the house itself was modest, the interior comforts and Clark's dress may have worked in concert with how the landscape around the home was experienced to present the Clark household as better off than in fact it was. That the refuse accumulation occurs downslope, facing the river, also speaks to the fact that Fredericksburg was not quite the town it would become by the 1730s (see

Levy 2013). Much of the riverfront property along this portion of the Rappahannock was planted with tobacco at that time (Levy 2013: 32). Slopes are convenient places to discard trash out of sight, especially when no one was present across the river to see it. Therefore, a sense of place within the landscape may not have been as influenced by an attachment to a local community in terms of keeping trash out of sight from the villagers across the river but instead was performed in reference to the laws and customs associated with a sense of the larger economic and social landscape of the Virginia colony and Clark's British homeland. In this regard, masking trash accumulations probably served the purpose of structuring the experiences of guests invited into the dwelling in ways that would enhance Clark's status.

Washington-era disposal areas are located directly behind the Washington home, hidden from the view from the Rappahannock. The distribution of domestic refuse around the Washington household (figure 4.3) appears to exhibit a shift in behaviors. Refuse accumulation occurs primarily behind the Washington home and not downslope facing the bustling town of Fredericksburg. This was a period when the Ferry Farm landscape was crossed by travelers using both the Kings Highway and the Ferry Road. Fredericksburg had also been established as an important trading port for ships arriving from as far away as Europe. The Washington household was a highly visible part of the landscape (see Levy 2013), and given Augustine's and later Mary's strategies to present their family as genteel and well versed in mannerly behavior, it is no surprise that the highly visible portions of the house and its setting were maintained in good order. The front of the house, facing Fredericksburg and the Rappahannock, would have hidden the area of densest refuse accumulation, which also would have been for the most part hidden by outbuildings and the detached kitchen east of the main house from the view of travelers along the two major roads. The Washingtons' concern with presenting their home as part of an ordered landscape reflects their awareness of being on display both to travelers and to the larger community. This was consistent with what some have termed the Georgian worldview; it served as an important tactic in the overall strategy of identity construction of the household within the context of the Fredericksburg social landscape and its customs and behavior. The care taken in disposing of domestic refuse in a discreet location signals their sense of how their household was connected to this larger social landscape.

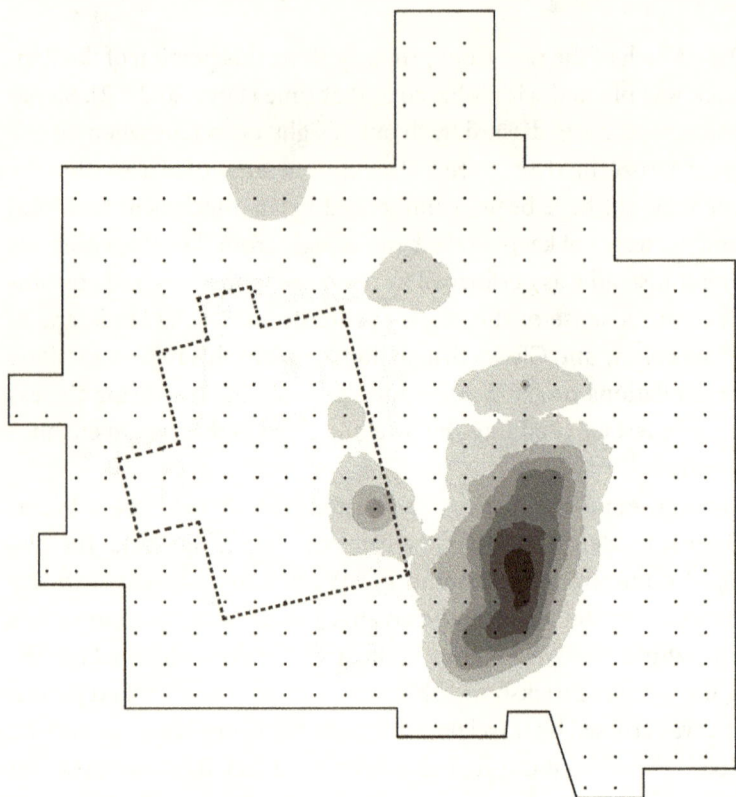

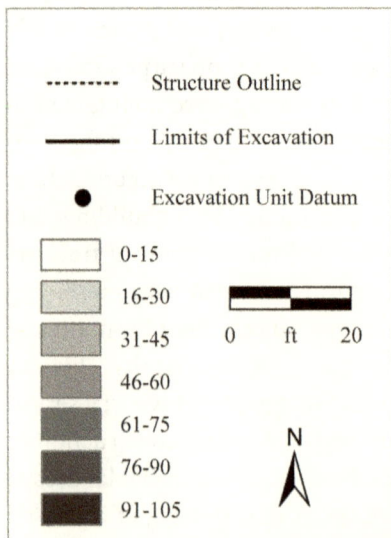

Figure 4.3. Distribution of recovered diagnostic ceramics around the Washington household.

Legend:
- Structure Outline
- Limits of Excavation
- Excavation Unit Datum
- 0–15
- 16–30
- 31–45
- 46–60
- 61–75
- 76–90
- 91–105

0   ft   20

N

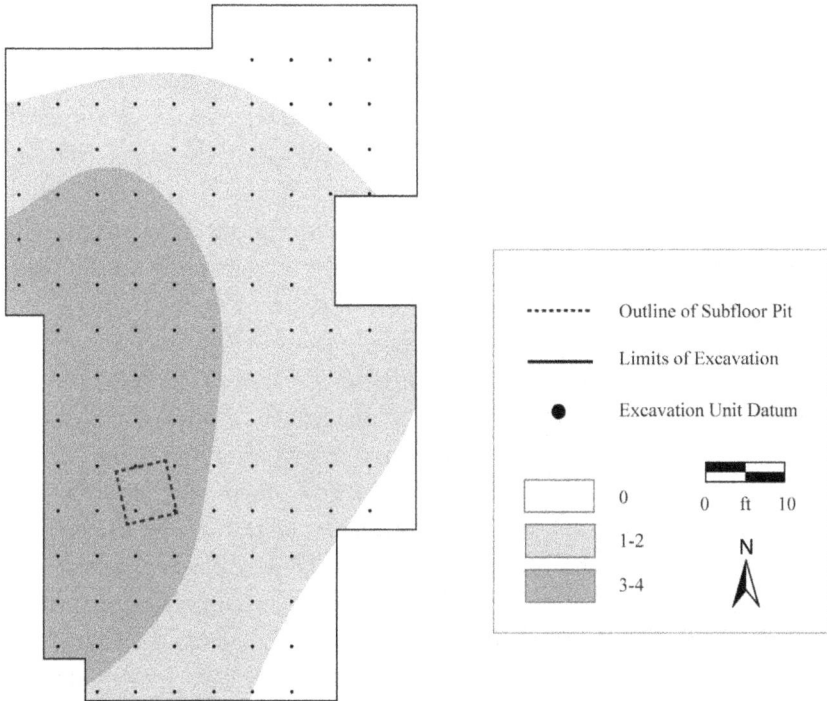

Figure 4.4. Distribution of recovered colonoware ceramics around the Washington-era domestic slave quarter.

In contrast to this pattern is the distribution of colonowares associated with the only known domestic servants' cabin at Ferry Farm that dates to the Washington occupation period (figure 4.4); it is located just north of the main house, in the area surrounding the remains of a subfloor pit. The enslaved African servants appear to have been discarding colonowares to the west of their cabin and partially down the slope facing Fredericksburg. This seems to imply that some of the Washingtons' slaves felt a different connection to the land and their place within the cultural landscape. It likely reflects the tensions stemming from their position of inequality in context with the Washington family and the larger Fredericksburg community. That refuse occurs downslope of the cabin may indicate this family's sense of detachment from the dominant urban community across the river, or possibly even resistance to following in line with the sense of household identity their owners were maintaining. It is also possible that east of the cabin was a more private activity area they were maintaining out of view from the community across the river. Regardless, the areas of refuse accumulation exhibited by both the Washington household and the home of their domestic servants seem to indicate that where trash was disposed of during this period implies two separate meaningful attachments to their sense of place and identity within the larger cultural landscape.

The antebellum-period distribution is harder to interpret within our framework; in part this is because much of the area around the cellar was disturbed and because excavations east of the Smither home have not been completed. As noted above, a large portion of the Smithers' house was destroyed by the construction of an icehouse in the twentieth century, but the existing evidence points to the main trash disposal area as lying south of the house, away from the ruins of the Washington home (figure 4.5). As noted previously, this era was marked by increasing tensions surrounding the institution of slavery and the coming Civil War. During the Smither occupation, however, Ferry Farm remained a place of veneration. It was still intimately linked with the Washington family and their history. Also, though this was not entirely uncommon across the South, the Smither family was of mixed race. It is not entirely clear how the larger Fredericksburg community felt about such households or whether the Smithers' common-law marriage was quietly tolerated or openly frowned upon. Regardless, the Smither family was in the process of constructing their household within this social and cultural landscape. It is interesting to note that domestic refuse does not occur in great quantities downslope facing the river and Fredericksburg. Likewise, middens were not located in areas that were too far away from the dwelling or strewn widely across the top of the bluff. During this period, the domestic behaviors associated with refuse discard appear to have been in line with those of lower- to middle-class rural families (see Groover 2004, 2001). It is possible that they were in part maintaining the site and in turn managing their household identity to remain discrete within the larger landscape in response to the constraints of the cultural conventions of the period. They may also have been taking strides to minimize their impact to the top of the bluff, given the presence of visitors making pilgrimages to the boyhood home of George Washington and the importance of the site to the national imaginaries of the postcolonial population.

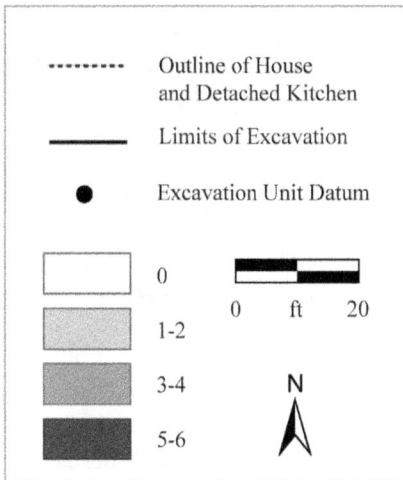

Figure 4.5. Distribution of recovered diagnostic ceramics around the Smither household.

Conclusions

Clearly, the legacy of dwelling across the Ferry Farm site reveals a dynamic assemblage of households, each having contributed to the formation of a sense of place in reference to the larger social, cultural, and historical constraints of their periods. These families actively made choices, including where trash would accumulate and where spaces would be clear, as part of their strategies to manage their identities and a sense of place. In this manner, they played an active role in shaping their environments and their worlds in the spirit of *landschaft*.

The different patterns of refuse discard we observed among the varied households across time seem to reveal how the different residents conceptualized place. That the daily routinized and ritualized practice of simply throwing out the trash was expressed differently during various periods of occupation implies that the residents conceptualized their household identities and places within the larger social and cultural landscape differently. Within each period, the residents of the Ferry Farm site simultaneously revealed and reproduced the meaning derived from place through a simple routinized activity. Across time, it seems that where people dispose of trash has as much to do with the meaning revealed to them through dwelling in place as it does with the practical concerns of simply keeping areas clean.

One might chalk up the patterns we observed simply to "keeping up appearances," but as innocuous as this concept may seem, we are convinced that such behaviors are ripe with both unconscious symbolic meaning and ritualized action reflected in the way each household dwelled within the land. What we have shown through this analysis is that where people dispose of their refuse within a landscape involves more than just practical considerations; it is inseparable from a symbolic dimension relating to the circumstances, both cultural and historical, in which household identities and a sense of place within the landscape are forged.

Acknowledgments

The authors are indebted to Dr. Laura J. Galke, Dr. David Muraca, the staff at Ferry Farm, and the George Washington Foundation for being extraordinarily accommodating. We would also like to thank Kevin Fogle and Mary C. Beaudry for their assistance, insight, and comments they provided on our chapter.

References Cited

Beaudry, Mary C.
2004 Doing the Housework: New Approaches to the Archaeology of Households. In *Household Chores and Household Choices: Theorizing the Domestic Sphere in Historical Archaeology*, edited by Kerrie S. Barile and Jamie C. Brandon, pp. 254–262. University of Alabama Press, Tuscaloosa.
1999 House and Household: The Archaeology of Domestic Life in Early America. In *Old and New Worlds*, edited by Geoff Egan and Ronald L. Michael, pp. 117–126. Oxbow Books, Oxford, U.K.
1993 Public Aesthetics versus Personal Experience: Worker Health and Well-Being in 19th-Century Lowell, Massachusetts. *Historical Archaeology* 27 (2): 90–105.
Beaudry, Mary C., and Stephen A. Mrozowski
1989 Archeology in the Backlots of Boott Units 45 and 48: Household Archeology with a Difference. In *Interdisciplinary Investigations of the Boott Mills, Lowell, Massachusetts*, vol. 3, *The Boarding House System as a Way of Life*, edited by Mary C. Beaudry and Stephen A. Mrozowski, pp. 49–82. Cultural Resources Management Series 21. National Park Service, North Atlantic Regional Office, Boston.
Bon-Harper, Sara
2010 Yard Space: Comparisons of General Activity Areas between Historic Period Social Groups. Poster presented at the 75th Annual Meeting of the Society for American Archaeology, St. Louis, Missouri.
Bon-Harper, Sara, and Sean Devlin
2012 Spatial Data and the Use of Exterior Domestic Space. Paper presented at the 45th Annual Meeting of the Society for Historical Archaeology, Baltimore, Maryland.
Bon-Harper, Sara, and Theresa McReynolds
2011 Who Swept Here? Site Maintenance and Cultural Tradition in Historic Contexts. Paper presented at the 44th Annual Meeting of the Society for Historical Archaeology, Austin, Texas.
Bourdieu, Pierre
1977 *Outline of a Theory of Practice*. Cambridge University Press, Cambridge.
Brück, Joanna
1999 Ritual and Rationality: Some Problems of Rationality in European Archaeology. *European Journal of Archaeology* 2 (3): 313–344.
Deetz, James
1996 *In Small Things Forgotten: An Archaeology of Early American Life*. Revised edition. Anchor Books, New York.
Edwards-Ingram, Ywone D.
1998 "Trash" Revisited: A Comparative Approach to Historical Descriptions and Archaeological Analyses of Slave Houses and Yards. In *Keep Your Head to the Sky: In-*

terpreting African American Home Ground, edited by Grey Gundaker, pp. 245–271. University Press of Virginia, Charlottesville.

Galke, Laura J.

2009 The Mother of the Father of Our Country: Mary Ball Washington's Genteel Domestic Habits. *Northeast Historical Archaeology* 38: 29–48.

George Washington Foundation

2012 George Washington's Ferry Farm. Electronic document, http://www.kenmore.org/ff_home.html, accessed March 24, 2014.

Glassie, Henry

1976 *Folk Housing in Middle Virginia: A Structural Analysis of Historic Artifacts*. University of Tennessee Press, Knoxville.

Groover, Mark D.

2004 Household Succession as a Catalyst of Landscape Change. *Historical Archaeology* 38 (4): 25–43.

2001 Linking Artifact Assemblages to Household Cycles: An Example from the Gibbs Site. *Historical Archaeology* 35 (4): 38–57.

Heath, Barbara J.

2010 Space and Place within Plantation Quarters in Virginia, 1700–1825. In *Cabin, Quarter, Plantation: Architecture and Landscapes of North American Slavery*, edited by Clifton Ellis and Rebecca Ginsburg, pp. 156–176. Yale University Press, New Haven, Connecticut.

Heath, Barbara J., and Amber Bennett

2000 "The Little Spots Allow'd Them": The Archaeological Study of African-American Yards. *Historical Archaeology* 34 (2): 38–55.

Hendon, Julia A.

2006 The Engendered Household. In *Handbook of Gender in Archaeology*, edited by Sarah Milledge Nelson, pp. 171–198. AltaMira Press, Lanham, Maryland.

Ingold, Tim

2005 Epilogue: Towards a Politics of Dwelling. *Conservation* and *Society* 3 (2): 501–508.

1993 The Temporality of the Landscape. *World Archaeology* 25 (2): 152–174.

Jamieson, Ross W.

2002 *Domestic Architecture and Power: The Historical Archaeology of Colonial Ecuador*. Kluwer, New York.

Journey Through Hallowed Ground Partnership

2014 The Journey Through Hallowed Ground: Gettysburg to Monticello. Electronic document, http://www.hallowedground.org/, accessed March 24, 2014.

King, Julia A.

1988 A Comparative Midden Analysis of a Household and Inn in St. Mary's City, Maryland. *Historical Archaeology* 22 (2): 17–39.

King, Julia A., and Henry M. Miller

1987 The View from the Midden: An Analysis of Midden Distribution and Composition at the van Sweringen Site, St. Mary's City, Maryland. *Historical Archaeology* 21 (2): 37–59.

Lawrence, Susan
1999 Towards a Feminist Archaeology of Households: Gender and Household Structure on the Australian Goldfields. In *The Archaeology of Household Activities,* edited by Penelope Allison, pp. 121–141. Routledge, London.
Levy, Philip
2013 *Where the Cherry Tree Grew: The Stories of Ferry Farm, George Washington's Boyhood Home.* St. Martin's Press, New York.
Lydon, Jane
2009 Imagining the Moravian Mission: Space and Surveillance at the Former Ebenezer Mission, Victoria, Southeastern Australia. *Historical Archaeology* 43 (3): 5–19.
Muraca, David, John Coombs, Phil Levy, Laura Galke, Paul Nasca, and Amy Muraca
2011 Small Finds, Space, and Social Context: Exploring Agency in Historical Archaeology. *Northeast Historical Archaeology* 40: 1–18.
Muraca, David, Paul Nasca, and Phil Levy
2011 *Report on the Excavation of the Washington Farm: The 2002 and 2003 Field Seasons.* Report on file at the George Washington Foundation, Fredericksburg, Virginia.
Olwig, Kenneth R.
1996 Recovering the Substantive Nature of Landscape. *Annals of the Association of American Geographers* 86 (4): 630–653.
Prosser, Lauren, Susan Lawrence, Alasdair Brooks, and Jane Lennon
2012 Household Archaeology, Lifecycles and Status in a Nineteenth-Century Australian Coastal Community. *International Journal of Historical Archaeology* 16: 809–827.
Rodman, Margaret C.
1992 Empowering Place: Multilocality and Multivocality. *American Anthropologist* 94: 640–656.
Schiffer, Brian M.
2002 *Behavioral Archaeology.* University of Utah Press, Salt Lake City.
1987 *Formation Processes of the Archaeological Record.* University of Utah Press, Salt Lake City.
South, Stanley
1977 *Method and Theory in Historical Archaeology.* Academic Press, New York.
Stewart-Abernathy, Leslie
1986 Urban Farmsteads: Household Responsibilities in the City. *Historical Archaeology* 22 (2): 5–15.
Thomas, Julian
2008 Archaeology, Landscape, and Dwelling. In *Handbook of Landscape Archaeology,* edited by Bruno David and Julian Thomas, pp. 300–306. Left Coast Press, Walnut Creek, California.
Van Dyke, Ruth M.
2008 Memory, Place, and the Memorialization of Landscape. In *Handbook of Landscape Archaeology,* edited by Bruno David and Julian Thomas, pp. 277–284. Left Coast Press, Walnut Creek, California.

Vickery, Amanda
2009 *Behind Closed Doors: At Home in Georgian England.* Yale University Press, New Haven, Connecticut.
Warren, Jack D., Jr.
1999 The Childhood of George Washington. *Northern Neck of Virginia Historical Magazine* 49 (1): 5785–5890.
Weems, Mason L.
1809 *The Life of George Washington; with Curious Anecdotes, Equally Honorable to Himself and Exemplary to His Young Countrymen.* Matthew Carey, Philadelphia.
Wesson, Cameron B.
2008 *Households and Hegemony: Early Creek Prestige Goods, Symbolic Capital, and Social Power.* University of Nebraska Press, Lincoln.
Wurst, Louann
1999 Internalizing Class in Historical Archaeology. *Historical Archaeology* 33 (1): 7–21.
Young, Amy L.
2004 Risk and Women's Roles in the Slave Family: Data from Oxmoor and Locust Grove Plantations in Kentucky. In *Engendering African-American Archaeology: A Southern Perspective,* edited by Jillian E. Galle and Amy L. Young, pp. 133–150. University of Tennessee Press, Knoxville.

5

....

Ranch as *'Ohana*

The Role of Ranching Station Households in the Formation of the Hawaiian Ranching Community

BENJAMIN BARNA

Modern Hawai'i has long been portrayed as a racial, ethnic, and cultural paradise, often explained by social scientists and Hawaiian residents as either an assimilationist "melting pot" (Adams 1934; Haas 1998; Hörmann 1952) or a multicultural "salad bowl" (Grant and Ogawa 1993). Anthropologists and sociologists increasingly question such characterizations (Edles 2004; Fu and Heaton 1997; Labov and Jacobs 1986; Lee and Baldoz 2010). An important critique of these characterizations notes that while the majority of Hawai'i's residents are multiethnic, many identify with particular ethnic groups and do so to take advantage of differences in socioeconomic status associated with those ethnic identities (Okamura 2008). Those differences derive mainly from working conditions on the sugar plantations that dominated Hawai'i's economy during the nineteenth and early twentieth centuries. Hiring and housing practices, for example, were intended to maintain social distance among immigrant laborers who came primarily from China, Japan, and the Philippines (Kinoshita 2006; Kraus-Friedberg 2008; Takaki 1983: 127).

Hawaiian Ranches as Multiscalar, Hybrid Households

Studies of Hawaiian multiculturalism tend to approach the problem at large social scales (such as Hawaiian society and ethnic groups), and doing so makes it difficult to fully explain the range of interactions that have led to such conflicting understandings as "melting pots" and "salad bowls." Narrowing one's focus, however, to the interactions within and among households, both domestic and industrial, can bring to light the role of these institutions in the socialization of immigrants in Hawai'i. For example, several generations of interaction among Hawaiians (that is, indigenous Hawaiians, or *kānaka maoli*), *haole* (Europeans and Euro-Americans), Chinese, Japanese, Portuguese, Filipino, and other ethnic and national groups in the ethnically segregated conditions of Hawai'i's sugar plantations led to their construction of the "Local" identity (Costa and Besio 2011; Labrador 2010; Okamura 1980; Trask 2000). In Hawai'i, "Local" is distinct from, and oppositional to, both Hawaiian and haole. It is the basic structural division in modern Hawaiian society, which at its broadest level is composed of people who are Locals and those who are not (Miyares 2008; Ohnuma 2002; Okamura 1998, 1994, 1980).

"Local" identity developed as groups of nonhaole immigrants adjusted to the polyethnic yet ethnically segregated living and working conditions of the sugar plantations and shaped their social world to match. In contrast, the community associated with Hawai'i's ranching industry emerged from the nineteenth century less ethnically stratified (Jiro Yamaguchi in Maly 1999: A57; Loomis 2006: 34–56). This may in part result from the fact that membership in the ranching community is not mutually exclusive to other Hawaiian social identities, be they kānaka maoli or "Local," but rather one that operates much like kinship. These family-like ties appear to derive in no small part from the way ranches have functioned, and continue to function, as work-centered extended households. Hawaiian ranches differ from other household forms in a few key ways that seem to have influenced the ranching community's development. Employees of ranches tend to be transient and dispersed, moving among headquarters, remote stations, grazing paddocks, and other places within and outside the ranch's borders, where they may have their own domestic households. Ranching stations are especially important to the socialization of ranch employees, as these are the domestic spaces to which ranch hands and cowboys return regularly and interact with other employees.

This chapter focuses on the socialization of immigrant ranch workers on a sheep and cattle ranch in the land division (*ahupua'a*) of Humu'ula on Hawai'i Island (figure 5.1). Between about 1862 and 2002, Humu'ula was used to graze sheep and cattle by a series of four ranching companies. Among the stations operated by these companies was one at a place called Laumai'a. Historical and archaeological evidence from the Laumai'a station provides a diachronic view of the process of incorporating immigrants

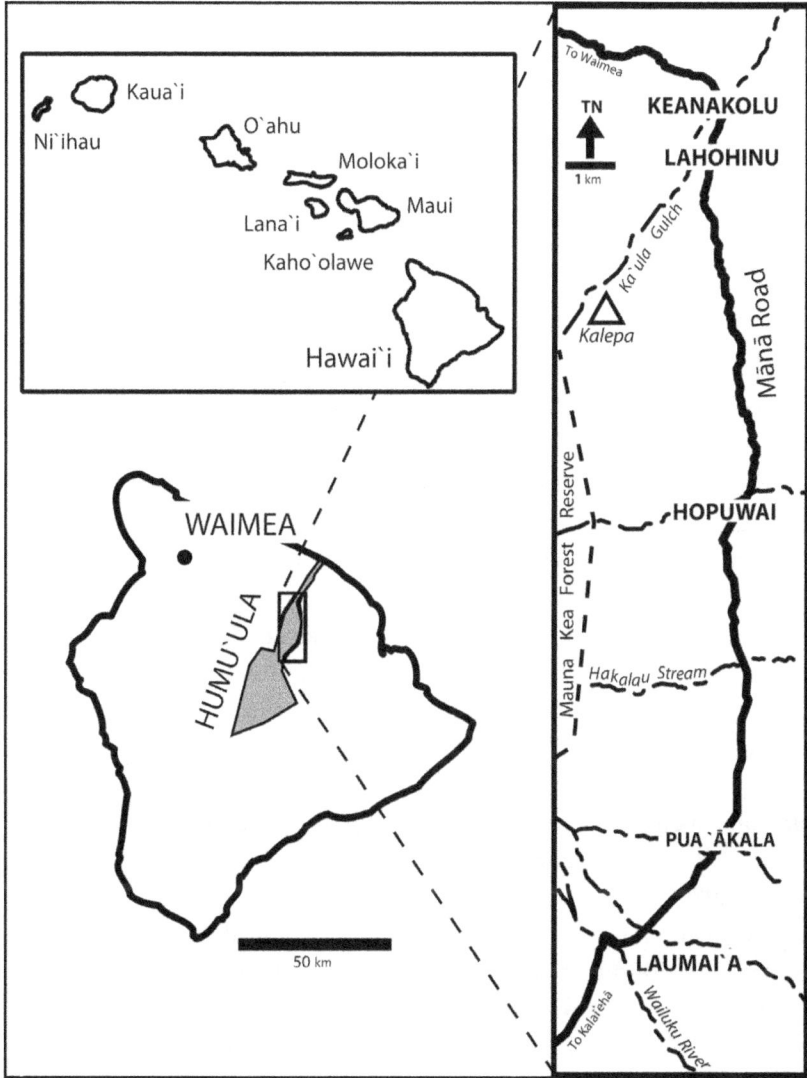

Figure 5.1. Map showing the *ahupua'a* of Humu'ula and ranching sites along the Mānā Road.

into the ranch-as-household and ultimately into the larger ranching community (Mills et al. 2013).

The Hawaiian Ranching Community of the Nineteenth Century

Goats, sheep, and cattle had been presented to Hawaiian chiefs and kings by explorers and merchants from Europe and the Americas in the eighteenth century, but only during the 1830s did the monarchy begin commercial exploitation of the wild herds that had grown from those gifts. Ranching was, like the sandalwood trade of the 1810s and 1820s, an indigenized form of capitalism organized and practiced according to a blend of Hawaiian and foreign social, political, and economic premises (Sahlins 1990). For example, Hawaiian ranching in those early decades combined indigenous traditions of animal husbandry (for example, management through *kapu,* or taboos) with technology and ranching techniques learned from Mexican vaqueros hired by the Hawaiian monarchy to bring its wild herds under control and to market as hides, tallow, and beef.

By the 1840s, most of this work had been accomplished, and most of the vaqueros left the islands. Their Hawaiian protégés, called *paniolo* or *paniola* after their "Spanish" mentors, continued to develop as a ranching community. From these "Spanish" origins, Hawaiian ranchers innovated customs and material culture. Typical examples include *noho lio*, a saddle designed for swimming cattle to ships at anchor, built with a saddle tree conceptually modeled after outrigger canoes, and *kaula ʻili*, a rawhide lariat built with a brass-ring hondo borrowed from rigging lines on the ships that called at Hawaiian ports (Bergin 2004: 189–198, 239–260, 273–304; Martin 1987).

The materiality of early Hawaiian cowboying illustrates the hybrid nature of the tradition, and that hybridity continued into the latter half of the nineteenth century. By the time commercial ranches were established in the 1850s, ranching companies and their employees routinely included Euro-American foreigners (*haole*) and part-Hawaiians (*hapa*), who brought their imported goods and the cultural practices associated with them to the ranches. In doing so, they engaged in household-level negotiations of cultural practices and identities that contributed to the evolving ranching subculture.

Plantations versus Ranches in Hawaiʻi

In the latter half of the nineteenth century, the vast majority of immigrants to Hawaiʻi were Chinese or Japanese men imported to work on sugar plantations under the terms of the Masters and Servants Act of 1850 (Sur 2008; Takaki 1983). Essentially enslaved to companies who arranged for their transit, these immigrants were placed into segregated working and living conditions within which race, national origin, and ethnicity limited employment opportunities and social standing. These practices created the conditions in which plantation workers constructed what is known today as the "Local" identity now shared by the majority of Hawaiian residents (Miyares 2008; Ohnuma 2002; Okamura 2008, 1980). Local identity developed as groups of laborers adjusted to the polyethnic character of the sugar plantations by opposing themselves to the haole ("white") plantation elite and management class.

On the ranches, however, many of these immigrants became incorporated into the already existing ranching community. Ranching was always a hybrid endeavor in Hawaiʻi, technologically, economically, and demographically. The ranching station household was one arena in which the Hawaiian, part-Hawaiian, and haole owners and employees of ranches were presented with opportunities to interact with imported Asian laborers and their descendants. Interactions on ranches differed enough from those on plantations to have resulted in a community characterized not by a division between Local and non-Local but rather, in the words of Hawaiian cultural practitioner Hannah Kihalani Springer, as *pili ʻana*, or connected (Barna 2013: 38–47). These connections arose from interpersonal efforts on the part of indigenes and newcomers to produce interactions that crosscut their populations and facilitated innovations in lifeways that drew from their varied backgrounds, beliefs, and worldviews (Lightfoot and Martinez 1995: 474). Not every station household, however, was amenable to *pili*—forming connections among immigrants and established ranch workers. In general, the philosophies guiding the management of the Humuʻula ranch can be categorized as either modeled on Hawaiian concepts of family or modeled on labor relations practiced on Hawaiʻi's sugar plantations. The former, "ranch as *ʻohana*," is associated with ranching companies owned or managed by descendants of the ranching community, while the latter, "ranch as plantation," was practiced by German transnationals who operated the ranch for a distinct period between 1876 to 1900.

Ranch as 'Ohana, Ranch as Plantation

Members of the ranching community often speak of their ranches in terms of 'ohana, or family (Friends of the Future 2005; Loomis 2006: 70–84; McClure 2008: 11–12). The concept of 'ohana appears to have developed in pre-Christian Hawai'i as an ascent group derived from the typical Polynesian house society (Anderson 2001: 59–60). Like sprouts (*'oha*) of a taro plant, 'ohana grow and disperse from an ancestor and thus are literally the "off-shoots of a family stock" (Handy and Pukui 1958: 3). Its current, semi-Westernized usage refers to extended networks of kin linked through blood relations (*pili koko*), adoption (*hānai*), and various "quasi-adoptive" (for example, *ho'okama*) relationships (Handy and Pukui 1958: 3–7, 15–17).

The fluctuating kinship relations of pili koko, hānai, and ho'okama within and between households were and continue to be recapitulated within Hawaiian ranches (Bergin 2004; Kimura 1969; Lee 1997; Loomis 2006: 70–84; McClure 2008: 11–12; Martin 1987; Nakano 1992). Bergin's (2004: 41–96) "foundation families"—Parker, Lindsay, Low, Bell, Stevens, and Purdy—include kānaka maoli and haole ancestors, but lesser-known figures like Francis Spencer and his son Ashford, who ran cattle and sheep in Humu'ula, married Hawaiian (or part-Hawaiian) women (Bird 1894: 223, 346; Siddall 1921: 369). In the twentieth century, Asian immigrants and their descendants began to marry into the extended ranching families. Recognizing the indigenous ideology of "ranch as 'ohana" draws attention to potential pathways for social and cultural pili through the literal and figurative kinship relationships that transform coworkers and their relatives into members of an occupational community (Applebaum 1981; Botwick and McClane 2005; Shackel 2004). Evidence from Laumai'a, Humu'ula, and other ranches in Hawai'i suggests that the degree of cultural pili in the ranching community varied with management personalities and the sociohistorical context of immigration.

Laumaiʻa and the Humuʻula Sheep Station

Although they are known as "cowboys," many paniolo also herded sheep as well as cattle. In 1857, the Waimea Grazing and Agricultural Company (WGAC), a venture grown out of early bullock hunter and businessman William French's sheep-grazing operation in Waimea, leased Humuʻula and other ahupuaʻa from the government on Mauna Kea for cattle and sheep ranching (Escott 2008: 34–39; Tomonari-Tuggle 1996). No company records of the WGAC are available at present, but some company activities can be discerned from a few government records and published descriptions by visitors to the area. The WGAC established a series of stations along the Mānā Road between the Mauna Kea saddle and Waimea. One of these stations was located at a place called Laumaiʻa, about eleven miles from the saddle between Mauna Kea and Mauna Loa. The company built a stone cabin, "Old Laumaiʻa" (site 26826), as its station there (figure 5.2).

In 1876, the financially struggling WGAC was outbid on its lease of Humuʻula and went bankrupt. Its successor, the Humuʻula Sheep Station Company (HSSC), abandoned the stone cabin, which may have been damaged by a series of earthquakes in March and April 1868, in favor of building a new wooden one, the "Laumaiʻa Cabin" (site 26825), across a gulch from the original site. The HSSC's wooden cabin was used continuously by the HSSC and two other companies that succeeded it until the early 1960s, when it was dismantled. Together, the two cabins at Laumaiʻa provide a diachronic look at work-related households associated with early (1860s) and later (1880s–1950s) commercial ranching in Hawaiʻi. Written and archaeological evidence of life at Laumaiʻa during each of these periods suggests that management strategies influenced the incorporation of immigrants into the ranching household. Companies with managers raised in the Hawaiian ranching community organized their labor, and thus the working households of their stations, according to the more inclusive philosophy of "ranch as ʻohana." Immigrants appear to have been more successful at incorporating into the community under this strategy than while employed by managers who attempted to run the ranch according to the precepts of Euro-American capitalism and racial and national prejudices. One way in which differences between these two strategies manifested themselves materially was in the architectural styles and techniques used to build each of the cabins at Laumaiʻa.

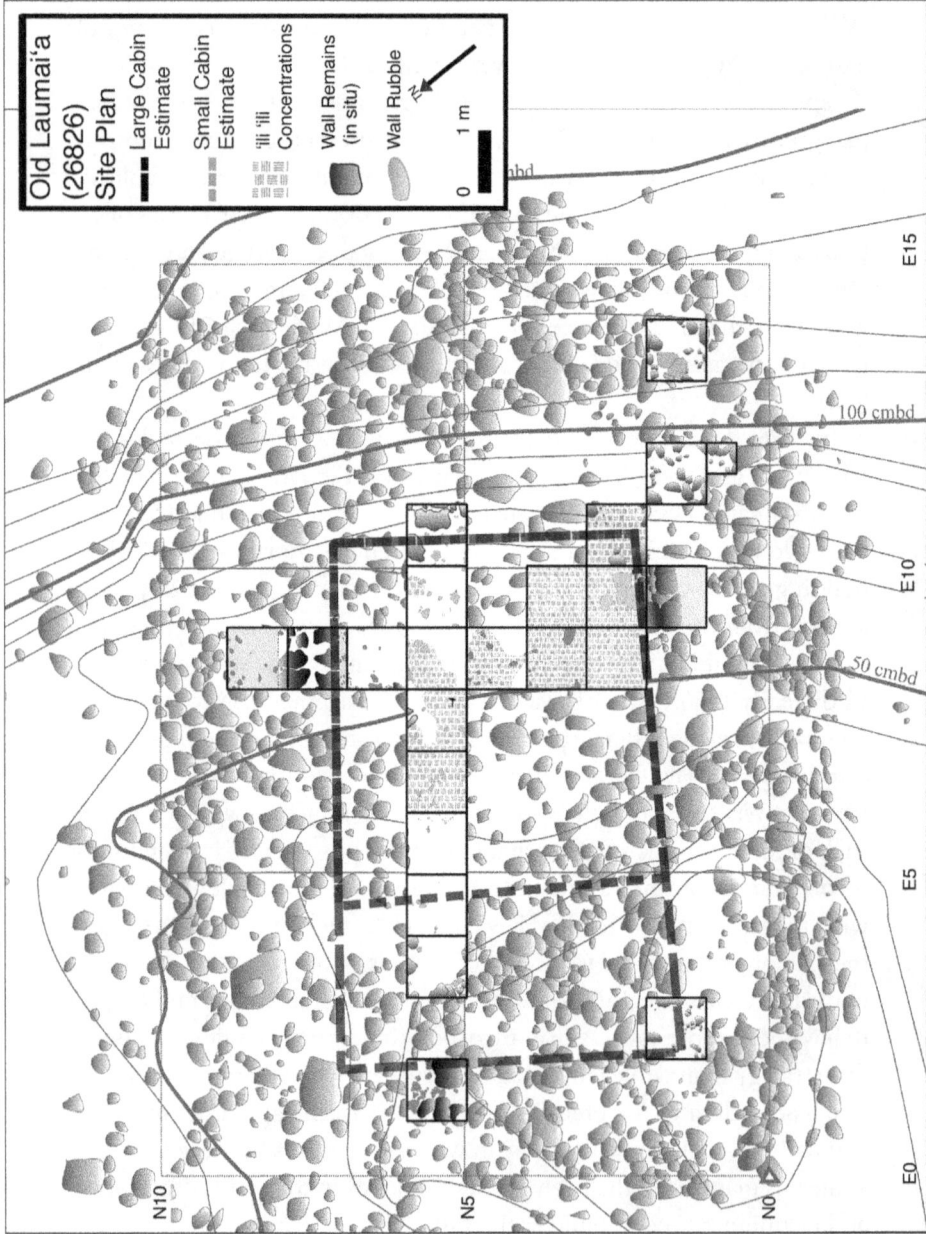

Figure 5.2. Plan of Old Laumai'a (50-10-24-26826), showing wall rubble and test units excavated in 2009. Figure by Peter R. Mills.

Pili ʻAna Architecture of the Two Laumaiʻa Cabins

In Hawaiʻi, changes in form and building materials conveyed evolving cultural meanings of social interaction (Mills 2009) through technological expressions of cultural hybridity (Bayman 2010, 2009: 141–147; Mills 2002: 163–164). The Old Laumaiʻa cabin (site 26826) was investigated through seventeen 1 × 1 meter test units by University of Hawaiʻi at Hilo and University of Nevada–Reno field school students in 2009 and 2011. At the Laumaiʻa Cabin (site 26825) in 2007 and 2009 students excavated fifteen 1 × 1 meter test units and eight 50 × 50 centimeter shovel probes. Differences in these two cabins' architecture suggest an early period of experimental hapa, or part-Hawaiian, construction followed by a coalescence of architectural choices favoring Western design but retaining emergent hapa practices.

Old Laumaiʻa (circa 1860–circa 1876)

The Old Laumaiʻa cabin represents an early use of Humuʻula for both permanent habitation and commercial ranching. It was large compared to other ranching cabins in Humuʻula, with a footprint of about 5 × 10 meters. Datable artifacts suggest an occupation during the mid-nineteenth century, no later than the mid-1870s. This date range is consistent with the period of the WGAC's lease on Humuʻula. The pattern of rubble around the site, shown in figure 5.2, indicates that the cabin was built with stone walls, as opposed to traditional Hawaiian thatched walls supported by a stone foundation (Apple 1971: 220–226; see Flexner 2010: 7.14). Roofing nails (n=7), a ball of lead sheeting with a cut nail embedded in it recovered from the cabin's interior, and a sheet of rusted iron near the cabin suggest that the cabin was roofed with tinplate over a wooden frame. No window glass was recovered. Low spots in the earthen floor were filled with ʻili ʻili (river-worn pebbles), a technique borrowed from hale construction.

One model that might be used to imagine this cabin is a similar stone cabin "on a side hill" on Mauna Kea described in the Pacific Commercial Advertiser on August 11, 1859. The log-roofed cabin had only three walls and housed a group of some thirty people identified as male and female cattle hunters in a space about one-fourth the size of Old Laumaiʻa. Its stone walls were plastered with mud and grass, and it was heated by a large open fire. The floor space available at Old Laumaiʻa suggests that it could have been used as a bunkhouse, and if inhabited by both sexes, it reflects the "compression" of Hawaiian architecture from dispersed *kauhale* complexes of functionally and gender-segregated houses and structures to single buildings after the abandonment of the Hawaiian state religion (*ʻaikapu*) in the 1820s (Anderson 2001; Kirch and Sahlins 1992: 175–177; Ladefoged 1998, 1991). These living conditions may also have promoted solidarity among bullock hunters and paniolo through communal living.

The stone construction of the Old Laumaiʻa cabin represents a break with temporary, seasonal-use architecture in the upper forests on Mauna Kea that housed bird catchers and bullock hunters. Even the permanent home of Ned Gurney, an English-born bullock hunter who lived in Humuʻula until the 1840s, had been constructed in the Hawaiian thatched style (Lyman 1906: 29–30). Early stone-walled domestic architecture in Hawaiʻi was often built for foreigners or used by Hawaiians to signal prestige or to associate themselves with Western power and influence, combining Hawaiian technologies with Western ones (Mills 2009). The arrival of ranching cabins in Humuʻula represents a form of "middle ground" architecture (see Bayman 2010), in which Hawaiian dry-stack masonry was innovated to create stone-walled buildings that met ranchers' desires for more-permanent structures in the wet and cold rangelands of Mauna Kea.

Laumaiʻa Cabin Site (1870s–1950s)

In 1876, the WGAC went bankrupt and transferred its Humuʻula lease to James W. Gay, a Honolulu businessman. Gay formed the Humuʻula Sheep Station Company (HSSC) to operate the ranch and made several changes to the ranch's infrastructure. One change was to abandon the stone cabin at Laumaiʻa and replace it with a new station less than half a mile down the road on the other side of the Wailuki River. In addition to the new cabin, Laumaiʻa included a sheep paddock, a horse pen, an "old stone pen," and later, a "Japanese camp" used by contract laborers (Haneberg 1891; see also Maly and Maly 2005: 394). Cowboys staying at the station also camped in tents during this later period, as they likely did during the earlier WGAC period (Eben Low, quoted in Hobbs 1939: 98).

In 1887, Gay hired two Prussian brothers named August and Armin

Haneberg to work as managers for the ranch. Within a year, August had become president of the HSSC, and he set about modernizing the ranch. In 1892, ranch employees and Japanese laborers installed a wooden water catchment tank at Laumaiʻa and wired the station into a telephone line that connected the other HSSC stations with the ranch's headquarters at Kalaiʻehā. The new station at Laumaiʻa remained in operation into the mid-twentieth century through two leaseholder changes. In 1900, Samuel Parker Sr., a member of the Parker family and formerly part owner of Parker Ranch, the island's largest cattle operation, purchased the HSSC. Fourteen years later, his son sold the lease to the Parker Ranch, which held the lease until 2002.

As at Old Laumaiʻa, no standing remains of the cabin survive. A foundation made of local basaltic cobbles partially covered by poured concrete was visible on the surface (figure 5.3). Excavations around the foundation revealed paving or a patio of cobble and ʻili ʻili extending toward Mānā Road from the platform. Three historical photographs of the cabin taken in the early twentieth century show that the exterior of the two-room building was clad with wooden battens. The cabin and lānai (patio) were roofed with corrugated tinplate. A plate-iron chimney hood visible in one of the photographs probably connected to the kitchen stove; the chimney hood was still located near the cabin foundation in 2011.

As is also the case at Old Laumaiʻa, the HSSC's cabin represented only a portion of the areas in which household activities took place. No associated outbuildings or work areas near the two cabins were identified during fieldwork, but heavy overgrowth of gorse (*Ulex europaeus*) and kikuyu grass (*Pennisetum clandestinum*) have obscured the areas around both cabins. Additional information about the cabin's households, however, can be discerned from artifact assemblages recovered in association with them. In particular, a trash deposit immediately behind the HSSC's cabin (Units 24N18W–24N21W; see figure 5.3) provides evidence of changing attitudes toward Japanese ranch hands that replaced their status as indentured foreigners by incorporating them within the ranching household— a necessary step before they could be perceived as part of the community.

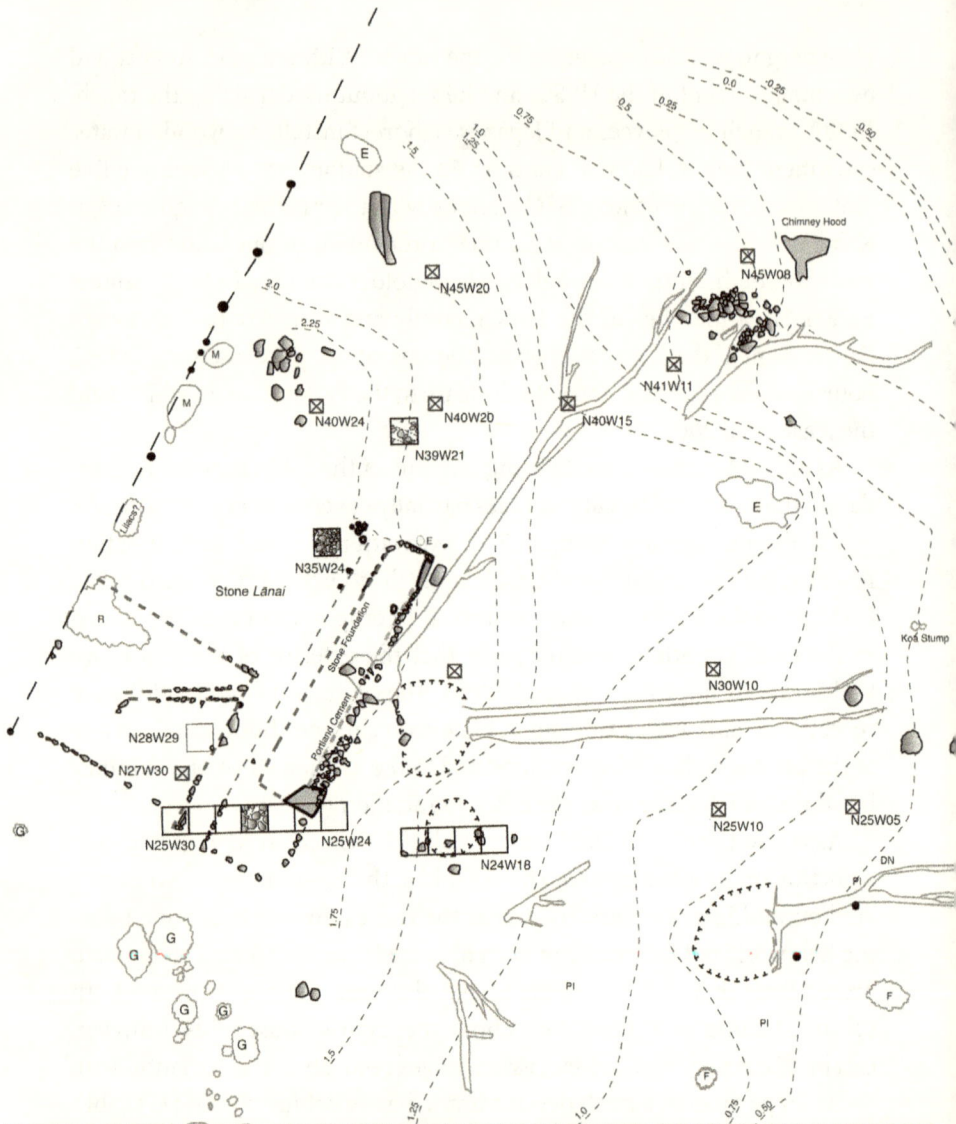

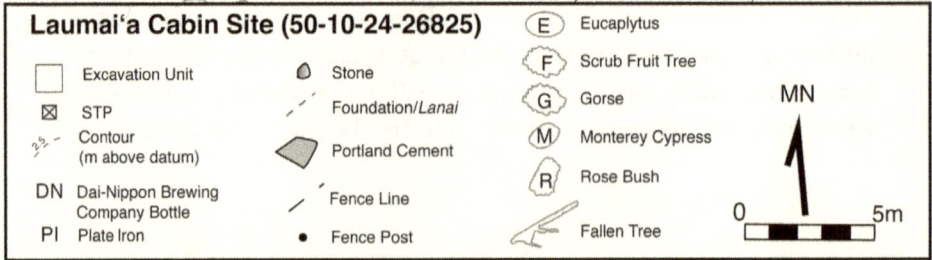

Figure 5.3. Plan of Laumai'a Cabin site (50-10-24-26825), showing cabin foundation and rubbish deposit containing Japanese-style export porcelains and fragments of alcohol bottles.

Pili ʻAna Working Households

While the architecture at Laumaiʻa became increasingly Westernized under the management of August and Armin Haneberg, vestiges of Hawaiian architecture such as the ʻili ʻili floor treatments, dry-stack masonry, and the presence of a lānai index the continuity and connections that early ranchers felt with Hawaiian traditions. Management strategies and philosophies followed a different trajectory, one in which the "ranch as ʻohana" attitude was interrupted by foreign ranch operators during the HSSC period. Whereas the Spencers, who lived as a family at the ranch headquarters during the 1870s, appear to have run their ranch as "ʻohana," the Haneberg brothers adopted practices used on sugar plantations to decrease the company payroll and increase employee efficiency. The HSSC had at least thirty Japanese and eleven Chinese employees working on the ranch in the 1890s. Four of them, three men and one woman, were imported on contract through the services of the Japanese Emigration Company of Hiroshima and K. Ogura and Company in 1895 (Humuʻula Sheep Station Company 1895), and there may have been others. Most manual labor tasks were assigned to employees designated "Japanese" and "Chinese" (Haneberg 1891; Humuʻula Sheep Station Company 1893, 1887; see also Maly and Maly 2005: 394). Some of Chinese workers cooked and hunted wild cattle, and both Japanese and Chinese workers occasionally herded sheep. Employees and contracted personnel from neighboring ranches with European and Hawaiian surnames conducted the bulk of the cowboying and supervisory work, although at least two Chinese men were performing cowboy duties in 1891. Japanese employees generally earned no more than half that of German, Hawaiian, and haole employees (Humuʻula Sheep Station Company 1893). Most of these Japanese employees were members of task gangs that roved the ranch repairing fences and carrying out other manual labor assignments. August Haneberg repeatedly refers to them as "Japanese" in his journal, and he notes that they slept in temporary tent camps and not in bunkhouses (Haneberg 1891). Despite this segregation of Japanese laborers from other ranch employees, both economically and physically, artifacts recovered from the HSSC's cabin indicate that after the HSSC was bought out by Samuel Parker Sr., social activities related to meals and recreation, especially social drinking, reversed Japanese workers' status as outsiders and facilitated their entry into the ranching community.

Tea and Alcohol at the Laumai'a Cabin

Two different drinking activities, both social in nature, appear to have involved Japanese ceramics at the Laumai'a Cabin. The ceramic assemblage includes one Western-style and five Japanese-style export porcelain cups (figure 5.4). These cups were probably used for drinking tea or coffee and perhaps sake or some other alcoholic beverage. All of these artifacts were recovered from the trash deposit located just behind the cabin.

The consumption of tea is represented in the assemblage by both Western and Japanese vessel forms. The two Western-style tea wares, a teacup and what is probably a saucer, were Japanese-style export porcelain with a "Phoenix Bird" pattern transfer print, a style that Ross (2012a: 19) dates to around 1914 in the United States. The five small Japanese-style cups with rim diameters between about 7 centimeters and 9 centimeters are similar in size and shape to *yunomi*, the handleless teacups used both in the elaborate tea ceremony and for everyday consumption with meals. Tea, as a mealtime drink, would have been consumed communally at the station. Served hot, it would have been welcome in the chilly and damp atmosphere of Humu'ula, and it would have provided opportunities to socialize with others around the table or campfire.

The five small cups also resemble *guinomi*, or sake cups. One fragment with an everted rim is similar to shallow, thin-walled sake cups identified by Ross (2012a: 10). If used for alcohol consumption, these cups would have played another, more complex social role within the Laumai'a household. Alcohol consumption among nineteenth- and twentieth-century Japanese ranch laborers was deeply embedded in social and ritual life, especially as a means of strengthening social bonds. As Ross (2012b: 42) has recently described, Japanese workers living abroad in the late nineteenth and early twentieth centuries consumed both sake and beer in all-male drinking parties. Because the Japanese workforce on the HSSC's ranch was almost exclusively male, it can be expected that the Japanese task gangs and other employees would have continued this custom once in Hawai'i.

While no *tokkuri* or *saka-bin* liquor bottles were represented in the assemblage, this should not be taken to mean that the small cups were used exclusively for tea. Sake bottles may have been thrown away in one of the two nearby river gulches that were almost certainly used for rubbish disposal. Pieces of waterworn ceramics and glass were found among the

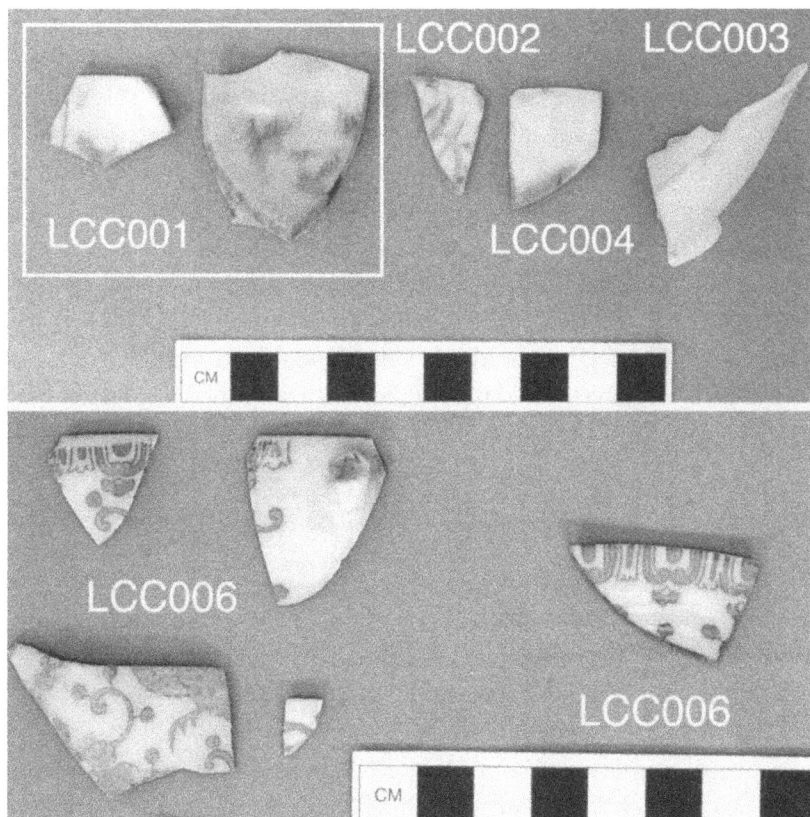

Figure 5.4. Japanese-style export porcelain cups recovered from Laumai'a Cabin site.

'ili 'ili in the cabin's foundation, which indicates that dumping rubbish in gulches was a common practice in Humu'ula. The workers at Laumai'a also had access to at least two other forms of alcohol.

The other two alcoholic beverages available to Laumai'a's workers are particularly intriguing as indicators of their pili, or connection to the ranching community: 'okolehao, a kind of Hawaiian "moonshine"; and patent and proprietary medicines. 'Okolehao is a fermented and distilled alcoholic beverage made from the roots of the ti plant (Cordyline fruticosa; kī in Hawaiian), which grew in the forest below Laumai'a. Rice supplied to workers on the ranch or the plantations lower on Mauna Kea could also have been used to distill 'okolehao.

Company documents and the archaeological record indicated that ranch employees also consumed alcohol in the form of patent medicines and flavoring extracts. In 1896, for example, eight Japanese laborers working at the ranch's Keanakolu station purchased "Pain Killer" and three others purchased lemon extract on account with the company (Humuʻula Sheep Station Company 1896: 23, 31, 37). Similarly, an invoice from 1901 shows that Samuel Parker Sr.'s managers purchased one dozen bottles of Burnett's Lemon Extract, possibly for its employees rather than for its cooks (H. Hackfeld and Company 1901). Fragments of bottles that once held alcohol were recovered in the rubbish deposits immediately behind and in front of the cabin. These included fragments of Dr. Collis Brown's Essence of Jamaica Ginger and Burnett's Standard Flavoring Extract. Either of these products would have sufficed as a substitute for "legitimate" liquor.

Social Drinking as an Indicator of Pili

Regardless of whether the small porcelain cups were used at Laumaiʻa for tea or for alcohol, they—and the alcohol bottles recovered with them—indicate that social bonds on the ranch were being created and reinforced through tea and alcohol drinking. Ross (2012b, 2010: 235–237) has described archaeological evidence of Japanese social drinking customs transported to overseas labor camps. The assemblages described by Ross were much larger than those at Laumaiʻa but contained small porcelain sake cups, which he implicates in the use of social drinking among transnational Japanese workers as a means of group identity formation and reinforcement. While those assemblages were located in primarily Japanese camps, the archaeological context of the Japanese porcelains at Laumaiʻa suggest that they were not being used solely to reinforce Japanese identity but also served as part of the process of incorporating Japanese workers into the ranch household and ultimately into the community.

Deposited on the ground less than 2 meters from the cabin, the porcelain cups and alcohol bottles suggest that whatever the people at the cabin were drinking, they were doing so in the open (see Beaudry and Mrozowski 1989: 121–140; Bond 1989). The presence of Jamaica Ginger or Lemon Extract in a worker's personal belongings would have belied their recreational use, despite their other accepted uses (see Adams 1907: 14).

The timing and location of the deposits containing the small cups and alcohol bottles also place their use within the context of the differences in attitudes toward ranch management between August Haneberg and

Samuel Parker Sr.'s managers. When he purchased the HSSC, Samuel Parker retained many of Haneberg's employees, including station foremen and paniolo (Bergin 2004: 233). He also continued to hire Chinese and Japanese employees as ranch hands and labor for sheep shearing and dipping (Blacksheep 1902). While any of these veteran employees could have engaged in Japanese-style social drinking at Laumai'a during the time that August Haneberg managed the ranch, manufacturing date ranges of the artifacts recovered immediately behind the cabin suggest otherwise.

The "Phoenix Bird" teacup, for example, probably arrived on the ranch after 1914, the year the Parker Ranch bought the Humu'ula lease from Samuel Parker Sr. The porcelain cups and alcohol bottles were also available during the Parker Ranch period, but the open disposal of these products is inconsistent with what is known about Parker Ranch management. A. W. Carter, the manager of the Parker Ranch during this period, was staunchly opposed to alcohol consumption and proved effective in enforcing temperance on the ranch (Bergin 2004: 182–183). Drinking at the station would most likely have been conducted in secret, and bottles would have been discarded away from the cabin—certainly not strewn on the ground.

Haneberg's management strategy also seems unlikely to have encouraged Japanese social drinking inside the station cabin. The "Japanese camps" described by Haneberg in his journal seem to have segregated these laborers, who were indentured and being paid less than half what other employees received. The location of the assemblage near the cabin contradicts the idea that these sake cups were used in the "Japanese camp" at Laumai'a, which would likely have been located away from the cabin itself. While haole and Hawaiian employees may have been using them, it seems more likely that recent Japanese immigrants would have been the ones to introduce the products and the practice to Laumai'a.

If A. W. Carter was effective at curtailing drinking on the ranch, and August Haneberg was able to segregate Japanese workers from other ranch employees, then it seems that the Japanese-style social drinking at Laumai'a was occurring during the years that Samuel Parker Sr. owned the ranch. Although friends with both royalty and sugar barons, and prone to social extravagance, Samuel Parker exhibited a business acumen and methods unlike those of the mercenary capitalism of August Haneberg (Bergin 2004: 165–163). He was close, socially, professionally, and by blood, with several cowboys (such as Eben and Jack Low, Ikua

Purdy, and Archie Kaʻaua) who contracted with the HSSC and worked as employees on his ranch (Bergin 2004: 263). Under this new management, the ranch's foremen and cowboys would have also played a significant role in reviving the sort of management practices associated with a "ranch as ʻohana" philosophy. While no documentary evidence places the HSSC's Japanese employees on the ranch after 1900, some likely remained in their old jobs, but as employees or contractors and not as indentured servants. This change of status may also have contributed to the acceptance of social drinking at Laumaiʻa.

Conclusion

Management philosophies, tradition, and family connections played important roles in structuring the social environments of the workplace, variously encouraging or impeding the incorporation of immigrants into the community. On the ranch in Humuʻula, de facto segregation of Japanese ranch hands by the HSSC's German managers and investors appears to have been driven by such ideological factors. Segregation between the working-class, workplace households at stations like Laumaiʻa and the roving "Japanese camp" had the effect of maintaining barriers to community membership based on ethnic difference. When Hawaiians who viewed their ranch as ʻohana took over and indenture was legally abolished, those barriers were removed. It should be noted, however, that the ethnic segregation was probably not absolute, especially at the stations down the line from ranch headquarters. Bonding over alcohol or tea and other activities that are less visible archaeologically very likely occurred as cowboys and ranch hands crossed paths and interacted outside the gaze of ranch managers. What really changed with the return of Hawaiians (in this case, members of the Parker family) to management of the ranch was the opportunity for formerly indentured laborers to find new roles in the ranch workforce and by extension in the ranching community itself. Once the institutional and social barriers imposed by the HSSC were removed, experimentation with the pragmatic and the preferred from the ranch workers' various cultures could again be used to meet their needs, as it had in the architecture of the older cabin at Laumaiʻa.

The (not entirely) metaphorical extended family of the ranch was organized into a work-centered household in which work and recreation guided interactions among its established members and newcomers toward incorporation into the larger Hawaiian ranching community. While the segregation imposed by haole plantation elites on immigrants in the sugar workforce has produced a multicultural but ethnically divided "Local" community, Hawai'i's ranches have produced a wholly different kind of identity among their workers. Without the unique dynamics within and among the workplace households on the ranches, interethnic relations probably could not have created opportunities for social inclusion of Asian immigrants within the community. By considering the ranch as household, we can observe some of the small, interpersonal relations that helped change transnational immigrants into community members whose lives became, in Hannah Springer's words, pili 'ana, or entwined.

Acknowledgments

Mahalo nui loa to Carolyn White and Peter Mills, Dr. Billy Bergin and the Paniolo Preservation Society, and Hannah Kihalani Springer for the opportunities and insights that led to this research. I would also like to thank James A. Nyman, Kevin R. Fogle, Mary C. Beaudry, Kerri Barile, and Mark Groover for their thoughtful comments. Any errors in fact or interpretation are purely my own.

References Cited

Adams, Romanzo
1934 The Unorthodox Race Doctrine of Hawaii. In *Comparative Perspectives on Race Relations*, edited by Melvin M. Tumin, pp. 81–90. Little, Brown, Boston.
Adams, Samuel Hopkins
1907 *The Great American Fraud*. P. F. Collier and Son, Chicago.
Anderson, Pia-Kristina Balboa
2001 *House of the Kama'aina: Historical Anthropology in a Rural Hawaiian Valley*. PhD dissertation, University of California, Berkeley.
Apple, Russell Anderson
1971 *Hawaiian Thatched House: Use, Construction, Adaptation*. Office of History and Historic Architecture, Western Service Center, Department of the Interior, National Park Service, San Francisco, California.
Applebaum, Herbert
1981 *Royal Blue: The Culture of Construction Workers*. Holt, Rinehart, and Winston, New York.

Barna, Benjamin

2013 *Ethnogenesis of the Hawaiian Ranching Community: An Historical Archaeology of Tradition, Transnationalism, and* Pili. PhD dissertation, University of Nevada, Reno. ProQuest, UMI Dissertations Publishing, 3566237.

Bayman, James M.

2010 The Precarious "Middle Ground": Exchange and the Reconfiguration of Social Identity in the Hawaiian Kingdom. In *Trade and Exchange: Archaeological Studies from History and Prehistory*, edited by C. D. Dillian and Carolyn L. White, pp. 129–148. Springer, New York.

2009 Technological Change and the Archaeology of Emergent Colonialism in the Kingdom of Hawai'i. *International Journal of Historical Archaeology* 13: 127–157.

Beaudry, Mary C., and Stephen A. Mrozowski (editors)

1989 *Interdisciplinary Investigations of the Boott Mills, Lowell, Massachusetts.* Vol. 3, *Life at the Boarding Houses.* Cultural Resources Management Series 21. National Park Service, North Atlantic Regional Office, Boston, Massachusetts.

Bergin, Dr. Billy

2004 *Loyal to the Land: The Legendary Parker Ranch, 750–1950.* University of Hawai'i Press, Honolulu.

Bird, Isabella L.

1894 *The Hawaiian Archipelago: Six Months among the Palm Groves, Coral Reefs, and Volcanoes of the Sandwich Islands.* 1st edition. G. P. Putnam's Sons, New York.

Blacksheep

1902 Sheep Raising in the Hawaiian Islands. *Paradise of the Pacific* 15 (12): 28–29.

Bond, Kathleen H.

1989 Alcohol Use in the Boott Mills Boardinghouses: Tension between Workers and Management, a Documentary and Archaeological Study. Unpublished master's thesis, Boston University, Boston, Massachusetts.

Botwick, Bradford, and Debra A. McClane

2005 Landscapes of Resistance: A View of the Nineteenth-Century Chesapeake Bay Oyster Fishery. *Historical Archaeology* 39: 94–112.

Costa, LeeRay, and Kathryn Besio

2011 Eating Hawai'i: Local Foods and Place-Making in Hawai'i Regional Cuisine. *Social and Cultural Geography* 12: 839–854.

Edles, Laura

2004 Rethinking "Race," "Ethnicity" and "Culture": Is Hawai'i the "Model Minority" State? *Ethnic and Racial Studies* 27: 37–68.

Escott, Glenn

2008 *Phase II Archaeological Investigations at State Sites 50-10-21-23499, 23515, 23517, and 23539 on Lands of the Ke'āmuku Sheep and Cattle Station Located in the Ahupua'a of Waikōloa, South Kohala District, Island of Hawai'i [TMK 3-6-7-001: 09].* Prepared for Directorate of Public Works, Environmental Division, U.S. Army Garrison, Hawaii (APVG-GWV), Honolulu, Hawai'i.

Flexner, James L.
2010 *Archaeology of the Recent Past at Kalawao: Landscape, Place, and Power in a Hawaiian Hansen's Disease Settlement*. PhD dissertation, University of California, Berkeley.
Friends of the Future
2005 *Paniolo House Stories: From the Kūpuna of Waimea, Hawai'i*. Friends of the Future / Xlibris, Philadelphia.
Fu, Xuanning, and Tim B. Heaton
1997 *Interracial Marriage in Hawaii, 1983–1994*. Edwin Mellen Press, Lewiston, New York.
Grant, Glen, and Dennis M. Ogawa
1993 Living Proof: Is Hawaii the Answer? *Annals of the American Academy of Political and Social Science* 530: 137–154.
H. Hackfeld and Company
1901 Invoice to Humu'ula Sheep Station. Paniolo Preservation Society Archives 1.D.35 HPA. Misc Accounting 1898–1907. Waimea, Hawai'i.
Haas, Michael
1998 *Multicultural Hawai'i: The Fabric of a Multiethnic Society*. Taylor and Francis, New York.
Handy, Edward S. C., and Mary Kawena Pukui
1958 *The Polynesian Family System in Ka-'ū*. Polynesia Society, Honolulu, Hawai'i.
Haneberg, August
1891 August Haneberg Journal. Paniolo Preservation Society Archives, Waimea, Hawai'i.
Hobbs, J. F.
1939 Our Fourth Industry Is Livestock. In *Hawaiian Annual*, pp. 97–101. Thomas G. Thrum, Honolulu, Hawai'i.
Hörmann, Bernhard Lothar
1952 Race Relations in Hawaii. In *Thrum's Hawaiian Annual*, pp. 130–160. Thomas G. Thrum, Honolulu, Hawai'i.
Humu'ula Sheep Station Company
1896 Keanakolu Sheep and Cattle Accounts. Box 3, Paniolo Preservation Society Archives, Waimea, Hawai'i.
1895 Memorandum of Agreement between Humu'ula Sheep Station Company and Japanese Immigration Company of Hiroshima, Japan, 21 Dec. 1895. Paniolo Preservation Society Archives 1.D.6a HPA. Waimea, Hawai'i.
1893 Time Book Beginning July 1st, 1893. Humu'ula File, Paniolo Preservation Society Archives, Waimea, Hawai'i.
1887 Accounts. Paniolo Preservation Society Archives 1.D.41. Waimea, Hawai'i.
Kimura, Larry
1969 Old Time Parker Ranch Cowboy. In *Hawai'i Historical Review: Selected Readings*, edited by Richard A. Greer, pp. 258–267. Hawaiian Historical Society, Honolulu.
Kinoshita, Gaku
2006 *Us, Hawai'i-Born Japanese: Storied Identities of Japanese American Elderly from a Sugar Plantation Community*. Routledge, New York.

Kirch, Patrick V., and Marshall Sahlins

1992 *Anahulu: The Anthropology of History in the Kingdom of Hawaii.* Vol. 1, *Historical Ethnography*. University of Chicago Press, Chicago.

Kraus-Friedberg, Chana

2008 *"Where You Stay?": Transnational Identity in Sugar Plantation Worker Cemeteries, Pahala, Hawaiʻi*. PhD dissertation, University of Pennsylvania. ProQuest, AAI3309461.

Labov, Teresa, and Jerry A. Jacobs

1986 Intermarriage in Hawaii, 1950–1983. *Journal of Marriage and Family* 48: 79–88.

Labrador, Roderick N.

2010 "We Can Laugh at Ourselves": Hawaiʻi Ethnic Humor, Local Identity and the Myth of Multiculturalism. *Pragmatics* 14: 291–316.

Ladefoged, Thegn N.

1998 Spatial Similarities and Change in Hawaiian Architecture: The Expression of Ritual Offering and *Kapu* in *Luakini Heiau*, Residential Complexes, and Houses. *Asian Perspectives* 37: 59–74.

1991 Hawaiian Architectural Transformations during the Early Historic Era. *Asian Perspectives* 30: 57–69.

Lee, Edgy

1997 *Paniolo O Hawaiʻi: Cowboys of the Far West*. Edgy Lee, producer, VHS. FilmWorks, Honolulu, Hawaiʻi.

Lee, S. S. H., and R. A. Baldoz

2010 "A Fascinating Interracial Experiment Station": Remapping the Orient-Occident Divide in Hawaii. *American Studies* 49: 87–109.

Lightfoot, Kent G., and Antoinette Martinez

1995 Frontiers and Boundaries in Archaeological Perspective. *Annual Review of Anthropology* 24: 471–492.

Loomis, Ilima

2006 *Rough Riders: Hawaiʻi's Paniolo and Their Stories*. Island Heritage Publishing, Waipahu, Hawaiʻi.

Lyman, Henry M.

1906 *Hawaiian Yesterdays*. A. C. McClurg, Chicago.

McClure, Michal

2008 *Hawaiian Cowboys: A Photographic Journal*. Island Heritage Publishing, Waipahu, Hawaiʻi.

Maly, Kepā

1999 *The Historical Puna Trail—Old Government Road (Keaʻau Section) Archival-Historical Documentary Research, Oral History and Consultation Study, and Limited Site Preservation Plan, Ahupuaʻa of Keaʻau, Puna District, Island of Hawaiʻi*. Prepared by Kumu Pono Associates for the Office of Mauna Kea Management, University of Hawaiʻi, Hilo. TDAR ID 305259. Electronic document, http://core.tdar.org/document/305259.

Maly, Kepā, and Onaona Maly

2005 *Mauna Kea—Ka Piko Kaulana O Ka ʻāina/Mauna Kea—The Famous Summit of the*

Land. Prepared by Kumu Pono Associates for the Office of Mauna Kea Management, University of Hawai'i, Hilo.

Martin, Lynn (editor)

1987 *Nā Paniolo O Hawai'i: A Traveling Exhibition Celebrating Paniolo Folk Arts and the History of Ranching in Hawai'i*. State Foundation on Culture and the Arts, Folk Arts Program, Honolulu.

Mills, Peter R.

2009 Folk Housing in the Middle of the Pacific: Lime Architecture, Cultural Power and Ideology in 19th-Century Hawaii. In *Materiality of Individuality*, edited by Carolyn L. White, pp. 75–91. Springer, New York.

2002 *Hawaii's Russian Adventure: A New Look at Old History*. University of Hawai'i Press, Honolulu.

Mills, Peter R., Carolyn L. White, and Benjamin Barna

2013 The Paradox of the Paniolo: An Archaeological Perspective on Hawaiian Ranching. *Historical Archaeology* 47: 117–138.

Miyares, I. M.

2008 Expressing "Local Culture" in Hawai'i. *Geographical Review* 98: 513–531.

Nakano, Jiro

1992 *Parker Ranch Paniolo: Yutaka Kimura*. United Japanese Society of Hawaii, dist. by University of Hawai'i Press, Honolulu.

Ohnuma, Keiko

2002 Local *Haole*—A Contradiction in Terms? The Dilemma of Being White, Born and Raised in Hawai'i. *Cultural Values* 6: 273–285.

Okamura, Jonathan Y.

2008 *Ethnicity and Inequality in Hawai'i*. Temple University Press, Philadelphia.

1998 *Imagining the Filipino American Diaspora: Transnational Relations, Identities and Communities*. Garland Publishing, New York.

1994 Why There Are No Asian Americans in Hawai'i: The Continuing Significance of Local Identity. In *Social Process in Hawai'i*, vol. 35, *The Political Economy of Hawai'i*, edited by Ibrahim G. Aoude, pp. 161–178. University of Hawai'i Press, Honolulu.

1980 Aloha Kanaka Me Ke Aloha 'Aina. *Amerasia Journal* 7 (2): 119–137.

Pacific Commercial Advertiser

1859 Cattle Hunting on Hawaii. August 11, 1859. Honolulu, Hawai'i.

Ross, Douglas E.

2012a Late Nineteenth and Early Twentieth-Century Japanese Domestic Wares from British Columbia. *Ceramics in America 2012*: 2–29. University Press of New England, Hanover, New Hampshire.

2012b Transnational Artifacts: Grappling with Fluid Material Origins and Identities in Archaeological Interpretations of Culture Change. *Journal of Anthropological Archaeology* 31: 38–48.

2010 Comparing the Material Lives of Asian Transmigrants through the Lens of Alcohol Consumption. *Journal of Social Archaeology* 10: 230–254.

Sahlins, Marshall

1990 The Political Economy of Grandeur in Hawaii from 1810–1830. In *Culture through*

Time: Anthropological Approaches, edited by Emiko Ohnuki-Tierney, pp. 26–56. Stanford University Press, Palo Alto, California.

Shackel, Paul A.

2004 Labor's Heritage: Remembering the American Industrial Landscape. *Historical Archaeology* 38: 44–58.

Siddall, John William (editor)

1921 *Men of Hawaii: A Biographical Reference Library, Complete and Authentic, of the Men of Note and Substantial Achievement in the Hawaiian Islands*, vol. 2. Honolulu Star-Bulletin, Honolulu, Hawai'i.

Sur, Wilma

2008 Hawai'i's Masters and Servants Act: Brutal Slavery? *University of Hawai'i Law Review* 31: 87–112.

Takaki, Ronald

1983 Pau Hana: *Plantation Life and Labor in Hawaii, 1835–1920*. University of Hawai'i Press, Honolulu.

Tomonari-Tuggle, M. J.

1996 *Bird Catchers and Bullock Hunters in the Upland Mauna Kea Forest: A Cultural Resource Overview of the Hakalau National Wildlife Refuge, Island of Hawai'i*. Prepared for U.S. Fish and Wildlife Service by International Archaeological Research Institute, Honolulu, Hawai'i.

Trask, Haunani-Kay

2000 Settlers of Color and "Immigrant" Hegemony: "Locals" in Hawai'i. *Amerasia Journal* 26 (2): 1–24.

6

·····················

Intimate Landscapes and Ideal Households

Nineteenth-Century Proslavery Reforms on a South Carolina Plantation

KEVIN R. FOGLE

The phrase *intimate landscape* refers to a photographic tradition that captures small portions of broad scenic landscapes while attempting to illustrate their interconnectedness. For photographers, the interpretation of *intimate* is twofold. First, the subject is physically closer to the lens. Second, the images are not passive; they reflect a personal involvement or familiarity that is not found in the grand landscape. Intimate landscapes are not idealized picturesque spaces, they are vibrant small-scale landscapes that have the ability to bridge scales and offer a meaningful viewpoint on the threads that connect these spaces (Tal 2004; Till 2012).

An intimate landscape perspective can offer historical archaeologists a useful analogy for conceptualizing landscapes on a smaller scale. Archaeological landscapes at the household scale, as a form of intimate landscape, can offer a realistic snapshot of a defined and very personal space. Over the past two decades, households have become a common data source for macro landscape research conducted at the settlement, community, and regional scales (Brandon and Barile 2004; Pluckhahn 2010; Spencer-Wood 2002). Less common are studies of the household scale from an explicit landscape approach (Trifkovic 2006). This perspective makes it possible to populate the landscape with individuals instead of monolithic social entities (Trifkovic 2006: 258). When considering the study of household landscapes, archaeologists face the challenge of not treating such spaces as unique isolates. Intimate landscapes in both the past and the present are intricately coupled to their local communities or regions. Definitions of a household and the landscape it embodies inevitably vary and should be flexible with regard to both the site and the goals of the archaeological research. Households across space and time are quite diverse, and no single definition will ever meet the multiplicity of household manifestations (Brandon and Barile 2004).

In this chapter I approach archaeological landscapes at the social and spatial household scale on Witherspoon Island, a nineteenth-century plantation site located in Darlington County, South Carolina. I examine intimate landscapes through the lens of influential proslavery reforms that were popularized during the last four decades of slavery in the United States. Reform literature promoted the image of ideal enslaved households operating as part of efficient modern plantations ruled by reason and benevolent management (Berlin 2003; Breeden 1980; Oakes 1982). The lives of enslaved individuals and their associated household landscapes at Witherspoon Island, as well as at many plantations throughout the South, were significantly influenced by a wide array of reforms related to housing, sanitation, diet, and Christian enlightenment.

Landscape as Discourse Materialized

The household landscapes considered here are approached from a discourse materialized perspective adopted from cultural geography. *Discourse materialized* is an analytical framework developed by Richard Schein to examine the processes behind cultural landscapes that work to naturalize, reproduce, and contest social practices (Schein 2009). For Schein, discourses are understood to be "shared meanings which are socially constituted ideologies, sets of 'common sense' assumptions" (Duncan 1990: 12). Discourse materialized builds upon the idea that cultural landscapes mediate ideology. According to Schein, every individual choice behind any cultural landscape is rooted within some form of discourse. When a choice results in a physical landscape expression, the landscape literally becomes discourse materialized (Schein 1997). Multiple discourses are present in all landscapes and offer "competing social and visual disciplines or strategies that combine to constrict or limit human action within and interpretation of any particular landscape" (Schein 1997: 663). Together these discourses create a conceptualization of cultural landscapes as dynamic palimpsests composed of past and present materialized discourses that never remain static (Schein 1997: 661).

The cultural landscape is both materially disciplined by specific discourses such as zoning laws or homeowners' association regulations and continuously engaged by individuals who can choose to accept, deny, or overlook these discourses. By acknowledging contestation through individual human agency, Schein provides a means to challenge and potentially change dominant discourses in all landscapes (Schein 1997).

The discourse materialized approach adopts a poststructuralist position while retaining a degree of the geographic empirical tradition using historically and spatially contextualized data to understand the social implications of the landscape (Schein 2004). Within this framework, cultural landscapes are not merely fixed representations of ideologies but also the product of dynamic social relations that are continuously changing the material face of everyday spaces (Mitchell 2002).

The strength of the discourse materialized approach is its inclusive nature that allows scholars to approach a wide range of concerns beyond traditional hegemonic power relations, including issues of gender, race, identity, and belonging. The flexible multiscalar nature of the discourse materialized framework allows broad global and national-level discourses to be studied fruitfully within landscapes at many scales (Schein 1997). Schein's approach clearly shows the importance of both temporal and geographic context for understanding the ever-changing landscapes that surround us all.

Both the historical contextualization and multiscalar implications of Schein's discourse materialized framework make this approach particularly well suited for historical archaeologists concerned with the social implications of cultural landscapes. The dynamic landscape of becoming that Schein envisions poses a significant challenge, however. It is a fundamental question of scale. For archaeologists, the multitude of competing discourses that impacted the archaeological landscape over a wide temporal span can be extremely difficult to discern at the site level. If they elect to conceptualize a cultural landscape as a dynamic palimpsest of multiple materialized discourses, archaeologists must achieve fine-grained control over landscape features.

Contemporary household archaeology may provide a solution to this issue. I believe that a contextual household methodology can be successfully merged with a discourse materialized landscape perspective to provide the necessary level of control over the archaeological landscape.

Contextual household approaches incorporate a broad range of interdisciplinary data "aimed at linking household cycles and family histories to the depositional histories of domestic sites through close attention to site formation processes and site structure" (Beaudry 1999: 117). Such a combined approach challenges the simplistic notion of landscape as built environment and can be used to bring a wide range of multiscalar discourses to bear on complex archaeological deposits across landscapes.

At Witherspoon Island, I apply a contextual methodology that attempts to synthesize the microhistorical record, microstratigraphy, and material culture studies to link archaeological deposits and features to discrete historical occupations or events. This level of detail can offer unprecedented insight into past behaviors with a wide range of social implications both at the household level and at the level of broader narratives (Walton et al. 2008). Such an approach offers vital clues to everyday household actions that can reveal individual variability that is a true hallmark of the archaeological record (Beaudry 1999).

Witherspoon Island Plantation

Witherspoon Island was an absentee plantation in the Pee Dee region of South Carolina that operated between 1808 and 1904. Only the slaves and a single overseer lived on the property before 1865, while the planter, J. D. Witherspoon, resided in Society Hill, a town 20 miles north of the plantation. Farm records and family letters indicate that the plantation was primarily used for the production of cotton, food crops, and livestock. Census records and slave lists suggest that Witherspoon Island grew from a small cotton operation into one of the largest plantations in the region, with a population of more than 250 slaves in the 1850s (Fogle 2012).

After Emancipation, the plantation continued to produce cotton and food crops. According to census data from the 1870s and 1880s, former Witherspoon slaves and families from neighboring plantations settled on the island as tenant farmers. The number of tenant-farming households on the island fluctuated in the second half of the nineteenth century, averaging around twenty families on a regular basis (Fogle 2012).

The household landscapes on Witherspoon Island plantation are understood to include both the physical dwelling and surrounding yard space. This is not an arbitrary household definition. Ethnographic and historical studies suggest that yard space was understood to be "an extension of the house" whereby "the limits of the yard represent the outer walls of the house itself" (Mintz 1974: 249). These exterior spaces served as the center of life for enslaved Africans and often contained dedicated areas for socialization, domestic chores, poultry, and small gardens (Mintz 1974; Westmacott 1992). Commonly known as yards or houseyards, these unique landscapes were a common feature of plantations in the Caribbean and the southern United States (Westmacott 2001; Wilkie 1996). The ubiquitous nature of such landscapes in both plantation and post-Emancipation settings suggests a continuity of these cultural landscapes, making them an important subject of anthropological and archaeological study.

Two neighboring household landscapes at one slave settlement on Witherspoon Island were excavated. Cabin 1 to the south was occupied from the 1840s to around 1900. Cabin 2 in the north is a little earlier and dates from the 1820s until the late 1880s. Both household landscapes are in unplowed contexts, meaning that the architectural and yard features for both the slave and the later tenant-farming occupations are undisturbed by mechanized cultivation (Fogle 2012). These intact conditions offer an excellent opportunity to examine the potential impact of nineteenth-century proslavery reforms on these intimate landscapes.

Proslavery Reforms

With the close of the international slave trade in 1808 and a growing abolition movement, the institution of slavery was under escalating scrutiny by the beginning of the nineteenth century (Ford 2009). In the face of increasing attacks on their slave-based economic systems, planters actively worked to defend their livelihoods (Finkelman 2007).

Slaveholders used a wide range of historical, moral, spiritual, and economic arguments to support a southern culture built around the ownership of other human beings. The core of the proslavery defense rested on the racist argument that "if southern slavery was humane and generous, and rooted in Christianity, then it could easily be justified to the entire world as an institution beneficial, not only to the master class, but to the slaves themselves" (Finkelman 2007: 105). Supporters argued that if slavery was to survive, it would have to shift from an aloof patriarchal system of total authority to a more paternalistic system in which masters functioned as sympathetic father-figures to dependent slaves (Ford 2009:

143–149; Morgan 1987: 76–79). Paternalistic planters would be responsible for providing slaves with Christian enlightenment and healthy environments in which obedient enslaved families could live happily and multiply (Ford 2009: 147).

By the third decade of the nineteenth century, the proslavery and paternalism propaganda had coalesced into a loosely organized but influential plantation reform movement focused on improving conditions for enslaved communities (Berlin 2003: 203–204). Popularized through agricultural societies, farming journals, church sermons, and plantation management books, this reform movement was part of a national- and regional-level discourse created by influential planters, proslavery advocates, and agricultural specialists throughout the country (Berlin 2003: 204–205; Ford 2009: 147; Vlach 1995: 119).

The circulation of this reform dialogue within agricultural networks and among peers significantly impacted the lives, dwellings, and associated landscapes of enslaved individuals with both material and symbolic ramifications. The reform discourse was implemented and modified at the local level in varying degrees by a range of individual agents including planters, overseers and drivers, and the slaves themselves (Vlach 1995).

In Darlington District, the local agricultural society advocated reforms both to slave housing and to management practices. For example, an 1857 meeting of the society was entirely dedicated to the proper design of slave housing. The meeting concluded with a strong recommendation that slave quarters be afforded more space than is traditional, in an attempt to improve the health and morality of the slaves (Darlington Agricultural Society 1846–1880). While it is not known whether J. D. Witherspoon was an active member of the district's agricultural society, he appears to have been well versed in scientific agriculture and occasionally submitted miscellaneous reports to national publications such as the *Monthly Journal of Agriculture* (Fogle 2012).

The progressive reform discourse promoted by the agricultural society and others was widely disseminated throughout the Southeast. Reports and articles by the Darlington Agricultural Society were regularly published in local newspapers such as the *Darlington Flag* and in prominent agricultural journals such as *DeBow's Review* and *The Southern Cultivator* (J. D. Witherspoon subscribed to some of these) (Fogle 2012). The prominence of the agricultural society in the Darlington area suggests that J. D.

Witherspoon would have been familiar with local reform publications and associated with society members on a regular basis.

As an absentee plantation, Witherspoon Island had no big house and was visited only occasionally by the planter. This was not a show plantation but a working farm set in a remote location where visitors would have been uncommon. Given that the plantation operated during the peak years of the reform movement, it is possible to examine the degree to which J. D. Witherspoon conformed to various aspects of the reform discourse and the impact this had on individual enslaved landscapes at the household level. I examine three elements of the multifaceted discourse: housing improvements, sanitation, and religious instruction.

Slave Quarter Reforms

Improvements to slave habitations and new construction of quarters constitute a major tenet of the reform discourse. Proponents argued that proper dwellings were essential to the health and well-being of slaves. A commentary published in an early nineteenth-century agricultural journal suggested that "negro cabins should be built of plank, have large glass windows and good chimneys, and . . . be elevated at least two feet above ground" (R.W.N.N. 1856, quoted in Breeden 1980: 130). Reformers argued that quarters in poor repair with leaky roofs, dirt floors, and improper ventilation and lighting constituted virtual "laboratories of disease" (*Southern Cultivator* 1850, quoted in Breedon 1980: 120). While not uniform in its recommendations, the reform dialogue followed the basic argument that providing slaves with proper shelter and a healthy living environment encouraged productivity and the development of stable slave families. The planters also "understood that housing had the potential to be used as a benign technique of coercion" (Vlach 1995: 118). Reform propagandists suggested that improved slave housing would lead to more-content slaves who were less likely to contest the plantation order (Vlach 1993: 93–94).

Documentary and archaeological evidence at Witherspoon Island suggests that the planter may have adopted certain aspects of the housing reform discourse that altered landscapes at both the settlement and the household scale.

Archaeological survey of this particular slave settlement on Witherspoon Island suggests that the cabins were neatly arranged in several rows with four to seven cabins in each row. Unfortunately, twentieth-century cultivation activity and logging disturbed the western two-thirds of this particular settlement, making determination of the exact placement and numbers of structures difficult, especially given the lack of historical maps or plats of the plantation. The settlement was not placed in the low swampy lands that surround the island—instead, it was set on higher ground near a freshwater spring that flowed year-round. The siting and organization of the settlement seem to have followed the best practices preached by reformers, with regularly spaced houses on high ground and immediate access to freshwater (Breedon 1980: 114).

Slave lists, census data, and house size suggest that the slave quarters were single-family dwellings, another hallmark of recommendations made in the reform literature. According to the slave schedule in the federal census, in 1860 J. D. Witherspoon owned forty-four slave quarters (U.S. Federal Census 1860). Forty or forty-one of these dwellings appear to have been on the plantation, with the rest situated near the Witherspoon residence in Society Hill. A slave inventory from 1860 breaks down the Witherspoon holdings into thirty-six family groups, which strongly suggests that dwellings were single-family (Sales and Appraisal Book 1860). The discrepancy between the number of family groups and the greater number of quarters is likely explained by the absence of slaves who had been gifted to the planter's children throughout the 1850s.

The slave quarters on the island were single-pen cabins made of local cypress logs with mud or brick chimneys (figure 6.1). Excavations have identified substantial sandstone piers showing that the dwellings were raised well above the ground level—which would have necessitated wooden flooring. Less than 150 grams of flat glass has been recovered in total from the entire settlement, suggesting that the structures had wooden shutters rather than glass windows. The elevation of the cabins, the floors, the single-family design, and the siting and dimensions of the cabins all conform to the reform housing ideals. The log construction (instead of plank) and lack of glass windows, however, suggest that not all of the prescribed reforms were implemented at Witherspoon Island. The planter's rationale for not employing plank construction or glass windows is ultimately unknowable, but it could be because of the additional cost or effort required to outfit the forty slave quarters on the island.

The cabin architecture may have changed as the dwellings were constructed throughout the first half of the nineteenth century. The earliest

Figure 6.1. Former slave cabins on the Witherspoon Island plantation circa 1912. By permission of the Darlington County Historical Commission, Darlington, South Carolina.

cabin (Cabin 2), which predates the 1830s, was built with a stick-and-mud (or "mudcat") chimney, while the majority of cabins that postdate the 1830s were built with substantial brick chimneys. As the slave population on the island increased, housing was constructed to meet these needs and new designs were implemented. The switch to brick chimneys could be evidence for implementation of reform ideals or may reflect increased access to bricks on the island.

After Emancipation there was a significant shift in the settlement land-scape from highly ordered spaces to more-haphazard arrangements as dwellings were relocated and physically moved around the settlement. At the household level, several habitations show evidence of cabins being merged to form larger dwellings. Where the cabins were merged, we find sandstone piers beneath the original cabin and brick piers placed beneath the additions. The alignment and spacing of the brick piers strongly suggest that the additions were extant cabins relocated from elsewhere in the settlement.

Sanitation Reforms

Cleanliness of a slave cabin and its surrounding yard was a second major issue addressed in reform discourse. Activists called for the slave quarter to be regularly cleaned and recommended the construction of plantation hospital buildings to improve the health of slaves (Kenny 2009: 4–5). Reform propaganda argued that slaves left to their own devices would naturally live in squalor and disorder, which was the root of illness (Vlach 1993: 96). The planters' concern for the health of slaves was not simply for the well-being of their bondsmen or for the immediate loss of productivity at a plantation. Rather, slaves represented a major capital investment, and planters could not risk losing such valuable assets (Ford 2009; Vlach 1993: 108–109).

Cleanliness in slave dwellings had been less of a concern under patriarchal systems of plantation governance, when quarters often were seen as semiprivate spaces to be managed by the enslaved laborers themselves (Vlach 1993: 92). With the shift toward paternalistic management, masters and their agents became more involved with the private lives of slaves and with the landscapes of the enslaved, challenging traditional understandings of private and public space on the plantation (Berlin 2003: 205; Morgan 1987: 76–79). Reformers (e.g., Clay 1833: 13–14) suggested that "dwellings of the negro should be arranged in some order favorable to the circulation of air, and to the cleanliness both of the paths leading to them, and of the surrounding ground. . . . They should be required to keep their houses clean by washing the floors at least once a week, and sweeping every day. . . . These matters require the frequent personal inspection of master or overseer." The sanitation reforms were implemented by planters, tasked to slaves, and enforced by overseers or drivers who were ordered to make weekly or monthly visits to slave quarters to inspect trash disposal locations and the sanitary conditions of the buildings, sometimes all the way down to kitchen utensils. The increased surveillance of the enslaved landscape worked to discipline slave behavior, curtailing unauthorized entrepreneurial endeavors and punishing slaves who did not meet the planter's standards (Joyner 1984: 124–125; Vlach 1993: 108–109).

According to family letters, Witherspoon maintained a plantation hospital and also mixed medicines for the slaves himself. These factors suggest that the planter was intimately concerned with health on the plantation and that this concern likely extended to cleanliness in and around the dwellings of enslaved families (Fogle 2012).

Archaeologically, sanitation reforms might be identified through trash disposal patterns across the enslaved landscape. Yard excavations at cabin site 1 revealed a shifting refuse disposal strategy between the periods of slavery and tenant farming. The earlier slave occupation was characterized by a relatively clean compacted sand yard surface with trash deposited in a midden south of a potential fence line. Above the compacted yard surface lay a series of mid- to late nineteenth-century sheet-midden trash deposits from the tenant-farming occupation. These tenant deposits extended from the southern midden up to the dwelling structure itself. The clean yard space and isolated trash from the earliest occupation indicate that the enslaved residents were being forced to follow the "best practices" preached in the sanitation reform literature. Excavations at cabin site 2 mirror this pattern of tenant-farming deposits in the yard with earlier trash being deposited on the outskirts of the houseyard. The question remains as to whether this disposal pattern was mandated by the planter or occurred independently.

Historical accounts provide examples of slaves ignoring or actively resisting their reform-minded planter's regard for organization and sanitation around the houseyard by putting off upkeep projects or leaving yards strewn with trash (Berlin 2003). Some opposition may be linked to different understandings of material culture in instances in which slaves used and reused objects in ways that challenged dominant white understandings. For example, seemingly random objects left in a yard that might be considered trash to a planter may have been specifically placed as part of commemoration or ritual activities (Edwards-Ingram 1998: 264–265). Another possibility is that certain bondsmen refused to recognize the slave quarter as a home and intentionally treated the landscape in ways that ran counter to traditional European and African aesthetic sensibilities (McKee 1992: 208–210).

Current archaeological and documentary evidence from the enslaved households at Witherspoon Island does not point toward resistance to housing or sanitation reforms. The biggest shift on these landscapes concerning sanitation was the transition that occurred after Emancipation, when houseyard upkeep and trash disposal choices appear to have become the sole responsibility of the former slaves. Without oversight, the houseyards were transformed from highly regulated landscapes to more-complex spaces characterized by large sheet middens and unsystematic trash disposal locations across the yards.

Moral Reforms

Another feature of reform discourse focused on encouraging Christian worship in enslaved populations. Unlike housing and sanitation reforms, the moral aspect of the reform discourse would not typically result in discrete material landscape manifestations at the household level. That being said, I argue that moral reforms may have significantly reinforced and influenced enslaved behaviors that shaped the intimate landscapes on Witherspoon Island. Moral reforms also provide an important line of historical evidence for the larger adoption of proslavery reforms on the plantation.

Advocates for moral reforms were not only concerned with the spiritual salvation of their bondsmen; many saw religion as an effective instrument of social control that would keep their slaves obedient and out of trouble (Berlin 2003: 206; Daly 2002: 31). Reformers understood that "religious instruction would lead them [the enslaved] to respect each other more, to pay greater regard to mutual character and rights; the strong would not so much oppress the weak; family relations would be less liable to rupture; in short, all the social virtues would be more honored and cultivated. Their *work* would be *more faithfully done;* their *obedience* more universal and more cheerfully rendered" (Jones 1842: 209; emphasis in original). These moral reforms can be traced to the early 1830s when an evangelical branch of proslavery ideology developed in response to abolitionist charges that slavery was a sin and that slaveholders were guilty of suppressing Christian worship among their slaves (Daly 2002: 3; Oakes 1982: 108). Working to counter these claims, a wide array of proslavery adherents including southern pastors, missionaries, and planters argued that the Bible ordained slavery as an acceptable institution, and they maintained that all slaveholders had a moral obligation to enlighten their mentally inferior bondsmen (Daly 2002; Finkelman 2007: 108).

The evangelical defense of slavery marked a shift from prevalent late eighteenth- and early nineteenth-century sentiments among planters, who were often suspicious about the relationship between their slaves and Christianity. The suspicion of planters was largely rooted in concerns about the antislavery leanings of many denominations and the Christian ideology of spiritual liberation, which were commonly linked to highly visible slave uprisings such as the Denmark Vesey plot in the Charleston area (Genovese 1976: 186; Montgomery 1993: 31; Touchstone 1988: 99–100).

During the three decades before the Civil War, both evangelical missions to slaves and church membership of enslaved individuals increased (Cornelius 1999: 21; Oakes 1982: 107; Touchstone 1988: 100). This concerted effort by churches and missionaries could not have succeeded without a reversal in planter attitudes regarding slaves and religion. Reformers touted the benefits of Christian instruction and argued that to avoid past issues, planters had to become more involved in the religious lives of their slaves. Planters, missionaries, and ministers had to work together to accommodate and emphasize proper messages for their sermons and lessons (Montgomery 1993: 31). These approved messages, they felt, would help counter the revolutionary influence of unsanctioned black preachers and private worship within the quarters (Berlin 2003: 206; Seabrook 1834). The contents of these sermons were "designed to instill in slaves their Christian duty to accept their appointed station in life" and to "obey their worldly and heavenly masters" (Montgomery 1993: 31–32).

Reformers suggested that slaves could receive religious instruction in several ways: on the plantation, at local churches where they were welcome, or a combination of both. Plantation-based instruction was to be led either by the planter reading passages or by a visiting preacher. Church-based instruction fell into two broad categories: integrated sermons or separate services for black and white congregations on the Sabbath (Berlin 2003; Daly 2002; Genovese 1976; Jones 1842).

Whether Witherspoon slaves were instructed in the Gospel either by the overseer or by the planter during his regular weekly visits is not known. It is clear that Christian morals were enforced by J. D. Witherspoon, according to a memoir written by a grandson of the planter. One account details Witherspoon giving a number of slaves to his daughter as part of her inheritance before she moved to the Alabama frontier in 1850 with her husband and family. The memoir suggests that among the slaves to be gifted, Witherspoon intentionally selected all of the unmarried mothers on the plantation as a punishment for their moral transgressions

(Dubose 1910). He chose to rip apart families and relationships of which he disapproved because of their perceived moral transgressions in the expectation that fear of these serious consequences was "to serve as an example to those left behind" on the plantation (Dubose 1910: 19).

Slaves from the Witherspoon plantation primarily attended a Baptist church located in the small community of Mechanicsville about 5 miles from the island. Planter J. D. Witherspoon was not affiliated with the Mechanicsville Baptist Church. Witherspoon, his family, and their household servants were members of churches near their homes in Society Hill.

From the late eighteenth century until the 1860s, Mechanicsville Baptist Church and its previous incarnations maintained a large enslaved congregation that throughout the nineteenth century regularly outnumbered the white members. According to membership rolls, over 600 slaves were baptized in the church by 1860, heavily outnumbering the nearly 250 whites who were baptized during the same period (Mechanicsville Baptist Church 1829–1867).

Most Baptist churches in Darlington District, including the Mechanicsville Baptist Church, held separate services and meetings for their enslaved members in the nineteenth century. The services for the black members usually occurred before or after the services for white members. Typically a slave deacon or exhorter approved by the church would preach while several white members attended both to supervise and to provide readings for the black congregation (Huger 1845: 27–28).

Richard Brockington, a neighboring planter, owned a slave named Adam who was licensed to preach by Mechanicsville Baptist Church in 1804 (Mechanicsville Baptist Church 1803–1829). Adam was a fixture at the church, delivering sermons to enslaved congregations for fifty years until his death in 1854 (Mechanicsville Baptist Church 1829–1867). The content of Adam's sermons or those any of the black deacons would likely have had to conform to a church-approved message that avoided certain controversial topics such as spiritual liberation and instead focused on the central message of servants obeying their masters.

In theory, the services and associated meetings for the black congregation would have always been overseen by white members. According to the Mechanicsville Church minutes, however, it was a common occurrence for slave services to be held with no white supervision. Every few years the church took white members to task for not attending the black services, suggesting that this was an ongoing issue (Mechanicsville Baptist

Table 6.1. Mechanicsville Baptist Church membership among J. D. Witherspoon slaves, 1803–1859

Decade	Adult slaves (age 11+)	Baptisms	Church members[a]	Church members in population
1800–1809	No data (1810 Census)	0	0	0%
1810–1819	57 (1820 Census)	0	0	0%
1820–1829	118 (1830 Census)	2	2	1.50%
1830–1839	103 (1840 Census)	12	14	17%
1840–1849	115 (1850 Census)	8	14	12.20%
1850–1859	153 (1860 Census)	35	45	29.40%

Source: Mechanicsville Baptist Church, 1803–1867.
[a] Membership numbers reflect recorded deaths, excommunications, and relocations by decade.

Church 1829–1867). These unsupervised gatherings were probably a welcome respite for the enslaved congregation, offering a rare chance to truly worship among themselves.

As a Baptist church, Mechanicsville practiced a believer's baptism and did not baptize infants and children (McGrath 2006: 271). Only adults who professed "faith in Christ" and provided "satisfactory evidence" of this faith could be received for the rite of baptism and immersed in the murky waters of the Great Pee Dee River (Mechanicsville Baptist Church 1829–1867: 3–4). This meant that Witherspoon slave children were not baptized until they reached late adolescence or full adulthood.

Plotting Witherspoon slave baptisms by decade reveals a trend that could reflect the adoption of religious reforms by the planter (table 6.1). Even though the Witherspoon Island plantation was actively producing crops by 1809, the first 2 Witherspoon slaves were not baptized at Mechanicsville until the mid-1820s. The 1830s and 1840s witnessed a slow increase in new members, followed by a surge in Witherspoon slave membership in the 1850s. In total, 57 slaves from Witherspoon Island were baptized as members of the church (Mechanicsville Baptist Church 1829–1867).

By 1860, 12 of the 57 members had died, had been excommunicated, or had been removed from the plantation, leaving 45 active members, which meant that 29.4 percent of the adult Witherspoon slaves were on the Mechanicsville Church rolls (Mechanicsville Baptist Church 1829–1867). Of the 36 slave families identified on the 1860 inventory, 24 are confirmed to have had 1 or more church members, meaning that 67 percent of households had church members present (12 had 2 or more members) (Sales and Appraisal Book 1860). It is also likely that children and non-members attended both meetings and sermons on a semiregular basis, such that the church's influence extended well beyond the official church members (Sparks 1988: 62–63).

A cornerstone of the Baptist faith and other southern evangelical denominations in the nineteenth century was the regulation of church members' personal behavior (Cornelius 1999: 36–37). Baptists felt that "it was the serious responsibility of the congregation as a whole and of each member as well, to keep watchful care over the daily activities of the brothers and sisters" (Raboteau 1978: 180). This meant that the personal lives of church members and their families were constantly being observed and monitored by other members.

Disciplinary violations were brought to the attention of the church by white members, enslaved members, unaffiliated planters, and occasionally the individual transgressors themselves (Cornelius 1999: 37). At Mechanicsville Baptist Church, meetings were held by white discipline committees once or twice a month to deal with cases of disorder among the black members and to evaluate new members. For discipline cases, the committee investigated the charges, heard testimony of the accused, consulted the black congregation or deacon, and set punishments that ranged from admonishment before the church to full excommunication (Mechanicsville Baptist Church 1829–1867).

For bondsmen, discipline went beyond basic moral tenets and controlled members' behavior on the plantation by enforcing elements of the slave code dealing with issues such as running away, disobeying their masters, and stealing food and other goods (Sparks 1988: 75–76). Reformers (e.g., Jones 1842: 218–219) saw this as an advantage and argued that "much unpleasant discipline will be saved to the churches. The offences of colored communicants against Christian character and church order are numerous, and frequently heinous; the discipline of delinquents is wearisome, difficult, and unpleasant." The minutes of the Mechanicsville Baptist Church show that five to ten slave discipline cases were typically heard most months throughout the nineteenth century. This figure does not include the numerous lesser infractions not reported to the white congregation that likely would have been settled directly by black deacons and committees made up of enslaved members. This internal system may have offered black members flexibility to deal with a wide range of disciplinary issues on their own terms. Local churches in the Darling-ton region were quite concerned with the abuse of power by their black discipline committees and enslaved deacons. These fears prompted some churches to regularly disband these committees only to reinstate them when they became tired of handling the details of every small infraction (Salem Baptist Church 1797–1930).

Discipline cases for Witherspoon slaves included charges of adul-tery, nonattendance, improper language, manifesting improper spirit, and abandoning planter-sanctioned marriages (Mechanicsville Baptist Church 1829–1867). Because the planter, his family, and his overseers were not affiliated with Mechanicsville Baptist Church, it is likely that most transgressions were reported by Witherspoon slaves about Witherspoon slaves.

The strong emphasis on watchful care worked to shape household be-havior on Witherspoon Island through both self-discipline and surveil-lance. This vigilant environment meant that households with enslaved church members may have been watching for infractions and trying to avoid unwanted attention by conforming to rules regarding their per-sonal behavior and that of their families. With respect to the household landscape, the system of surveillance likely worked to reinforce accepted behaviors associated with sanitation, health, and maintenance in the slave yards and dwellings with material ramifications. The moral code also regulated activities that took place on Sundays, the traditional day off for slaves, and treated gardening, fishing, hunting, and any profit-creat-ing activities as improper behaviors that broke the Sabbath (Jones 1842): "The labor which the overwhelming mass of the Negroes perform in the South, especially in the cotton growing districts, leaves them abundant time for their own domestic affairs, if they have any disposition to im-prove it. Hence the general fact that the Negroes who keep the Sabbath, are the most thrifty and well-to-live" (Jones 1842: 138). I do not mean to suggest that all churchgoing Witherspoon slaves would have actively par-ticipated in this cycle of church discipline. Many slaves on the plantation were nonmembers, and some members may have ignored or not partici-pated in this aspect of church life. Evidence from the Mechanicsville Bap-tist Church minutes clearly shows that at least some Witherspoon slaves worked to create a disciplining landscape through moral surveillance and adherence to both plantation and church rules.

Slaves were not oblivious to the flagrant "Servant, obey your masters" indoctrination that official church sermons attempted to convey (Berlin 2003: 207). Slaves attended church for many reasons beyond a sincere concern for their spiritual enlightenment or because their masters required it. Membership in religious communities likely offered significant advantages for bondsmen. In the simplest sense, the trip to church may have been seen as a break in the monotony of everyday plantation life. Services, meetings, and other church activities offered slaves a chance to network, socialize, and form relationships with slaves from the broader region in an environment beyond the direct purview of their individual owner or overseers (Berlin 2003).

Within several years of Emancipation, most black church members in the Darlington region had been dismissed from their former church congregations (Salem Baptist Church 1797–1930). They joined the new black churches that sprang up quickly after the war; these often were organized by former deacons and preachers who drew on experience and training from their time in antebellum churches (Cornelius 1999).

Discussion

Archaeological and documentary evidence from the plantation strongly suggests that J. D. Witherspoon adopted elements of the reform discourse advocated in the agricultural literature and by his peers. While the plantation did not meet every aspect of the reform ideals, certain principles of housing design and moral instruction were implemented on Witherspoon Island over time.

At the household landscape level, the lives of the enslaved inhabitants became less private with the adoption of moral and sanitation reforms. Watchfulness by neighbors and regular inspections by overseers and drivers meant that at Witherspoon Island, slave quarters and their yards were no longer sheltered landscapes separate from the slaves' daily labors on the plantation.

The nineteenth-century reform discourse attempted to create a duplicitous landscape that projected humanitarian and moralistic ideals, while in reality, the core of reform discourse aimed to develop a better means to control slaves and to protect the planters' investment. The true nature of this reform discourse was recognized by the enslaved laborers, who took what advantages they could from the improved environments, while attempting to resist the planters' ulterior motives, aimed at creating a visually and spatially disciplining landscape (Vlach 1995: 126–127).

Landscapes analyzed through a discourse materialized framework can offer archaeologists a distinct perspective on intimate domestic spaces while not treating them as isolated entities. The reforms examined in this study are just one aspect of the discourses that shaped the lives of enslaved individuals and the material appearance of household landscapes on Witherspoon Island. All cultural landscapes in the past, as in the present, were constantly in flux, in Schein's (1997) sense representing multiple, competing materialized discourses.

References Cited

Beaudry, Mary C.
1999 House and Household: The Archaeology of Domestic Life in Early America. In *Old and New Worlds,* edited by Geoff Egan and Ronald L. Michael, pp. 117–126. Oxbow, Oxford, U.K.
Berlin, Ira
2003 *Generations of Captivity: A History of African-American Slaves.* Belknap Press of Harvard University Press, Cambridge, Massachusetts.
Brandon, Jamie C., and Kerri S. Barile
2004 Introduction: Household Chores; or, The Chore of Defining the Household. In *Household Chores and Household Choices: Theorizing the Domestic Sphere in Historical Archaeology,* edited by Kerri S. Barile and Jamie Brandon, pp. 1–14. University of Alabama Press, Tuscaloosa.
Breeden, James O.
1980 *Advice among Masters: The Ideal of Slave Management in the Old South.* Greenwood Press, Westport, Connecticut.
Clay, Thomas S.
1833 *Detail of a Plan for the Moral Improvement of Negroes on Plantations.* Privately printed, Georgia.
Cornelius, Janet
1999 *Slave Missions and the Black Church in the Antebellum South.* University of South Carolina Press, Columbia.
Daly, John Patrick
2002 *When Slavery Was Called Freedom: Evangelism, Proslavery, and the Causes of the Civil War.* University Press of Kentucky, Lexington.
Darlington Agricultural Society
1846–1880 Minutes of the Darlington Agricultural Society (S.C.). South Caroliniana Library, University of South Carolina, Columbia.

Dubose, John Witherspoon
1910 *The Witherspoons of Society Hill.* Hartsville Publishing, Hartsville, South Carolina.
Duncan, James
1990 *The City as Text: The Politics of Landscape Interpretation in the Kandyan Kingdom.* Cambridge University Press, New York.
Edwards-Ingram, Ywone D.
1998 "Trash" Revisited: A Comparative Approach to Historical Descriptions and Archaeological Analyses of Slave Houses and Yards. In *Keep Your Head to the Sky: Interpreting African American Home Ground,* edited by Grey Gundaker, pp. 245–271. University Press of Virginia, Charlottesville.
Finkelman, Paul
2007 The Significance and Persistence of Proslavery Thought. In *The Problem of Evil: Slavery, Freedom, and the Ambiguities of American Reform,* edited by Steven Mintz and John Stauffer, pp. 95–114. University of Massachusetts Press, Amherst.
Fogle, Kevin R.
2012 Boundaries of Enslaved Life on Witherspoon Island. Dissertation proposal, on file, Department of Anthropology, University of South Carolina, Columbia.
Ford, Lacy
2009 *Deliver Us from Evil: The Slavery Question in the Old South.* Oxford University Press, New York.
Genovese, Eugene
1976 *Roll, Jordan, Roll: The World That the Slaves Made.* Random House, New York.
Huger, Daniel E.
1845 *Proceedings of the Meeting in Charleston, S.C., May 13–15, 1845, on the Religious Instruction of the Negroes: Together with the Report of the Committee, and the Address to the Public.* B. Jenkins, Charleston, South Carolina.
Jones, Charles C.
1842 *The Religious Instruction of the Negroes in the United States.* Thomas Purse, Savannah, Georgia.
Joyner, Charles
1984 *Down by the Riverside: A South Carolina Slave Community.* University of Illinois Press, Urbana.
Kenny, Stephen
2009 "A Dictate of Both Interest and Mercy"? Slave Hospitals in the Antebellum South. *Journal of the History of Medicine and Allied Sciences* 64: 1–47.
McGrath, Alister
2006 *Christianity: An Introduction.* Blackwell, Malden, Massachusetts.
McKee, Larry
1992 The Ideals and Realities behind the Design and Use of 19th-Century Virginia Slave Cabins. In *The Art and Mystery of Historical Archaeology: Essays in Honor of James Deetz,* edited by Anne E. Yentsch and Mary C. Beaudry, pp. 195–213. CRC Press, Boca Raton, Florida.

Mechanicsville Baptist Church
1803–1829 Minutes of Mechanicsville Baptist Church 1803–1829 (Darlington County, S.C.). South Caroliniana Library, University of South Carolina, Columbia.
1829–1867 Minutes of Mechanicsville Baptist Church 1829–1867 (Darlington County, S.C.). South Caroliniana Library, University of South Carolina, Columbia.
Mintz, Sidney W.
1974 *Caribbean Transformations.* Aldine, Chicago.
Mitchell, Don
2002 Cultural Landscapes: The Dialectical Landscape—Recent Landscape Research in Human Geography. *Progress in Human Geography* 26: 381–389.
Montgomery, William
1993 *Under Their Own Vine and Fig Tree: The African-American Church in the South, 1865–1900.* Louisiana State University Press, Baton Rouge.
Morgan, Philip D.
1987 Three Planters and Their Slaves: Perspectives on Slavery on Virginia, South Carolina, and Jamaica, 1750–1790. In *Race and the Family in the Colonial South*, edited by Winthrop Jordan and Sheila Skemp, pp. 37–80. University Press of Mississippi, Jackson.
Oakes, James
1982 *The Ruling Race: A History of American Slaveholders.* Knopf, New York.
Pluckhahn, Thomas
2010 Household Archaeology in the Southeastern United States: History, Trends, and Challenges. *Journal of Archaeological Research* 18: 331–385.
R.W.N.N.
1856 Negro Cabins. *Southern Planter* 16: 121–122.
Raboteau, Albert
1978 *Slave Religion: The "Invisible Institution" in the Antebellum South.* Oxford University Press, New York.
Salem Baptist Church
1797–1930 Minutes of Salem Baptist Church 1797–1930 (Marlboro County, S.C.). South Caroliniana Library, University of South Carolina, Columbia.
Sales and Appraisal Book
1860 Darlington District Sales and Appraisal Book. Darlington County Historical Commission, Darlington, South Carolina.
Schein, Richard H.
2009 Belonging through Land/scape. *Environment and Planning A* 41: 811–826.
2004 Cultural Traditions. In *A Companion to Cultural Geography*, edited by James Duncan, Nuala C. Johnson, and Richard H. Schein, pp. 9–23. Blackwell, Malden, Massachusetts.
1997 The Place of Landscape: A Conceptual Framework for Interpreting an American Scene. *Annals of the Association of American Geographers* 87: 660–680.

Seabrook, Whitemarsh

1834 *An Essay on the Management of Slaves and Especially, on Their Religious Instruction: Read before the Agricultucal* [sic] *Society of St. John's Colleton*. A. E. Miller, Charleston, South Carolina.

Southern Cultivator

1850 Houses of Negros—Habits of Living, &c. *Southern Cultivator* 8: 66–67.

Sparks, Randy

1988 Religion in Amite County, Mississippi, 1800–1861. In *Master* and *Slaves in the House of the Lord: Race and Religion in the American South, 1740–1870*, edited by John B. Boles, pp. 58–80. University Press of Kentucky, Lexington.

Spencer-Wood, Suzanne

2002 The Historical Archaeology of Nineteenth Century American Cultural Landscapes: A Review. *Landscape Journal* 21: 173–182.

Tal, Guy

2004 Intimate Landscapes. *Nature Photographers Online Magazine,* July. Electronic document, http://www.naturephotographers.net/articles0704/gt0704-1.html, accessed September 30, 2014.

Till, Tom

2012 The Forgotten Intimate Landscape. *Outdoor Photographer* (May): 48–53.

Touchstone, Blake

1988 Planters and Slave Religion in the Deep South. In *Master and Slaves in the House of the Lord: Race and Religion in the American South, 1740–1870*, edited by John B. Boles, pp. 99–126. University Press of Kentucky, Lexington.

Trifkovic, Vuk

2006 Persons and Landscapes: Shifting Scales of Landscape Archaeology. In *Confronting Scale in Archaeology: Issues of Theory and Practice*, edited by Gary Lock and Brian Molyneaux, pp. 257–271. Springer, New York.

U.S. Federal Census

1860 U.S. Federal Census, 1860. Microfilm on file, South Carolina Department of Archives and History, Columbia.

Vlach, John M.

1995 "Snug Li'l House with Flue and Oven": Nineteenth-Century Reforms in Plantation Slave Housing. *Perspectives in Vernacular Architecture* 5: 118–129.

1993 Not Mansions . . . But Good Enough: Slave Quarters as Bi-cultural Expression. In *Black and White Cultural Interaction in the Antebellum South*, edited by Ted Ownby, pp. 89–114. University Press of Mississippi, Jackson.

Walton, John, James F. Brooks, and Christopher R. N. DeCorse

2008 Introduction. In *Small Worlds: Method, Meaning, and Narrative in Microhistory*, edited by James F. Brooks, Christopher R. N. DeCorse, and John Walton, pp. 3–12. School for Advanced Research, Santa Fe, New Mexico.

Westmacott, Richard

2001 Gardening, Yard Decoration, and Agriculture among Peoples of African Descent in the Rural South and in the Cayman Islands. In *Places of Cultural Memory: African*

Reflections on the American Landscape, edited by Bruce D. Joyner, pp. 135–138. U.S. Department of the Interior, National Park Service, Atlanta, Georgia.

1992 *African-American Gardens and Yards in the Rural South.* University of Tennessee Press, Knoxville.

Wilkie, Laurie

1996 House Gardens and Female Identity on Crooked Island. *Journal of Bahamas Historical Society* 18: 33–39.

7

Households of the Overseas Chinese
in Aurora, Nevada

EMILY DALE

In 2011, the U.S. Forest Service conducted excavations of a Chinese-occupied section of Aurora, Nevada, a late nineteenth-century mining boomtown. Research into the town's past as well as investigations of the artifacts recovered during excavation revealed that what had been excavated were Chinese households. Here I attempt to integrate the archaeology of Chinese immigration in the western United States with studies of household activities through a case study in northern Nevada.

Household archaeology attempts to understand the day-to-day life of the domestic sphere (Allison 1999: 1). Definitions of household archaeology that deemphasize kinship as a determining factor (Beaudry 1999: 121; Laslett 1972: 24) are especially important for the archaeology of Chinese immigrants, who were mostly men discriminated against by federal legislation restricting Chinese immigration, conditions that precluded the formation of extended or even nuclear families. Hence, in nineteenth-century America, the living situations of Chinese immigrants seldom revolved around familial or kin ties. While numerous archaeologists have attempted to understand the domestic activities of Chinese immigrants (e.g., Greenwood 1996; Ritchie 1993; Valentine 1999), only a few have taken a household archaeology approach (e.g., Greenwood and Slawson 2008; Stapp 1993). Voss has criticized the manner in which scholars have applied a household archaeology framework to their interpretations of Chinese sites, noting that archaeologists focusing on the household "privilege normative, middle-class European American practices related to the family unit, property ownership, and refuse disposal" (2008: 37), disregarding Chinese notions of household forms and functions. Taking these concerns into consideration, I argue that by studying Chinese immigrants at the household level and by framing interpretations at the scale of daily activity, archaeologists can de-exoticize the lives of Chinese immigrants, contest troubled theoretical perspectives arising from the application of acculturation and assimilation models, and attempt to comprehend Chinese households from an emic, insider perspective.

Historical Overview

Aurora, one of Nevada's first and biggest mining boomtowns, was founded in 1861. By 1864, the town boasted a population of 6,000 to 10,000 people. Later that same year, the mining industry in the town collapsed and Aurora began to fade. Additional booms, dependent on the resurrection of mining interest in the area, and busts, caused by the inevitable failure of the mines, occurred throughout the rest of the century. One of the more successful later booms took place in the late 1870s and early 1880s. This second boom, however, was much smaller than Aurora's first, and the town was home to only 500 residents. In 1920, the census recorded only 6 men in the town (U.S. Census Bureau 1920); Aurora's last resident died in the 1930s (Shaw 2009: 158). Aurora also contained one of the state's earliest Chinese populations, which waxed and waned in conjunction with Aurora's successes and failures.

Combining historical research, archaeological data, and geographic analysis, I discuss the presence of the Chinese and their households in Aurora both demographically and spatially. I focus on the results of archaeological research and the interpretations these allow regarding architectural, demographic, and consumer material culture recovered from these households.

Aurora had an Overseas Chinese population throughout its history, as evidenced by mention of them in newspaper articles, tax assessment rolls, census records (e.g., County of Esmeralda 1875; U.S. Census Bureau 1870, 1880, 1900, 1910), and other documents. In 1863, two Chinese men were jailed for fighting in the street (*Aurora Daily Times* 1863). In the 1870s and 1880s, Aurora was host to lively Chinese New Year celebrations. And in 1920 two of Aurora's six recorded remaining residents were Chinese (U.S. Census Bureau 1920). Aurora remained, through good times and bad, a viable community for the Chinese.

While most of Aurora's records describe the activities of Chinese men who made the town their home, as well as the value of their lots and homes in the assessment rolls and their exploits and business advertisements in the local newspapers, Aurora was also home to a few Chinese women. These women were recorded in the censuses, married at the courthouse (*Esmeralda Herald* 1881), nearly kidnapped (*Esmeralda Herald* 1878b), involved in knife fights in the street (*Esmeralda Herald* 1878a), and worked as prostitutes (*Esmeralda Daily Union* 1864c).

Aurora's Chinese also held a variety of jobs over time. A "China Doctor" was practicing in Aurora in 1864, while other Chinese operated washhouses, a Chinese store, and a restaurant on the town's main street owned by Chee Kwong. Chinese gardens were common throughout Aurora's history, and Chinese laundries persisted throughout the decades. The Chinese also worked as cooks, woodchoppers, servants, and, in the case of some women, prostitutes.

One thing that united Aurora's Chinese in the town's early years was the 1864 passage of Ordinance 32. Possibly passed by the board of aldermen as a response to public outcry against Chinese brothels (*Esmeralda Daily Union* 1864c), Ordinance 32 limited Chinese residence to the northwest section of Aurora on Spring Street west of Roman Street. Until this point, Spring Street was a highly populated part of town. According to the 1863 and 1864 Mono County Assessment Rolls and the 1864 Esmeralda County Assessment Roll, nearly all of the lots on Spring Street were occupied by Euro-Americans as both residences and businesses (County of Mono 1864, 1863; County of Esmeralda 1864). The ordinance, passed in March 1864, went into effect in April that same year. A June trial for a Chinese individual who violated Ordinance 32 called the legality of the bylaw into question (*Esmeralda Daily Union* 1864b). No information is available on the outcome of the trial, but by late 1864, as the *Esmeralda Union* reported, "nearly all the houses on [Spring] street [were] occupied by Chinese" (*Esmeralda Daily Union* 1864a).

Most of the historical records from the late 1860s and early 1870s are missing, likely the result of Aurora's economic downturn in 1864 and 1865 and the numerous relocations of those records throughout the ensuing decades. Therefore, there is no way to determine the exact date when Ordinance 32 was no longer in effect. Historical documentation from the 1880s and 1890s, however, indicates that residential patterns in Aurora shifted dramatically in the 1870s and 1880s.

The town's dwindling population was concentrated on the blocks around downtown's Pine Street, and the Chinese were no exception. Assessment rolls and newspaper articles from this time period note the presence of the Chinese around the courthouse and on Pine Street. Besides a Chinese garden and mills at Spring Street's far end, near the town's western boundary, and a few residences east of Roman Street, Spring Street was apparently uninhabited. Ordinance 32, then, seems to have held little sway over later Chinese populations, a hypothesis I tested through historical research and archaeological investigations in the area of Aurora set aside by Ordinance 32 for Chinese occupation.

Excavations and Households

In June 2011, with the assistance of the U.S. Forest Service and their volunteer-based Passport in Time community outreach program, I led excavations on Spring Street to discover how Ordinance 32 affected Chinese occupations of Aurora and for how long. We placed ten 1 × 1 meter excavation units along Spring Street, west of Roman Street, in the physical outlines of five separate domestic household platforms. We excavated five houselots along Spring Street in 2011; the majority of the data on the home lives of Aurora's 1860s and 1870s Chinese immigrants came from two distinct, neighboring habitations. A combination of historical and artifactual data confirmed an 1860s to 1870s residential occupation of this portion of Spring Street by Chinese householders. Our excavations focused on these two households.

In Aurora's first years, numerous businesses were set up along Spring Street, mostly in the form of stables, a brewery, and mills. But houses were also present. The 1864 Assessment Roll records these numerous domestic spaces as "cabin," "residence," and "house" (County of Esmeralda 1864). The same reference to "house" appears in the 1865 Assessment Roll for the Chinese-occupied lots and buildings (County of Esmeralda 1865), and a newspaper article from 1864 refers to the structures on Spring Street as "houses" (*Esmeralda Daily Union* 1864b). This differs from mentions of Chinese-run businesses. The 1864 Assessment Roll refers to a Chinese laundry, a potential brothel, and a store as "buildings" or by their purpose, such as "store" or "Wash House." The difference in language, "house" versus "building," suggests an acknowledgment of different functions and perhaps served as a way for the county assessor to organize the entries and assess taxes appropriately. Since the entries for Chinese businesses mention no other buildings on the lots in question or additional lots owned by the Chinese who operated the businesses, it seems likely that the buildings functioned as both businesses and residences. The same is clearly not true for the structures along Spring Street, which, again, were referred to solely as houses.

Additionally, the highly domestic character of the Spring Street archaeological assemblages, which include faunal remains, apparel fragments, and personal items, along with a lack of industrial or commercial objects associated with Chinese laundries, stores, or other businesses, points to a residential use of these Spring Street lots. Therefore, we can presume that these Spring Street Chinese used their lots for residential rather than business purposes. The archaeological deposits were shallow, and Chinese artifacts were mixed with Euro-American artifacts throughout all levels and down to sterile. I concluded that the excavated assemblage represented the Chinese occupation of these premises and not the Euro-American households previously located on Spring Street, who may have disposed of their rubbish differently than later Chinese inhabitants.

I framed the assemblage in terms of household activities, rather than solely as a reflection of the Chinese identity of the individuals who used and discarded the artifacts. By combining these two aspects, households and ethnicity, we can derive a more holistic, context-driven, and in-depth view of the physical space inhabited by the households. In doing so we are able to approximate the demographics of the households, and determine the types of activities in which members of the household participated. I discuss below the architectural, demographic, and consumptive information gleaned from the excavated assemblage of these Chinese households.

Architecture of the Household

A household by one definition is bounded by the physical space its members share "for the purposes of eating, sleeping, [and] taking rest and leisure" (Laslett 1972: 24; see also Beaudry 1999: 121). One question that emerges when discussing Aurora's Spring Street Chinese, then, is what were the physical characteristics of the household spaces inhabited by the Chinese on Spring Street?

Spring Street was occupied prior to the passage of Ordinance 32, and the Chinese who relocated here moved into houses constructed by Spring

Street's earlier Euro-American residents. The Chinese were given only one month to move after the passage of the ordinance, so inhabiting previously constructed houses would have been more practical than building new homes.

The historical record offers little information about the buildings on Spring Street, though the 1864 Assessment Roll mentions a few "frame" or "wood" houses (County of Esmeralda 1864). Architectural artifacts recovered during excavations included cut nails, plaster, mortar, a brick, milled wood, foundation stones, and window glass, all of which are appropriate components of the sort of frame and wood houses recorded in the assessment roll.

The historical information, coupled with the archaeological record, suggests that the Chinese lived in simple wood cabins or dugouts, perhaps with one or two windows. The Chinese, then, lived in Euro-American built houses, and the spaces these households afforded were not necessarily of Chinese design or construction. This does not mean, however, that the Chinese on Aurora's Spring Street declined to make alterations to houses they did not construct. We recovered examples of painted wood and plaster during our excavations that led us to infer that the Chinese added finishing touches to the buildings in keeping with their own aesthetic sensibilities.

The writings of Mark Twain offer additional information on the domestic architecture of Aurora. Before adopting his famous moniker, Samuel Clemens came west with his brother Orion to try his luck in Nevada's and California's goldfields. Eventually, he settled for a few months in Aurora, where he lived for a time with his friend Calvin Higbie on the latter's Spring Street lot (Stewart 2004: 85–90) in the area that would in a few years' time be set aside for the Chinese by Ordinance 32. Twain's *Roughing It* chronicles his western adventures, including his time spent in Aurora. He included an illustration of a "floorless, tumble-down" cabin (Twain 1995: 260) with a "broken [window] pane" (Twain 1995: 267) (figure 7.1).

No Chinese were recorded as living in Higbie's cabin after his 1864 departure from Aurora, and in order to preserve any Twain-related artifacts for future excavators who might wish to explore the famous author's time in Aurora, we did not excavate the house platform that was most likely Higbie's lot. We do not know whether the Chinese lived in homes like the cabin Twain described or illustrated, but the picture and descriptions offer a brief glimpse into the state of housing and buildings on Spring Street.

Figure 7.1. Mark Twain and Calvin Higbie in Higbie's Spring Street cabin in Aurora (Twain 1995: 260). Note the wooden walls and canvas roof.

Demographics of the Household

The composition of households varies and does not necessarily correspond to a family unit based on kinship. For example, households can take the form of coresident groups such as boardinghouses or corporate households where economic ties bind the residents (Beaudry 1999: 121; Hardesty 1994: 137). It is therefore necessary to explore the internal composition of households. The archaeological assemblage contains information about the demographics of Spring Street's Chinese. For the most part, the Chinese households of Spring Street were male dominated. This was determined both through the lack of female- and child-associated artifacts and through the frequent mention of Chinese men in the documentary record. Analysis and interpretation of the largely male demographics of Aurora's excavated Chinese households contribute to the broader archaeological discussions of gendered households. Hardesty (1994) and Pappas (2004) contend that archaeologists must explicate the gendered dynamics of households, as household patterns created by gender-based organizations of space can be found archaeologically. Without an understanding of who made up these households, the nuances of artifact assemblages (as discussed below) are muddled or even lost.

Only one mention of a Chinese woman living on Spring Street was found in the historical record, in the 1863 Mono County Assessment Roll (County of Mono 1863), and no artifacts specifically associated with women, whether Chinese or Euro-American, were recovered from the Spring Street excavations. The lack of evidence for Chinese women is not surprising, as very few Chinese women immigrated to the United States. In 1860, for example, there were 18 Chinese men for every woman (Wegars 1993: 233), and by 1890, the imbalance had increased to 28 Chinese men for every woman (Voss and Allen 2008: 13). Additionally, many of the artifacts associated with Chinese women, such as clothing and fans, are ephemeral and seldom survive in the archaeological record. While Aurora's historical records clearly document the presence of Chinese women in the mining town, especially in other parts of the town and later in time, the archaeological record of Spring Street does not.

There is a similar lack of evidence for Chinese children. No children were recorded in the censuses, and the only mention of a Chinese youth in the historical record comes from two 1879 newspaper articles noting the antics of "Pete the China Boy," a young servant at the Del Monte mine's boardinghouse (*Esmeralda Herald* 1879a, 1879b). Excavations on Spring Street recovered no artifacts definitively tied to children. It should be noted, however, that a lack of evidence from the historical and archaeological records does not preclude the presence of women or children on Spring Street.

Historical records hold some clues regarding the male population of Spring Street's Chinese households. The 1865 Esmeralda County Assessment Roll includes three Chinese-occupied lots that coincide with the boundaries of Ordinance 32. Two of these lots are associated with specific Chinese individuals: Ah Ken owned his own lot and house, while Chung Lee lived on a Euro-American's lot. Meanwhile, a Euro-American policeman owned a lot that contained "2 china houses" (County of Esmeralda 1865). Again, no women are recorded on these lots, although in 1864 Wa Kee's Esmeralda Street lot was listed with "property of 3 girls" (County of Esmeralda 1864). Men, then, formed the backbone of these households. The documents do not answer the question of how many males made up the average Chinese household during Aurora's first boom. So while vague demographics are known, precise population counts are not.

Consumption Habits of the Household

A third topic addressed by household archaeology studies is that of consumption and production. Household studies concerned with consumption discuss a range of topics, including household economics, diet, social relationships, and consumer choice (Allison 1999: 8–9; Barile and Brandon 2004; Beaudry 1999: 119). The artifacts recovered from Spring Street provide a window into the lives and consumer choices of the Chinese who lived and worked there during the mid-1800s. Specifically, they provide evidence for the Chinese immigrants' transnational behaviors and habits.

Transnationalism emphasizes the role of both the home and the host society in the lives of immigrant populations. Transmigrants bring values, customs, habits, and culture from their homes with them to the host country, where those values, customs, and habits are maintained, changed, and/or adapted. For the Overseas Chinese, transnationalism encompassed both those who returned to China and those who stayed in America (Smits 2008: 112). Earlier theoretical approaches examined immigration through the lenses of acculturation and assimilation, relying on assumptions about Chinese traditionalism and aversion to change (e.g., Chung and Wegars 2005; Staski 1993). In the past decade, however, historical archaeologists have argued against using assimilation or acculturation models in Overseas Chinese archaeology (e.g., Kraus-Friedberg 2008; Liu 2002; Voss 2005). These scholars employ transnational models to examine a community as a whole, working with both Chinese and non-Chinese influences to explain the material assemblage. In the following section, I analyze the archaeological record of Spring Street through a transnational lens to examine the consumer choices and consumption habits of Aurora's Chinese.

Some of the artifacts reflect the traditional preferences and practices carried with the immigrants from China and maintained in their new homes. A bone toothbrush and opium paraphernalia (figure 7.2), all excavated from Spring Street, were brought or shipped to America from China and Hong Kong before they made their way to Aurora to be purchased by members of the households. As neither opium nor toothbrushes are common on non-Chinese sites (though they can be present without Chinese occupation), past archaeologists have used these artifact categories to discuss the foreignness of Chinese immigrants, implying that "the most important topic that could be addressed through archaeological research

Figure 7.2. Opium paraphernalia. Clockwise from the top: metal opium pipe bowl, intact opium tin lid, partial opium tin lid, and opium lamp part.

at Overseas Chinese sites was the ethnic boundary between Chinese and non-Chinese peoples" (Voss 2005: 427). Other interpretations have used such artifacts to prove Chinese immigrants' inability to assimilate or their resistance to acculturation as a way to grant agency to the Chinese (see, e.g., Staski 1993). In both of these cases, the Chinese can only be understood in contrast to other groups, rather than as people or households in their own right. By viewing these objects from an emic perspective, however, transnational approaches recognize opium and toothbrushes as common, everyday items that reflected a personal consumer choice on the part of the household's members who sought to maintain traditional practices and familiar material culture. Toothbrushes and opium pipes were familiar items from home that the Chinese migrants on Aurora's Spring Street wished to continue using, so they purchased, used, and discarded these items as they would any other desired or necessary goods.

Other artifacts from the assemblage, such as Euro-American style leather shoes, an Ayer's Cherry Pectoral bottle (figure 7.3), and wine or

Figure 7.3. Ayer's Cherry Pectoral bottle.

champagne bottles, represent adoption of Euro-American goods. They also represent an acceptance of certain non-Chinese practices that were more practical in the American West. For example, leather shoes would have been sturdier than traditional Chinese cloth shoes in occupations like mining and wood chopping. Issues of availability may also have contributed to the adoption of certain Euro-American goods. In only one year, 1864, is a "China doctor" listed on any of the tax assessment rolls or census records for Aurora (County of Esmeralda 1864), suggesting that traditional Chinese medicines may not have been available and that American remedies may have been substituted.

Lastly, some parts of the artifact assemblage constitute a combination of American and Chinese artifacts. Most notably, a blend of American and Chinese preferences exists in the food-related assemblage. Four large

Chinese storage jars (figure 7.4), one smaller jar, a soy-sauce spout, and sherds of a ginger jar, all used to ship and store Chinese foods, were found in association with numerous tin cans, used to store Western foods. The Chinese immigrants had access to their traditional fare as well as to food-stuffs typical of their new home, and they chose to consume both.

The faunal assemblage, which is quite diverse, especially points to the mixing of traditional Chinese habits and adopted American lifeways. Sur-prisingly, cow bones constituted more than half of the identifiable faunal assemblage, with pig bones, which generally make up the bulk of Over-seas Chinese archaeological faunal assemblages, accounting for only 10 to 15 percent. Aurora was located in the Sierra Nevada and consequently

Figure 7.4. Large Chinese stoneware storage vessels. Vessel 1, at top left, consists of the base and rim fragments. Note the distinct heel. Vessel 2, made up of the rim and base fragments in the middle and lower right, displays a sloping heel. The rim in the up-per right constitutes Vessel 3. Chinese characters impressed into the surface translate to "Tung Ho" and most likely represent a company name (Frank Lai and Chris Wu, personal communication 2011). These characters are slightly visible to the left of the handle.

was cold for much of the year. As a result, farmers and ranchers raised few pigs near the town (Kinchloe-Smith 2001: 108), indicating that the town's Chinese residents had little access to their favored protein. The higher number of cow bones than pig bones in the faunal assemblage, therefore, indicates dietary adaptation on the part of the Chinese. When their preferred meat was not obtainable, the immigrants turned to the readily available beef supplies in town. Overall, the integration of locally available meat cuts and canned foods with imported traditional Chinese foods points to the transnational combination of traditional consumption habits and newly acquired Euro-American practices.

There are, of course, alternative explanations beyond transnational ones for the blended archaeological assemblage recovered from Spring Street. Adapting the linguistic theories of double consciousness and code switching, some archaeologists have argued that in situations of culture contact, groups consciously navigate the public/private domains to cultivate acceptance in their new communities while simultaneously maintaining traditions at home (Deagan 1998, 1983; Ferguson 1992). For Aurora's Chinese, then, consumer choices manifest in the archaeological assemblage may reflect more than practicality; they may reflect deliberate social strategies employed by the Chinese to successfully navigate both public and private arenas. If the Chinese employed public displays of Euro-American consumption habits to foster positive reactions, the near-universal lack of racialized negative portrayals of the Chinese in Aurora's newspapers, coupled with articles sympathetic to their troubles, suggests that their strategies worked.

Finally, it is important to remember that these Auroran Chinese households were part of larger transnational households that spanned the Atlantic and connected the immigrants to their families back home in China. The American- and Chinese-situated households were enmeshed in kinship and economic relationships that transcended state and national boundaries. While the archaeology in Aurora grants insight into the lives of Chinese households in Nevada, the excavations reveal only part of the picture. The larger picture of transnational households and the familial relationships that bridged an ocean is still missing. Acknowledging this gap in the historical and archaeological record may ameliorate some of Voss's concerns regarding the European ideals of households placed on Chinese sites and help archaeologists theorize about emic perspectives of Chinese households and family.

Conclusions

Household archaeology places "people and their practices and differences at the center of archaeological interpretations of the past, rather than subsuming these in the 'noise' of passive and depersonalized depictions of . . . social systems" (Robin 2003: 307). In this chapter I attempt to focus on the Chinese as individuals, rather than as members of a faceless mass, by focusing on Chinese households from the late 1800s.

The 1860s and 1870s Chinese residents along Aurora's Spring Street lived in homes constructed by Euro-Americans that may have been adapted by Chinese individuals to suit their needs and tastes, male-dominated demographics, and transnational consumption choices. Only by understanding and explicitly exploring the roles of ethnicity, gender, and agency in the day-to-day activities and choices of Aurora's early Chinese community can we obtain a fuller and more meaningful picture of Chinese households.

The day in the life of one of these men may have included tidying up his American-built log cabin, brushing his teeth with a familiar bone toothbrush, indulging in some opium, wine, or champagne, and dressing in Western-style clothing before heading off to work as a laundry employee, restaurant owner or chef, gardener, or woodchopper, and then coming home to eat a dinner that consisted of beef, canned foods, and vegetables grown in one of the many Chinese gardens that operated in the area. Because of historical biases against the Chinese and gaps in the historical record, the names and identities of these Chinese individuals have been lost, but the remains of their household activities can still offer a glimpse into their daily lives.

Acknowledgments

I would like to first thank James Nyman and Kevin Fogle for organizing the symposium at the 2013 SHA meetings that led to this book and for allowing me to be a part of it. To Mary Beaudry, Mark Groover, and Kerri Barile, thank you for your insightful and helpful comments. I would also like to thank Carolyn White, my advisor, for all of her advice, support, and edits. Finally, thanks must go to Cliff Shaw for his love of Aurora and to Fred Frampton, who funded this project; without these two, I could not have undertaken this research. Any errors or omissions are my own.

References Cited

Allison, Penelope M.
1999 Introduction. In *The Archaeology of Household Activities*, edited by Penelope M. Allison, pp. 1–18. Routledge, London.

Aurora Daily Times [Aurora, Nevada]
1863 [No title.] 27 November. Aurora, Nevada.

Barile, Kerri S., and Jamie C. Brandon (editors)
2004 *Household Chores and Household Choices: Theorizing the Domestic Sphere in Historical Archaeology*. University of Alabama Press, Tuscaloosa.

Beaudry, Mary C.
1999 House and Household: The Archaeology of Domestic Life in Early America. In *Old and New Worlds*, edited by Geoff Egan and R. L. Michael, pp. 117–126. Oxbow Books, Oxford, U.K.

Chung, Sue Fawn, and Priscilla Wegars
2005 Introduction. In *Chinese American Death Rituals: Respecting the Ancestors*, edited by Sue Fawn Chung and Priscilla Wegars, pp. 1–17. AltaMira Press, Lanham, Maryland.

County of Esmeralda [Nevada]
1875 *Esmeralda County Census*. On file at the Nevada State History Museum, Reno.
1865 *Esmeralda County Tax Assessment Roll*. On file at the Esmeralda County Recorder's Office, Goldfield, Nevada.
1864 *Esmeralda County 1864 Assessment Roll*. On file at the Nevada State History Museum, Reno.

County of Mono [California]
1864 *Mono County 1864 Assessment Roll*. On file at the Mono County Museum, Bridgeport, California.
1863 *Mono County 1863 Assessment Roll*. On file at the Mono County Museum, Bridgeport, California.

Deagan, Kathleen A.
1998 Transculturation and Spanish American Ethnogenesis: The Archaeological Legacy of the Quincentenary. In *Studies in Culture Contact: Interaction, Culture Change, and Archaeology*, edited by J. G. Cusick, pp. 23–43. Occasional Paper 25. Center for Archaeological Investigations, Southern Illinois University, Carbondale.
1983 *Spanish St. Augustine: The Archaeology of a Colonial Creole Community*. Academic Press, New York.

Esmeralda Daily Union [Aurora, Nevada]
1864a The Chinese for Little Mack. 1 November. Aurora, Nevada.
1864b City Ordinance 32. 16 June. Aurora, Nevada.
1864c Report to Grand Jury: *To the Honorable District Court*. 31 March. Aurora, Nevada.

Esmeralda Herald [Aurora, Nevada]
1881 Celestial Wedding. 26 November. Aurora, Nevada.
1879a A Little Spread. 1 November. Aurora, Nevada.
1879b He Didn't Know It Was Loaded. 4 October. Aurora, Nevada.

1878a [Story about a knife fight.] 17 August. Aurora, Nevada.

1878b The China Gardens. 15 June. Aurora, Nevada.

Ferguson, Leland

1992 *Uncommon Ground: Archaeology and Early African America, 1650–1800*. Smithsonian Institution Press, Washington, D.C.

Greenwood, Roberta S. (editor)

1996 *Down by the Station: Los Angeles Chinatown, 1880–1933*. Monumenta Archaeologica 18. Institute of Archaeology, University of California, Los Angeles.

Greenwood, Roberta S., and Dana N. Slawson

2008 Gathering Insights on Isolation. *Historical Archaeology* 42: 68–79.

Hardesty, Donald L.

1994 Class, Gender Strategies, and Material Culture in the Mining West. In *Those of Little Note: Gender, Race, and Class in Historical Archaeology*, edited by Elizabeth M. Scott, pp. 129–146. University of Arizona Press, Tucson.

Kinchloe-Smith, Jessica

2001 The Best the Market Could Afford: Food Consumption at the Merchants' Exchange Hotel, Aurora, Nevada. Unpublished master's thesis, Department of Anthropology, University of Nevada, Reno.

Kraus-Friedberg, Chana

2008 Transnational Identity and Mortuary Material Culture: The Chinese Plantation Cemetery in Pahala, Hawai'i. *Historical Archaeology* 42: 123–135.

Laslett, Peter (editor)

1972 *Household and Family in Past Time*. Cambridge University Press, Cambridge.

Liu, Haiming

2002 The Social Origins of Early Chinese Immigrants: A Revisionist Perspective. In *The Chinese in America: A History from Gold Mountain to the New Millennium*, edited by Susie Lan Cassel, pp. 21–36. AltaMira Press, Walnut Creek, California.

Pappas, Efstathios I.

2004 Fictive Kin the Mountains: The Paternalistic Metaphor and Households in a California Logging Camp. In *Household Chores and Household Choices: Theorizing the Domestic Sphere in Historical Archaeology*, edited by Kerri S. Barile and Jamie C. Brandon, pp. 159–176. University of Alabama Press, Tuscaloosa.

Ritchie, Neville A.

1993 Form and Adaptation: Nineteenth Century Chinese Miners' Dwellings in Southern New Zealand. In *Hidden Heritage: Historical Archaeology of the Overseas Chinese*, edited by Priscilla Wegars, pp. 335–373. Baywood, Amityville, New York.

Robin, Cynthia

2003 New Directions in Classic Maya Household Archaeology. *Journal of Archaeological Research* 11: 307–356.

Shaw, Clifford Alpheus

2009 *An 1864 Directory and Guide to Nevada's Aurora: Embracing a General Directory of Businesses, Residents, Mines, Stamp Mills, Toll Roads, etc., Including an Account of the Grand Celebration of July 4, 1864, and a Brief History of the Wide West Mine*. C. A. Shaw, privately published, n.p.

Smits, Nicholas J.

2008 Roots Entwined: Archaeology of an Urban Chinese American Cemetery. *Historical Archaeology* 42: 111–122.

Stapp, Darby C.

1993 The Documentary Record of an Overseas Chinese Mining Camp. In *Hidden Heritage: Historical Archaeology of the Overseas Chinese*, edited by Priscilla Wegars, pp. 3–31. Baywood, Amityville, New York.

Staski, Edward

1993 The Overseas Chinese in El Paso: Changing Goals, Changing Realities. In *Hidden Heritage: Historical Archaeology of the Overseas Chinese*, edited by Priscilla Wegars, pp. 125–149. Baywood, Amityville, New York.

Stewart, Robert E.

2004 *Aurora: Nevada's Ghost City of the Dawn*. Nevada Publications, Las Vegas.

Twain, Mark

1995 *Roughing It*. University of California Press, Berkeley.

U.S. Census Bureau

1920 *United States Census*. On file at the Nevada State History Museum, Reno.

1910 *United States Census*. On file at the Nevada State History Museum, Reno.

1900 *United States Census*. On file at the Nevada State History Museum, Reno.

1880 *United States Census*. On file at the Nevada State History Museum, Reno.

1870 *United States Census*. On file at the Nevada State History Museum, Reno.

Valentine, David

1999 American Canyon: A Chinese Village. In *Community in the American West*, edited by Stephen Tchudi, pp. 107–130. Nevada Humanities Committee, Reno.

Voss, Barbara L.

2008 Between the Household and the World System: Social Collectivity and Community Agency in Overseas Chinese Archaeology. *Historical Archaeology* 42: 37–52.

2005 The Archaeology of Overseas Chinese Communities. *World Archaeology* 37: 424–439.

Voss, Barbara L., and Rebecca Allen

2008 Overseas Chinese Archaeology: Historical Foundations, Current Reflections and New Directions. *Historical Archaeology* 42: 5–28.

Wegars, Priscilla

1993 Besides Polly Bemis: Historical and Artifactual Evidence for Chinese Women in the West, 1848–1930. In *Hidden Heritage: Historical Archaeology of the Overseas Chinese*, edited by Priscilla Wegars, pp. 229–254. Baywood, Amityville, New York.

8

....

Traditions and Tasks

Household Production and the Internal Economy
at Dean Hall Plantation, South Carolina

NICOLE ISENBARGER AND ANDREW AGHA

The recent archaeological work at Dean Hall Plantation has produced
some of the most compelling evidence for on-site colonoware production ever recovered in South Carolina (Agha et al. 2012). From this evidence, we are able to explore the ways this ceramic tradition was used
to venerate and maintain core West African cultural systems, as well as
how the household production of colonoware strengthened ties and created competition and differences among households within the community. We show how the production of this ancestral craft stimulated the
household's engagement with the internal economy that thrived during
the antebellum period of Charleston's past (Isenbarger 2006; Joseph 1987;
Morgan 1982).

Our analysis employs anthropological approaches to household archaeology and household production to bring colonoware into the realm
of not just the potter but also the whole household as a productive unit.
This perspective allows us to place colonoware within a new context that
includes the entire assemblage recovered from one house to look at how
market access and exchange was affected by the fact that the enslaved
could produce their own ceramics for multiple functions and purposes.
Our analysis departs from typical colonoware studies, in that we focus on
how colonoware was made, who was involved, and how this ware fit in
with other material culture, rather than emphasizing the core West African cultural elements of the pottery (e.g., religion, medicine, resistance to
dominant social structures, African foodways) that are typically reviewed.
Our study, then, affords a better understanding of how each household

at Dean Hall Plantation became a part of a strong and vibrant enslaved community.

Defining Households within an Enslaved Community

Household archaeology has evolved over the past thirty years as an anthropological lens to the archaeological study of past peoples (Allison 1999; Barile and Brandon 2004; Pluckhahn 2010). Richard Wilk and William Rathje summarized the archaeological study of households quite eloquently in the first major publication on the subject: "Material culture can be thought of as a shell whose form reflects the demographic shape and the activities of households" (1982: 618). Building upon Wilk and Rathje's work a few decades later, Foster and Parker observed that "households are the dynamic loci of repetitive actions where personal identities and economic, social and ideological interests of family or co-habitant groups intersect with and shape the trajectory of communities" (2012: 4). This definition summarizes perfectly the historical situation at Dean Hall, a nineteenth-century rice plantation near Charleston, South Carolina, and helps to sharpen our focus on the households and the traditions of their inhabitants, who created this distinctive enslaved community. The "repetitive actions" Foster and Parker mention are the daily customs of preparing, processing, and consuming food and drink; activities involved with both plantation-related and household-related labor that took place in the houses and houseyards of the enslaved; care of family members; and production of crafts and utilitarian objects wanted and needed in enslaved households.

Although the two definitions provided above are thirty years apart, they both stress that we excavate the material remains of a dwelling, or a "house," from which we then extrapolate an interpretation of the "household" that produced and created an archaeological record that reflects the past function of the household (Foster and Parker 2012: 4; Wilk and Rathje 1982: 620). While at Dean Hall we excavated "houses" as components of the slave village, we did not excavate the "households." One particular duplex that we identified as House 15 is the subject of this study, and it is the "house" that we studied as a "household."

When defining *household*, then, we ask, what was the composition of the household at House 15? Technically speaking, a household's members can live under one roof or occupy multiple structures within a compound

(Wilk and Rathje 1982: 620–621). House 15 was a duplex of two rooms under one roof: were there two separate households here, one in each room, or did the duplex serve as the living quarters of one unified household? Did each room house a unique family unit, or did kin ties cross the center wall? Our household study allows us to place enslaved Africans with specific plantation and community roles at House 15. Were House 15's residents involved in different types of household production that may have created social and cultural ties or separations? If two separate households existed here, did they work together to better their condition, or did the benefits from their productiveness as a household drive them apart?

A household analysis at House 15 gives us the opportunity to look at the artifact assemblages from each room with greater intensity than we could devote to our initial study of the slave village as a whole. When we are placing a household within a community, the artifact assemblage representative of the household allows us to "discern how households harness or diffuse opportunities for *distinction* and *social differentiation* within a community" (Foster and Parker 2012: 4; emphasis ours). This notion allows us to question whether the artifacts recovered from House 15 reflect the special distinction or privilege afforded to individuals, and concomitantly to the households they headed or live in, through the unique positions they may have occupied in the labor hierarchy that existed at Dean Hall. It also allows us to question whether social differentiation within the community may have resulted from individuals occupying skilled or specialized labor positions on the plantation and to assess whether that differentiation generated distinctions in privilege, access, and respect within the enslaved community. If social separation was present, can it be rendered visible through analysis of the artifacts we recovered?

Furthermore, we have the opportunity to explore how household production influenced the lives of the enslaved within House 15 and whether it was a factor that fostered "social differentiation" between them and the rest of the village. If House 15 was able to engage in production that was different from that of the other households, was it a benefit to their lives or a burden? Did the community need the goods and crafts House 15 produced, or were members of that household shunned for their ability to engage in household production, activities that members of other households lacked the expertise to perform or were perhaps prevented from undertaking? Or did other households in the village create a competitive situation by producing their own goods?

Historical Background and Setting

Dean Hall Plantation was nestled in the center of a vibrant riverine plantation landscape. Established on the west bank of the Cooper River, nearly 25 miles upriver from Charleston, Dean Hall and its neighbors all existed for one reason: tidal rice cultivation. Historians, anthropologists, and historical archaeologists have shown that West Africans played a role in the technology and methods involved in the success of rice as an export crop (Carney 2001; Carney and Rosomoff 2009; Ferguson 1992; Littlefield 1981; Wood 1996). With success came profits, and those profits prompted accumulation of land and enslaved Africans.

Shortly after Scotsman Alexander Nesbitt founded Dean Hall in 1725, he oversaw the modification of its freshwater swamps into inland rice fields. Nesbitt's grandson Alexander relocated the plantation sometime in the 1790s to a prominent seat on the bank of the Cooper River, where it was flanked by new tidal rice fields. The move was in keeping with the historical shift regionally to tidal rice cultivation dependent on the tidal surges of the rivers that flow through the South Carolina Lowcountry. The plantation's 174 enslaved people were resettled in this new location as well. Grandson Alexander died in 1813, leaving his widow to continue managing and maintaining Dean Hall until she and his older brother, John, agreed to terms of sale for the plantation to William Carson in 1820.

William Carson was a successful merchant and investor in Charleston but was fascinated with rice culture. When he purchased the plantation, the sale included all the original Nesbitt enslaved Africans already there. He constructed a new 50-foot-square mansion, a mill yard on the river, a formal garden with dependencies, and new roads as well as improvements to the existing rice fields—both the newer tidal and the older inland impoundments. The improvement he made that most affected the enslaved community was the razing of the twenty-one single-pen cabins in which they had lived for nearly thirty years. The demolition made way for the construction of sixteen new duplexes, possibly over the period 1821 to 1827, on top of the remains of the old village. He later added a road crossing the center of the village; it was lined with twelve additional duplexes, four of which were two-story homes. Figure 8.1 is a plan view of the pre- and post-1837 village.

This improvement was enclosed within an intricate ditch/embankment drainage system that encircled the settlement, which had come to include

L   K

J   I

Berm   H   G   Berm

Berm

13   11   9   7   5   3   1

16   15   14   12   10   8   5   4   2

Berm   Berm

F   E

D   C

B   A   North

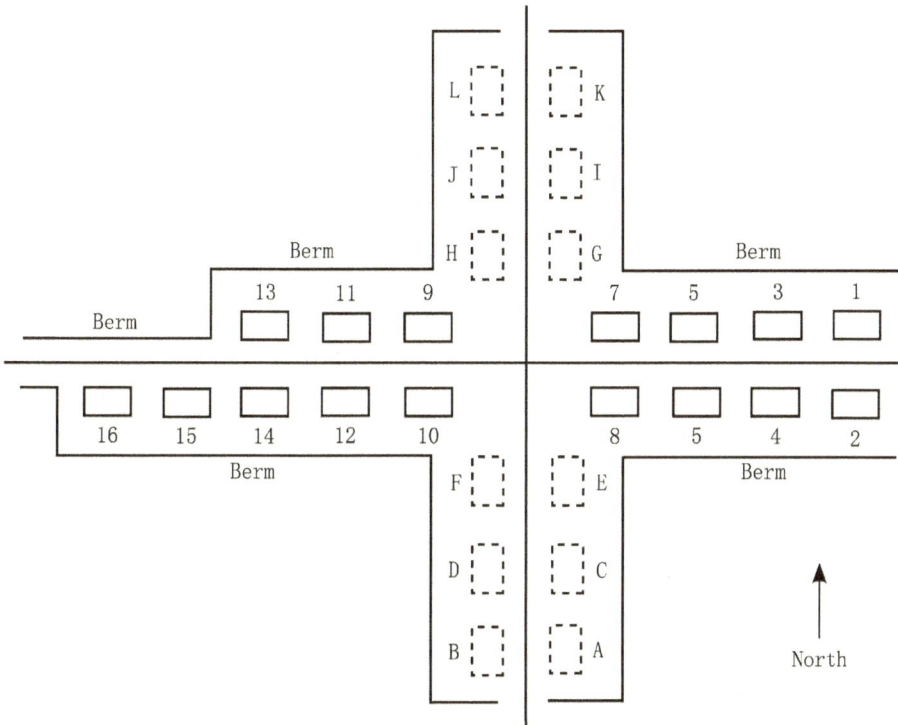

Figure 8.1. Layout of the 1827 and 1837 village (solid line) and post-1837 additions (dashed line). The berm, the roads, and nearly all of the houses were located through archaeology with plat confirmation.

the overseer's house, a work yard, and the complex of plantation buildings as well as the "improved" slave village. The drainage system would have helped protect the village from flooding and is evidence of Carson's concern with hygiene and sanitation—something almost all of his many visitors commented on. Famed Scottish geologist Charles Lyell and Edmund Ruffin both noted in 1843 that the village was clean and orderly and had the appearance of a "town" (Agha et al. 2012: 53–55).

Carson died in 1856, and with his death came the only disruption or change to the enslaved African population in the roughly 125 years of the plantation's existence: the splitting up of some, but not all, of the families through sale. The historical records are quite complete for the plantation and provide no evidence of sales or new purchases of people throughout Carson's thirty-six-year period of ownership. This fact meant that we had the rare opportunity to excavate a site where a community of enslaved

Africans had lived for nearly four decades and where they developed, re-membered, and shared traditions through the formative eighteenth cen-tury, survived an occupation of the plantation by British forces in 1781 and the death of their original owners, and were, ultimately, transferred to a new and unknown owner.

When we were given the opportunity to excavate such a large and in-tact slave village, we focused on how these African descendants practiced traditions that helped to create a community. We concentrated on three historically important areas of practice at Dean Hall that allowed us to comprehend the village as a whole and to identify the "glue" that held everyone together: the production of colonoware, rice cultivation, and the use of African/Gullah names.

The expansion of virgin land into rice fields meant new clay sources for quarries, which we linked to the continued practice of colonoware pro-duction and its use until the end of the nineteenth century. Nesbitt's 1754 inventory of his slaves lists only a few traditional West African and Gullah names (see Turner 1949), but the lists for 1813 and 1820 have both a greater number and a greater variety of names, showing a marked increase over time. Carson's 1857 estate inventory contains the final list of slaves, which records even more African/Gullah names, in both number and variety, than the previous lists combined. This community of African descendants was not forgetting its legacy of languages, potting skills, or centuries-old agricultural practices.

Our examination of the excavated contexts brought us to an under-standing and interpretation of the Dean Hall slave village as a collective community unified through its members' differing African pasts. The thousands and thousands of artifacts we recovered from each house we sampled bear witness to their many years of occupation in these places. We also learned that colonoware, a traditional ceramic commonly found on slave settlements across the South Carolina Lowcountry, was made in great quantities until almost 1900 and, of special note, that many of the colonoware pots made here were decorated with unique, possibly Afri-can-derived decorations and motifs (Agha et al. 2012). The decorations increased in variety and complexity through time and, when considered in tandem with the increasing trend of giving newborns African names, indicate that African traditions were alive, well, and strong at Dean Hall.

Although we excavated at nearly all of the cabins and their yards, we did not scrutinize the cabins at a household level with the same focus we gave to studying the community as a whole. The roughly 125,000 artifacts recovered from all units were collected based on their spatial distribution within each house or in its respective yard and were examined broadly to interpret the village as a community and to examine the ways in which the 59,020 sherds of colonoware could be interpreted as contributing to the continuation of communal traditions. Analyzing one particular duplex, House 15, through the anthropological lens of household archaeology brings forth new information and a much richer understanding of the enslaved community.

Household Production at Dean Hall

We can readily see traditional practices in a smaller, personal family set-ting and can envision the lives of enslaved Africans at Dean Hall not as total unknowns but as people with strong, productive households who harnessed their natural and built environment for their own benefit, to offset the harsh realities of slavery. There were 234 African descendants by 1850, and they lived in thirty duplexes, or sixty rooms. When we were faced with the enormous amount of discarded material generated by such a large labor force, it is easy to claim that we examined the site as a whole, but we also acknowledge that many households were rendered invisible when we aggregated data from the site as whole.

Barile and Brandon (2004: 4) point out the issues involved in examin-ing households as components of larger systems, whereby the household represents a "cultural pattern" that can be compared and contrasted with other household patterns. Here, similarities among household artifact assemblages can help reveal patterns that are representative of cultural processes. This approach is problematic when studying a village of en-slaved Africans: the architecture may have been identical, the institution of slavery may have unified all Africans under it through the common-ality of bondage, but several culturally unique and distinct people were on a plantation at any given time, and with them and their variety came different languages, pottery, foodways, religions, and spatial control. It is impossible to study one house/household of a village and think that all others within the settlement were the same. Our studies at Dean Hall show just what a fallacy it is to think enslaved Africans were as restricted in practices of daily life and cultural expression as they were with regard to the layout of their village or in the construction and layout of their dwellings. House 15 alone proves that enslaved households in a common village setting cannot be "pigeonholed into patterns" (Barile and Brandon 2004: 5).

Our analysis of House 15 shows it as unique among all other duplexes studied archaeologically. Furthermore, each of the two rooms evinced unique distinctions that prevent us from looking at the duplex as a whole, making us abandon any assumptions that the residents on either side of the shared central wall were the "same." It is clear that people of different ages, abilities, and proclivities lived in the two parts of the duplex. Most important to our study is that each household represented at House 15 is distinguished from other duplexes in the village by evidence of artisanal production of coarse earthenware, or colonoware; this they had in common, but there is also evidence of two different potters working at their craft in somewhat different ways.

Our analysis of the colonoware benefits greatly when looking at it in terms of household production, because the "household figures in typologies of craft specialization as a place where production occurs, as a means of organizing production, and as a level of output" (Hendon 1996: 52). Isenbarger's previous analysis of colonoware production among family units, or households, touches on the idea that an enslaved African's "access to resources, potters, and laborers" would have "determined the effect that Colonoware production had on enslaved families" (2005: 6). Besides analyzing evidence of colonoware production within households, we need to consider the constraints and affordances of the spaces available before thinking about how the household production of colonoware affected the positioning of a particular household within the larger village setting.

How were colonoware potters thought of in the community? Did colonoware production create the sort of "social differentiation" that Foster and Parker remark upon (2012: 4)? Creating crafts "can generate, reinforce, or challenge relations of power between individuals and groups" (Carballo 2011: 144). If we take this idea further, colonoware could have empowered the makers and the members of their household in their community, strengthening their ethnic identity and African heritage, while at the same time creating separation between potting and nonpotting households. Our focus is primarily on how colonoware production empowered households and their members by making it possible for them to engage in the internal economy in the greater Charleston area in which enslaved Africans participated.

To properly understand the tasks involved in craft making, we need to look closely at production and distribution (Wilk and Rathje 1982: 622). Wilk and Rathje's definitions of these terms in relation to household archaeology studies work extremely well for the interpretation of the material culture recovered from the duplex at the heart of this study. In the most basic terms, household production in this nineteenth-century plantation setting involved labor of two kinds: linear tasks that were single-person oriented; and simultaneous tasks that were performed by several people at the same time (Wilk and Rathje 1982: 622). Further, Wilk and Rathje define simple and complex simultaneous tasks: simple simultaneous tasks involve people all doing the exact same thing, while complex simultaneous tasks involve separate components that combine to get the job done (1982: 622). Here household archaeology lets us look at the task system of slave labor through these terms, affording a perspective on how household and community-oriented production influenced the acquisition and accumulation of material culture.

It is more than likely that Carson managed his labor force on the task-system model, which was introduced into Lowcountry plantations sometime in the 1740s and had been fully adopted across the South Carolina and Georgia coasts by 1800 (Morgan 1998, 1982). In this system, enslaved workers were given a set task or amount of work to complete each day, and if they finished early, they had "free time" to do as they pleased within the confines of planter acceptance. If some people finished their tasks early, they could assist others in finishing their tasks early, too. Work in the rice fields can be seen as a series of *simple simultaneous* tasks performed by many households in concert—planting rice seed, hoeing weeds, several men ditching and rebuilding embankments, and so forth. If one woman completed her task of planting her assigned rows with seed and then helped another woman who was not done, she was technically helping out that other household.

If on the one hand fieldwork was a simple simultaneous task, colonoware production, on the other hand, was a *complex simultaneous task*, whereby the potter employed members of his or her household to help with all of the tasks. Children may have fetched the water that was needed or may have helped collect wood for the fire. The potter may have had her daughter process the clay, recover it from clay storage pits, or sort sand for tempering. If the potter worked alone, however, the *linear production* mode of working may have resulted in decreased output, but it had the advantage of giving her complete control over the potting process from start to finish. Viewing plantation tasks through household production allows us to consider the ways that the enslaved chose to maximize their free-time endeavors and to delegate tasks within their own households.

Free time also allowed the enslaved to participate in the slaves' internal economy, a market/barter system in which enslaved Africans in and around Charleston participated. During their free time the enslaved were able to tend to their own garden plots and raise livestock, hunt, fish, or gather wild foods, make handicrafts, and hire out their own labor. They were able to sell or barter whatever they made in the free time they had made for themselves, along with other goods or services, for a profit that allowed them to supplement the basic provisions that their owners provided them. Families would have been able to delegate free-time activities to try to maximize the few benefits they could from these extra endeavors. An analysis of household items allows us to look not only at what free-time activities, if any, they may have participated in but also at the decisions they made as family units. Each family would have had different tastes and needs. By looking at the items and foods that a household acquired, we can glimpse evidence of personal preferences and tastes and what each household deemed necessities or considered important (Berlin and Morgan 1991; Hudson 1997; Isenbarger 2006; Joseph 1987; McDonald 1993; Morgan 1982; Wood 1995).

Well-organized rice labor at Dean Hall meant more free time, which meant more time to tend to household production that involved hunting/trapping animals for family food and to sell to the planter, tending yard animals and garden plots (for sale or consumption), more-successful colonoware production, and a myriad of other beneficial tasks with potentially profitable outcomes. Such outcomes from production resulted ultimately in the creation of the archaeological record. The abundance of material culture recovered from Dean Hall is proof that tasks were being completed and that the enslaved were allowed to express themselves through acquisition and accumulation of goods.

Based on specific artifacts, the plats, the historical setting, and the village layout, we believe that one or possibly two colonoware potters lived at House 15. Artifacts found here make it likely that a servant for hire lived in the west room. The following artifact discussion pairs significant historical facts and situations with the material culture to demonstrate how we arrived at this interpretation. Household analysis of both rooms brings us to a better understanding not only of House 15 but also of the community as a whole.

Archaeological Analysis of House 15

The Carson-era duplex was 32 × 16 feet in plan with chimneys on the west and east elevations; the north elevation faced the "street," while the south elevation faced the backyard. We imagine that there was a loft for each room and possibly a door between the rooms in the center wall of the duplex. Archaeological evidence from other cabins shows the presence of a porch that faced the backyard; such a porch may have been present at House 15. We excavated four 2 × 2 meter units at the ends of each room. Excavations at House 15 exposed robbed chimney features for both rooms of the duplex. Figure 8.2 is a plan of excavated units and identified architectural features.

Since the stratigraphy was intact at House 15, we were able to demarcate the Nesbitt-period occupation level from the Carson-period occupation. The Carson-period soil midden overlies a thin layer of very pale silt, apparently deposited by a flood. Under it was a rich, greasy black midden that had accumulated toward the end of the Nesbitt tenure (circa 1790–1820). The brick piers that supported the frame of the house were built on top of the lower midden, indicating that the midden existed before the duplex was built. Therefore, the contexts involved in our study of House

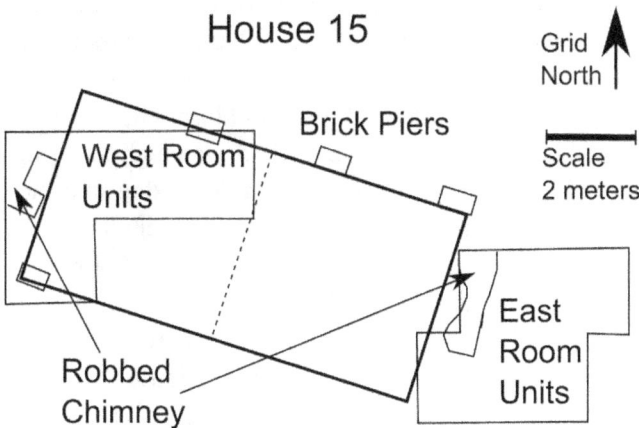

Figure 8.2. The excavated units and identified architectural features of House 15.

15 date strictly to the first twenty to twenty-five years of Carson's tenure; control over the proveniences allows more fine-grained interpretations of the activities of the duplex's enslaved African residents from 1820 to 1845.

Carson built House 15 sometime between 1821 and 1827. Heavy flooding, evidenced by the silt lens described above, may have been the impetus for Carson to have the duplexes built. The west end of the slave village was nearly 14 feet lower in elevation than the eastern end, and the original single-pen cabins built there may have sat lower to the ground. Hence their wooden posts may have been rotting rather speedily because they were exposed to intermittent but regular flooding. Based on the *terminus post quem* (TPQ) date of 1840 from the western robbed chimney and the scant number of ceramics postdating the 1840s, we believe Houses 15 and 16 were razed when the twelve additional cabins on the new road were built after 1837. This gives us a fairly tight twenty-year time period to investigate and interpret, whereas some of the other duplexes we excavated were occupied into the late 1890s.

Colonoware Production at House 15

The most exciting element of this household analysis, particularly with regard to household production, is that we believe there is evidence that colonoware firing took place in both rooms of House 15. Several vessel and nonvessel forms of colonoware were identified from both rooms. Two unidentifiable colonoware objects were found in the east room, along with the two colonoware pipe fragments. Some archaeologists have interpreted colonoware pipes as proof of on-site colonoware production (Anthony 1986; Ferguson 1992); we concur. Also found were twenty-two spalls and four fractured spalls in the west room and forty-eight spalls in the east room. A spall occurs when a vessel is not dry enough for firing, resulting in steam buildup inside the wall of the vessel, causing an explosion on the baked surface that creates circular or oblong craters. The spalls fly away from the vessel, landing in unpredictable locations. We believe that the colonoware produced at Dean Hall was fired in the fireplaces of the duplexes (Agha et al. 2012) and that the presence of these spalls, from contexts located on and near the old chimneys of the House 15 duplex, provide unmistakable evidence of firing within each room of House 15.

Besides ceramic evidence, we recovered two burnishing stones from the west room and one from the east. These stones were used to polish and compact the clays of the vessels to help them retain water/liquid better. Burnishing also helped to promote safer firing of the vessel, as rubbing the stone on the surface of an unfired pot would have helped remove air bubbles in the clay. Lastly, there are 4.3 grams of baked clay in the west room and 242.9 grams in the east room. This baked clay resembles colonoware paste but is unformed and occurs in random lumps and shapes. While we are uncertain of the function and purpose of these clay lumps, they are some of the most important evidence for on-site production. Taken together, these artifacts convincingly support late-term, post-1820 colonoware production at Dean Hall.

More evidence to support our interpretations of potters working in both rooms comes from the specific decorations that occur on some of the colonoware at House 15 that are not represented in the minimum number of vessels (MNV) analysis. In each household we found a vessel bearing a unique punctate mark not seen elsewhere in the settlement. From the west household we recovered a colonoware sherd that is marked with a sign resembling a typeset letter "v" with a dash above its right arm. From the east household there is a colonoware sherd impressed with an unhulled rice seed, showing a link between rice cultivation and colonoware production. Colonoware sherds marked with an X occur in both households, but the east room had a higher number of X-marked vessels. The west room had only one X-marked sherd, and it is burnished and punctated. The east room had three X-marked colonoware sherds, including two that are incised and one that is punctated. Even though both households had X-marked vessels, the manner of executing the X varies greatly, showing a difference in individual style of the potters or possibly even in the intended function of these vessels. At present, we are unable to decipher the meanings of these, but the variety and seeming importance of these marks leads us to believe that the enslaved living in House 15 produced these vessels for personal use.

Getting back to definitions of household production, was colonoware production a *linear* or *complex simultaneous* task? Since we can assume that the residents of both rooms of House 15 had families, we can suggest both scenarios. Here, Hendon's notion that "any change in the occupation of some members of the household will have an impact on the household as a whole" is important as we consider the family as a potting family (1996: 52). It is common, especially in colonoware studies of potters, to focus on the individual, which differentiates the "'artisan' and 'rest of the household,'" automatically (Hendon 1996: 53). Viewing the household as a productive unit engaged in a complex simultaneous task, however, places the "hidden producers" next to the potter, not behind him or her (Hendon 1996: 53). Even though the rest of the family may not have made pottery, their role in its production could be obvious if seen in the following way.

If the potters were elderly, they may have relied on their immediate family for help with collecting clay from the quarries, water for clay preparation, and wood for the fire. Or if they were younger, they may have performed all tasks alone. Here, the issue of free time comes into play. A younger potter may have been strong in the field and also may have had time to access a clay source that existed in the rice ditches and canals. Or potters may have directed someone else to collect clay because they were too busy in their task. In the free time spent after tasks, she may have had the time needed to prepare clays and form the vessels on which her family and others within the community relied. Here we have considered only a few of the possibilities that may have existed on plantations in the past, but through these examples we are able to show how household studies can strengthen analysis of household material culture from House 15 at Dean Hall as well as at other sites throughout South Carolina.

The Influences of the Internal Economy

Colonoware enriches the study of all ceramics in new and powerful ways. Here, colonoware production was a free-time task that eliminated the need to purchase manufactured ceramics or other kitchen or personal goods. Pottery produced on the plantation may have been sold to or bartered with other enslaved Africans through the internal economy, furthering the opportunities to purchase desired goods for the household. Ceramics play an important role in our interpretations of how much free time the people at House 15 had. Free time allowed for personal/household production that may have resulted in profits; such profits may have been spent at the local market on ceramics. We performed an MNV analysis on the 169 manufactured ceramic sherds from the west room and on the 412 manufactured ceramic sherds from the east room as well as on 298 nonresidual colonoware sherds from the west room and 455 nonresidual sherds from the east room. Only ceramics from the Carson-era proveniences were selected for this analysis. Even though the sherd counts differ, our analysis indicates that the two households owned almost equal numbers

Table 8.1. Minimum number of vessels analysis by vessel form at 38BK2132 House 15, Carson era

Ceramic vessel form	West room	East room	Total
MANUFACTURED WARES			
Bowl	1	4	5
Plate	11	8	19
Cup/mug	2	2	4
Hollowware	3	7	10
Jar	1	2	3
Crock	—	1	1
Chamber pot	—	3	3
Black ink bottle	—	1	1
Unidentifiable form	7	2	9
COLONOWARES			
Bowl	21	26	47
Jar	15	8	23
TOTALS	61	64	125

of vessels (west room, $n=61$; east room, $n=64$). Further, when we focus on the manufactured plates and bowls and colonoware bowls and jars, we see that they, too, have a roughly equal distribution (west room, $n=40$; east room, $n=43$). Table 8.1 displays the MNV data.

In order to look at market interactions and buying power within the slaves' internal economy, we are particularly interested in comparing the frequencies of decorated and undecorated manufactured wares and of colonoware within and between the two rooms. Both households' ceramic assemblages are dominated by colonoware vessels. The ratio of manufactured wares to colonowares is 1:2.9 in the west room and 1:2.8 in the east room. We take these ratios as further evidence that colonowares were made by members of the two households living at House 15 (Agha et al. 2012).

The residents of the east room may have had a greater preference for bowls over plates than did the residents of the west room. This difference could, however, be a reflection of the number of individuals in each room or household unit, since more people would require more individual vessels. The ratio of plates to bowls in the west room (1:2) is almost twice as high as that from the east room (1:3.75). The east room inhabitants also preferred colonoware bowls (n=26) over manufactured bowls (n=4), with a ratio of the latter over the former at 1:6.5. As noted earlier, archaeology at Dean Hall Plantation produced a colonoware assemblage that is one of the largest ever recovered in South Carolina (n=59,020). Ferguson's insistence that colonoware was a continuation of ancestral African foodways is not challenged here; rather, it is supported, given that we see a clear preference for bowls over plates that we take as evidence that the family living in House 15's east side was preparing food according to African customs (Ferguson 1992, 1991; Otto 1984).

Although the west room had slightly more plates (n=11) than the east room (n=8), the west side had a higher number of colonoware jars (n=14) than the east side (n=8). We believe that the jar, as a cooking vessel, was also a continuation of past African foodways (see Ferguson 1992). Interestingly, the east room had fragments (n=12) of iron cook pots that may have been used in place of colonoware jars. Ferguson theorized that even as (or if) iron cook pots replaced colonoware jars, African foodways could still have been practiced, and the preference for bowls, whether of colonoware or of European manufacture, seems to support this interpretation.

In summary, we have evidence from both rooms that the people who lived here practiced African foodways, based on the vessels identified. The participation of these households in the internal economy dictated what ceramics were available to them, but their selections were also influenced by the fact that they chose to prepare and consume their food in a manner customary in traditional African foodways.

Decorated Ceramics as Reflections of Household Choices

Decorated ceramics allow us the chance to take an in-depth look at the personal preferences among the enslaved. These preferences were contingent upon their own creative drive, through colonoware, internal economy activities, and personal tastes. Ceramic vessels from both households have a similar distribution of undecorated to decorated vessels (west=1:1.3, east=1:1.8), indicating that the access of both households to the market was perhaps equal. We identified twenty-seven unique decorative elements on ceramics in the west room and thirty-two in the east room. We believe that these designs reflect personal preference and market consumption and that the ceramics were not supplied by Carson or given by him as

Table 8.2. Minimum number of vessels analysis by broad decoration types at 38BK2132 House 15, Carson era

Decoration type	West room	East room	Total
MANUFACTURED WARES			
Creamware, undecorated	1	4	5
Creamware, annular	—	1	1
Pearlware, undecorated	—	1	1
Pearlware, annular	1	1	2
Pearlware, blue hand painted	—	1	1
Pearlware, polychrome hand painted	1	—	1
Pearlware, blue transfer printed	3	1	4
Pearlware, blue shell edged	—	2	2
Whiteware, undecorated	1	3	4
Whiteware, annular	2	1	3
Whiteware, polychrome hand painted	1	1	2
Whiteware, blue transfer printed	2	2	4
Whiteware, black transfer printed	1	1	2
Whiteware, blue shell edged	3	3	6
Whiteware, green shell edged	2	—	2
Yellowware, green mocha	—	1	1
COLONOWARES			
Bowl, scalloped rim	5	4	9
Bowl, incised	1	1	2
Jar, incised	1	—	1
Jar, punctate	2	—	2
Jar, incised and punctate	1	—	1
Jar, drag and jab/roulette	1	—	1
TOTALS	29	28	57

hand-me-downs. Besides the decorations on manufactured ceramics, we have decorations or marks on colonoware to consider as well. Colonoware is found in thousands of contexts across the South Carolina Lowcountry, but it is almost always undecorated (see, e.g., Ferguson 2007). We are not suggesting that the marks found on the colonoware hold the same decorative value as the manufactured wares; we refer to them as decorations here simply because they are additions to the clay surface beyond the forming process. Decorations and surface treatments can serve functional purposes and hold both utilitarian and symbolic meanings (Rice 1987: 144, 232). Table 8.2 lists the ceramic decorations identified.

From the Dean Hall enslaved village site we recovered the largest number (n=1,118) of marked colonoware vessels reported from any site in South Carolina; this assemblage is possibly larger than any other from the southeastern United States (Agha et al. 2012). The MNV analysis of the Carson-era colonoware shows that the west household had twice as many decorated colonoware vessels (n=10) as the east household (n=5), and the decorations on the pots found in each differ dramatically. For instance, both households had colonoware bowls with scalloped rims (west, n=5; east, n=4), but the types of scalloping varied between rooms. The scallop decoration types in the west room include finger-impressed (n=3), object-impressed (n=1), and cut (n=1) scalloping. The east room had peaked (n=1), fingernail-impressed (n=1), finger-impressed (n=1), and angled-object impressed (n=1) scalloping. We identified a colonoware bowl with incising along or near the rim from each room as well.

Furthermore, five of the fourteen colonoware jars identified in the west room are decorated: one is incised, one is marked with round punctates, one has triangular punctates along the shoulder, one has both incised lines and round punctate marks, and one has evidence of rouletting (that looks similar to drag and jab designs), which is an African pottery decorative motif and/or surface treatment (Gosselain 2000; Haour et al. 2010; Soper 1985). These marks on the jars are important because none of the eight individual jars identified from the east room has any decorative elements. Figure 8.3 displays four different decorative motifs identified on the colonoware from House 15. Are the decorated jars in the west room evidence of a potter living there? Do the strong differences in decorations on pots in the two rooms provide evidence of potters living in both? Or are the differing decorative motifs and elements reflective of the two households' preferences regarding ceramic variety and tastes?

The east household shows a preference for creamware ceramics (n=5) over the west household (n=1), perhaps because these vessels would have been outdated at the time, making them cheaper to buy. Both creamware and pearlware were out of fashion and out of production by 1820 (Neale 2005; Noël Hume 1969: 130); this supports the notion that the enslaved may have been able to buy outdated, out-of-fashion wares at lower prices, which brought more decorative types into their households. These wares may also have been obtained prior to Carson's tenure, which would have allowed the enslaved to spend profits made after 1820 on other items once they were housed in the new duplexes. We identified five pearlware vessels

Figure 8.3. Examples of decorated colonoware vessels from House 15. West room: *top left*, possible typeset punctate; *bottom left*, triangular punctate jar. East room: *top right*, unhulled rice seed punctate; *bottom right*, punctate X on interior base.

in the west room and six in the east room. In addition, 11 whiteware vessels were recovered in each room. Whiteware was newly invented and available by 1820 (Noël Hume 1969: 130). Was it more expensive than the pearlware and creamware? Even if it was, the enslaved were able to obtain more whiteware than anything else. Does a preponderance of fashionable and pricey ceramics reflect buying power and the profits obtained through free-time production?

Limited access to markets and finding affordable wares hindered the choice of which manufactured ceramics to purchase. Despite these restrictions, we see a great deal of diversity in the ceramics throughout the entire settlement at Dean Hall, so we have to assume that at least some choices reflect personal tastes. Each room had one annular pearlware bowl. The west room additionally had one polychrome hand-painted pearlware flatware vessel and three blue transfer-printed vessels, including one cup with a chinoiserie design. The east room had one blue hand-painted hol-lowware vessel, one blue transfer-printed bowl, and two blue shell-edged plates.

There were nine whiteware plates in the west room, and each has a different decorative motif—in other words, no two are alike. The plates unique to the west room include two green shell-edged plates, two blue transfer-printed plates, and one brown-banded plate. The decorative mo-tifs on the blue transfer-printed plates are chinoiserie and floral. Decora-tive motifs on the six whiteware plates from the east room include a black-and-purple polychrome hand-painted example with a scalloped rim and two blue shell-edged examples with an impressed bud motif.

The manufactured wares found at House 15 are reflective of market in-teractions, given that the occupants of the duplex likely would have traded or bartered for them or purchased them. As noted earlier, we are able to look at differences in the decorations, not just among the manufactured wares but also in the colonowares. Because of the variety of decoration on vessels in the colonoware assemblage, we believe that the marks represent the personal tastes of the individuals using them and possibly even rep-resent different cultural identities or ethnicities. The differences in deco-rations between the rooms, then, reflect the varied individual tastes and participation in the internal economy by the enslaved at Dean Hall.

Household Decisions and Personal Tastes

The household choices and personal tastes of the enslaved can further be seen in the non-kitchen-related items that they acquired. It is through these material goods that we can see not only how they expressed their individuality but also the decisions they made as a household about how to meet their needs. Clothing items were represented by buttons only. The majority of the brass buttons are plain or simply gilded; these could have been further embellished, however, if wrapped with colored string. In the west room we found thirteen brass buttons and one pewter button. One of the brass buttons has an unidentifiable stamped design, and one is domed. We identified four military buttons from House 15 (in both rooms: three brass and one pewter button), suggesting that the enslaved were given old uniforms, perhaps by Carson. We recovered eight buttons from the east household: one is bone, two are white pressed porcelain Prosser-type buttons (Sprague 2002), and five are brass. Both of the Prosser buttons are four-holed, and one has a piecrust edge. This array of clothing items may indicate that the enslaved purchased clothes different from what Carson provided them or that they purchased or found other ways to obtain buttons to repair and mend their shirts and coats.

Personal items included glass beads, faux gemstones, and chamber pots. The west household had two faceted glass beads—one aqua and one blue—as well as a green cut-glass "gemstone." The east household had a blue faceted bead. Beads were some of the most commonly purchased clothing items among enslaved populations (Heath 1999: 50).

The east household also had three undecorated chamber pots: one of creamware, one of pearlware, and one of whiteware. The presence of chamber pots could represent necessity or preference. These items could have been acquired because residents of House 15 East preferred not to have to go outside at night or because someone living there was old or ill and not physically able to make it outside to relieve him- or herself. Another possibility is that the chamber pots were not used for their intended purpose. Excavations in downtown Charleston resulted in the recovery of a colonoware vessel in the form of a chamber pot that had sooting on it, suggesting that it had been used for cooking or over a fire (Isenbarger 2001: 8.23–8.24). The individuals in the east room may have simply liked the vessel form and used it for another purpose, perhaps as a large serving dish or a mixing bowl.

Leisure items consist solely of tobacco pipe fragments. The west room had ten molded white ball-clay pipe stems bearing decorations we found throughout the settlement, suggesting that these types were readily available for sale locally. The enslaved living in the west room also had one green-glazed ball-clay pipe stem. The east room produced two colonoware tobacco pipe fragments. When the community as a whole is being looked at, these can be used as evidence for on-site production at the village; however, when the separate households are analyzed, more-complex relations may become apparent. Moving beyond the mere presence of a potter, we can ask, were these pipes seen as a sign of prestige and reverence to someone who held a special position within the community? Or were these made out of necessity because the residents could not afford to purchase tobacco pipes? Pipe fragments of any kind mean that the enslaved smoked tobacco that they obtained through purchase using the profits from household production, by growing it in their own garden plots, or as rations or rewards from the planter.

Discussion

When we considered the entire enslaved settlement at Dean Hall in our initial community approach, we were able to see that there were differences in the material culture found in the houses. This household analysis allowed us to take a closer look at one cabin in particular and to explore at least some of the ways in which each family unit made use of their free time and participated in the internal slave market. We have archaeological evidence that at least one colonoware potter fired pots in each room of House 15. Other evidence for use of free time, choices made as a family unit, and individual tastes comes from the objects and material culture the residents of House 15 were able to make and acquire.

Further, the recovery of a slave hire tag from deposits in the west room indicates that one of the people living there had in 1821 been hired out as a servant. It is unclear whether money this individual earned would have been paid directly to the enslaved worker or to the owner, William Carson, or split between them in some manner. Alternatively, perhaps Carson hired a servant because of his or her special skills or abilities and that servant came to live at Dean Hall, perhaps staying there permanently. Either scenario means that a resident of the west room was probably receiving money and could have participated in the slaves' internal economy, using cash to make purchases at the market in nearby Strawberry Ferry. If hired by Carson, this servant may have worked for him only in 1821—we recovered only one slave hire tag—or may have continued to work for Carson in subsequent years. Most important, a servant, whether hired in or hired out, who may have earned his or her own money, may have been able to be away from the plantation more frequently than other members of the enslaved community. Such a person may have had access not just to the nearby market but also to markets farther away, perhaps even as far afield as urban Charleston.

The personal tastes and decisions of the household units can be seen in the ceramic assemblage. From both rooms of the duplex we recovered a similar ratio of manufactured to colonoware vessels. Creamware was more prevalent in the east room. Residents of both rooms had access to pearlware and whiteware vessels. Variation was also seen in the shell-edged decorated ceramics: in the west room we found examples of both green and blue shell-edged whiteware but no shell-edged pearlware, whereas the east room produced examples of blue shell-edged pearlware as well as whiteware. From west room deposits came twice as many decorated colonoware vessels as were found in the east room. The east room had more X-marked colonoware vessels than the west. Do greater numbers of X-marked vessels, which are generally thought to have been used for medicinal and ritual purposes, as well as the presence of chamber pots, perhaps mean that someone among the enslaved living in the east room may have been sick or elderly?

The artifact assemblage shows evidence that the enslaved in both rooms showed a continuance of more-traditional African foodways. The ways in which residents of the two sides of the duplex maintained these traditions differed, however. Residents of both rooms showed a preference for bowls. Jars were present in each room, but the west room had more colonoware jars and the east room more iron cook pots. People living in the west room seem to have retained traditional foodways using colonoware cooking vessels.

Further evidence that negates notions of assimilation or acceptance can be seen in the material culture differences between the rooms. The residents of the west room, where the servant lived, had more marked colonoware vessels. A servant presumably had more money and hence readier access to goods. The residents of the east room had iron cook pots, greater numbers of manufactured plates, chamber pots, a greater variety of buttons, and Masonic pipes. The only extra personal item we saw from the west room is a faux gemstone. These differences are likely reflections of the decisions each household made as to how to allocate time and money and the personal tastes of individuals—difference that only a household-level analysis can bring to light.

Traditions are honored and sustained through a community of unified individuals, because "without a community . . . traditions could not exist" (Thomas 2001: 32–33). The fact that we can see traditions in the material culture, the historical record, and the rice landscape at Dean Hall shows that the community was strong and that William Carson, rather than thwart the preservation of traditions, created situations that allowed the enslaved to express themselves through continuous reference to their ancestral past. We witness these expressions through our study of the households that created the community at Dean Hall, where it is clear that household-level production allowed the formation of a distinct enslaved community, some of whose members were able to participate in the internal slave economy. Household archaeology has permitted us to investigate the subtle nuances of daily life and to come away with a much better understanding of this site than our initial broader analysis afforded.

Through the lens of household archaeology we were able to look at the ways in which enslaved families used the task system and internal economy to their own advantage and how by using traditional skills to produce wares for their own use and for sale or barter they both influenced and were influenced by these systems. We examined colonoware as an aspect of household production, affording a richer and more comprehensive interpretation of past enslaved households in the South Carolina Lowcountry. The Dean Hall slave community's involvement in the internal economy gave them limited control of their own labor, the very thing for which they had been enslaved, allowing them to make their own choices and decisions as to ways in which they would work for themselves. Not only does our analysis give us a glimpse into decisions made about how to spend free time, but it also permits us to consider what items the residents of House 15 acquired or created in their efforts to better their living conditions despite lives defined by bondage. By looking at the material goods on which they chose to spend their profits, we are able to better understand what they found important in their daily lives.

References Cited

Agha, Andrew, Nicole Isenbarger, Charles F. Philips Jr., Kandice Hollenbach, Eleanora A. Reber, and Jessica Allgood
2012 *Traditions in Rice and Clay: Understanding an Eighteenth–Nineteenth Century Rice Plantation, Dean Hall Plantation (38BK2132), Berkeley County, South Carolina.* Brockington and Associates, n.p. (tDAR ID: 391016) DOI: 10.6067/XCV8ST7QP4.

Allison, Penelope (editor)
1999 *The Archaeology of Household Activities.* Routledge, London.

Anthony, Ronald
1986 Colono Wares. In *Home Upriver: Rural Life on Daniel's Island*, edited by Martha Zierden, Leslie Drucker, and Jeanne Calhoun, pp. 7-22–7-55. Manuscript on file, South Carolina Department of Highways and Public Transportation, Columbia.

Barile, Kerri S., and Jamie C. Brandon (editors)
2004 *Household Chores and Household Choices: Theorizing the Domestic Sphere in Historical Archaeology.* University of Alabama Press, Tuscaloosa.

Berlin, Ira, and Philip D. Morgan
1991 Introduction. In *The Slaves' Economy: Independent Production by Slaves in the Americas*, edited by Ira Berlin and Philip D. Morgan, pp. 1–23. Frank Cass, London.

Carballo, David M.
2011 Advances in the Household Archaeology of Highland Mesoamerica. *Journal of Archaeological Research* 19: 133–189.
Carney, Judith
2001 *Black Rice: The African Origins of Rice Cultivation in the Americas*. Harvard University Press, Cambridge, Massachusetts.
Carney, Judith, and R. N. Rosomoff
2009 *In the Shadow of Slavery: Africa's Botanical Legacy in the Atlantic World*. University of California Press, Berkeley.
Ferguson, Leland G.
2007 Early African-American Pottery in South Carolina: A Complicated Plainware. *African Diaspora Archaeology Network Newsletter* June 2007. Electronic document, http://www.diaspora.illinois.edu/news0607/news0607.html#1, accessed September 1, 2014.
1992 *Uncommon Ground: Archaeology and Early African America, 1650–1800*. Smithsonian Institution Press, Washington, D.C.
1991 Struggling with Pots in Colonial South Carolina. In *The Archaeology of Inequality*, edited by Randall H. McGuire and Robert Paynter, pp. 28–39. Blackwell, Oxford, U.K.
Foster, Catherine P., and Bradley J. Parker
2012 Introduction: Household Archaeology in the Near East and Beyond. In *New Perspectives on Household Archaeology*, edited by Bradley J. Parker and Catherine P. Foster, pp. 1–12. Eisenbrauns, Winona Lake, Indiana.
Gosselain, Olivier P.
2000 Materializing Identities: An African Perspective. *Journal of Archaeological Method and Theory* 7: 187–217.
Haour, Anne, Olivier Gosselain, Robert Vernet, Kevin MacDonald, Katie Manning, Anne Mayor, Susan McIntosh, Alexander Livingstone Smith, Ndeye Sokhna Gueye, Franziska Barth, Ross Thomas, Annabelle Gallin, and Noemie Arazi (editors)
2010 *African Pottery Roulettes Past and Present: Techniques, Identification and Distribution*. Oxbow Books, Oxford, U.K.
Heath, Barbara J.
1999 Buttons, Beads, and Buckles: Contextualizing Adornment within the Bounds of Slavery. In *Historical Archaeology, Identity Formation and the Interpretation of Ethnicity*, edited by Maria Franklin and Garrett Fesler, pp. 47–70. Colonial Williamsburg Foundation Research Publications, Richmond, Virginia.
Hendon, Julia A.
1996 Archaeological Approaches to the Organization of Domestic Labor: Household Practice and Domestic Relations. *Annual Review of Anthropology* 25: 45–61.
Hudson, Larry E., Jr.
1997 *To Have and to Hold: Slave Work and Family Life in Antebellum South Carolina*. University of Georgia Press, Athens.
Isenbarger, Nicole M.
2006 Potters, Hucksters, and Consumers: Placing Colonoware within the Internal Slave

Economy Framework. Unpublished master's thesis, Department of Anthropology, University of South Carolina, Columbia.

2005 Potters, Hucksters, and Consumers: Introducing Colonoware into the Slaves' Internal Marketing Economy. Paper presented at the 62nd Annual Meeting of the Southeastern Archaeological Conference, Columbia, South Carolina.

2001 Analysis of Colonoware in the Eighteenth Century Deposits. In *Excavations at 14 Legare Street, Charleston, South Carolina*. Archaeological Contributions 28. Charleston Museum, Charleston, South Carolina.

Joseph, Joseph W.

1987 Highway 17 Revisited: The Archaeology of Task Labor. *South Carolina Antiquities* 19: 29–34.

Littlefield, Daniel C.

1981 *Rice and Slaves: Ethnicity and the Colonial Slave Trade in South Carolina*. Louisiana State University Press, Baton Rouge.

McDonald, Roderick A.

1993 *The Economy and Material Culture of Slaves: Goods and Chattels on the Sugar Plantations of Jamaica and Louisiana*. Louisiana State University Press, Baton Rouge.

Morgan, Philip D.

1998 *Slave Counterpoint: Black Culture in the Eighteenth-Century Chesapeake and Lowcountry*. University of North Carolina Press, Chapel Hill.

1982 Work and Culture: The Task System and the World of Lowcountry Blacks, 1700–1880. *William and Mary Quarterly*, 3rd ser., 39: 563–599.

Neale, Gillian

2005 *Miller's Encyclopedia of British Transfer-Printed Pottery Patterns, 1790–1930*. Miller's, London.

Noël Hume, Ivor

1969 *A Guide to Artifacts of Colonial America*. Knopf, New York.

Otto, John Solomon

1984 *Cannon's Point Plantation, 1794–1860: Living Conditions and Status Patterns in the Old South*. Academic Press, Orlando, Florida.

Pluckhahn, Thomas J.

2010 Household Archaeology in the Southeastern United States: History, Trends, and Challenges. *Journal of Archaeological Research* 18: 331–385.

Rice, Prudence M.

1987 *Pottery Analysis: A Sourcebook*. University of Chicago Press, Chicago.

Soper, Robert

1985 Roulette Decoration on African Pottery: Technical Considerations, Dating and Distributions. *African Archaeological Review* 3: 29–51.

Sprague, Roderick

2002 China or Prosser Button Identification and Dating. *Historical Archaeology* 36: 111–127.

Thomas, Brian W.

2001 African-American Tradition and Community in the Antebellum South. In *The

Archaeology of Traditions: Agency and History before and after Columbus, edited by Timothy Pauketat, pp. 17–33. University Press of Florida, Gainesville.

1998 Power and Community: The Archaeology of Slavery at the Hermitage Plantation. *American Antiquity* 63: 531–551.

Turner, Lorenzo Dow

1949 *Africanisms in the Gullah Dialect*. University of South Carolina Press, Columbia.

Wilk, Richard R., and William L. Rathje

1982 Household Archaeology. *American Behavioral Scientist* 25: 617–639.

Wood, Betty

1995 *Women's Work, Men's Work: The Informal Slave Economies of Lowcountry Georgia*. University of Georgia Press, Athens.

Wood, Peter H.

1996 *Black Majority: Negroes in Colonial South Carolina from 1670 through the Stono Rebellion*. Norton, New York.

9

The Spooky Entanglements
of Historical Households

CHARLES R. COBB

Household studies in archaeology have now been around long enough that we do have some tacit agreement, even if not universal consensus, on some fundamental issues related to what households are (or are not) and what they do (see Barile and Brandon 2004; Hendon 1996; Pluckhahn 2010). This allows one to contemplate broader issues represented in this volume without having to necessarily reinvent the wheel. We know that households and individual domestic buildings are not isomorphic. We know that archaeological remains of structures and activity areas represent static remnants of lengthy, oscillating trajectories of domestic interactions. We know that households are not modular, self-sufficient units. We know that households may be the loci of tension and oppression rather than cores of harmony. In short, we know that even within modest communities households are incredibly variable and dynamic entities with complex histories.

Nevertheless, we feel obliged to study households, challenging as they are to define and demarcate, for the simple reason that they represent central elements of biological, material, social, and ideological reproduction. Households are where cultural notions of domesticity are constructed and contested; where the pedagogical practices of habitus are rehearsed and passed on; where norms surrounding social personae intersect and are played out. These are all themes that have been at the forefront of anthropological theorizing over recent decades, even if the household has not always been the point of departure.

Now that households have been the subject of archaeological study for several decades, what more do we have to learn from this vantage point?

The answer as seen in this collection of studies is "plenty." In particular, I have found two provocative threads running throughout these chapters.

The first relates to the continual discovery of new perspectives for modeling the household as a liminal point between local and external relations. Many of the studies here explicitly emphasize the ways in which households mediate the local and the global—a goal that is shared with microhistorical perspectives, the Annales school, and other multiscalar approaches.

The second thread relates to how households may be situated in the history of modernity. Case studies in this volume span the seventeenth to twentieth centuries in North America and Hawai'i, an interval when people throughout the world arrived and intermingled through intricate phases of colonialism, mercantilism, capitalism, and globalization. Political and economic forces in the guise of nation- and empire-building precipitated many of these interminglings. Yet these exchanges were also foundational to the emergence of modernity (or, more appropriately, modernities) as a function of the mutual constitution of the worldviews of colonizer/colonized, capitalist/worker, and other dyads—all of which we know are reductions of more-complex collations of interest groups. Households are where the practices and beliefs embedded in modernity were variously imposed, rejected, ignored, and rephrased. For this reason, case studies involving households are a starting point for addressing what Bruce Knauft (2002) has referred to as "micromodernity."

My ensuing reflections on household microhistories and micromodernities are predicated on the fact that the case studies fall under the rubric of historical archaeology in the North American sense. That is, they coincide with and postdate the era of European and Euro-American expansionism beginning in the late fifteenth century C.E. Further, it is presumed that the forces associated with the era of modern colonization and imperialism played a central role in the constitution of the households. Thus, my discussion is couched in many ways within historical events and processes over the past five centuries. At the same time, I do not want to forgo a comparative stance. There are intriguing similarities between some of the studies despite the distance and time separating many of them. Moreover, some of these similarities are recapitulated in earlier times and other places. I find it worthwhile to touch on some of these broad patterns and what they mean in terms of general statements that we can make about households.

Households and Microhistories

It is now received wisdom that the household is a crucible for the blending of domestic relations and a nebulous outer world characterized by myriad forces linked to religious systems, political formations, class and gender ideologies, regional or global economic systems, and other domains often subsumed under "structure." Although broad structural networks always impinge upon the household, much of the social change we observe is rooted in the choices and decisions that are made by individuals living and working within households (King 2006: 299). Diana Wong's (1984) recognition of this two-way avenue in her study of the household led her to argue both for its potential and for its limits as a unit of analysis. As she pointed out, households are never completely autonomous; their reproduction is dependent on external as well as internal ties. They are invariably articulated with some larger field of relations. For these reasons Matthew Johnson (2006: 318) has asserted that "the major task facing . . . historical archaeology in general, is not to shift focus to an exclusively larger scale, but to grasp the relationship between the small-scale and local, wider processes of transformation, and the colonial experience."

Yet from the perspective of archaeological modeling and theorizing, our understanding of the reactions within the household crucible is still governed largely by principles of alchemy rather than science or even humanistic interpretation. We know from countless observations that the domestic and the global are in some way arbitrated through the household, but how that occurs continues to challenge us. From an explanatory viewpoint we seem to be in the same boat as quantum physicists, who have found that two widely separated particles may be inextricably bound such that the behavior of one affects that of the other. How this occurs is still mysterious enough that the relationship is referred to as a "spooky entanglement." Interestingly, the metaphor of "entanglement" has become an increasingly popular term in colonial studies in archaeology (e.g., Jordan 2009; Stahl 2002; Thomas 1991), although I would argue that, just as in physics, this concept tends to cover a lot of descriptive ground without a lot of deep understanding.

One of the key ingredients for achieving a greater insight into these entanglements is delineating with greater precision the nature of the larger arena in which households are enmeshed. In part this is a function of one's research question: activities related to the gendered division of labor may situate a household in networks that may be somewhat different from networks related to a household's role in ritual practices. Furthermore, the historical contexts of households obviously must be taken into consideration as well. One may find common ground by studying household gender relations in Bronze Age Scandinavia and in feudal England, but it would be problematic to ignore the surrounding milieu of those households. Thus, on the one hand it is useful for historical archaeologists engaged in household studies to at least browse the literature of households connected to panregional or world systems in other times and places, but on the other hand, allowances must be made for historical and geographic difference.

There have been, for example, a number of insightful studies of the ways that households under Classical Roman rule were linked to the imperial order. In Britain it has been shown that the culinary habits of Romanized households were an outgrowth of local practices and widespread eating conventions throughout the empire (Hingley 1990), and in northern Europe the imposition of Roman rule led to increasing standardization of household organization throughout communities to facilitate tax collection and centralized management of resources (Therkorn 1987). At the same time there was enough variability in Roman households that one can question how commensurate they truly were (Herlihy 1984). These kinds of issues, including the contradictions between structural norms of empire and diverse practices emanating from household agency, are certainly of interest to historical archaeologists dealing with households under mercantile and capitalist regimes. The structures of domination of Roman rule, however, were obviously quite different from those of modernity and must be approached on different theoretical and historical grounds.

Nevertheless, in the same manner in which physicists have devised some common ways to study their own kinds of diverse entanglements lacking a unified theory, so too have archaeologists adopted a variety of overlapping approaches to the entanglements of domestic and global relations. Many have advocated some form of multiscalar approach that recognizes the hierarchical nature of social and cultural interactions, a perspective that seems to apply equally well to both sides of our normative divide of prehistoric and historical archaeologies (e.g., Anderson 1999; Lock and Molyneaux 2006; Marquardt 1992). Laurie Wilkie and Paul Farnsworth's (1999) study of Bahamian plantations is a particularly good example of the articulation of the household (how enslaved families leveraged market access to ceramics into constructions of community identity) with regional trade networks (the factors that impacted the variable composition of ceramic assemblages available to plantation owners). They demonstrate, as have others (e.g., Lenik 2009), that consumption practices in enslaved households were richly layered manifestations of opportunity and constraint.

This pattern is clearly a leitmotif of all of the studies in this volume. The authors amply demonstrate the partible nature of households as a function of the mix of multiscalar ties in which they were enmeshed. Achieving this kind of understanding, however, remains a theoretical and logistical hurdle. Criticisms of the Annales school in history, the epitome of multiscalar research, reflect some of the difficulties inherent in attempting to develop a focus that is simultaneously large and small (Bintliff 1991: 14; Fletcher 1992: 38–39; Lucas 2006: 37–39). Despite our best efforts, we either become mired in the detail of the everyday or else find it difficult to descend from the Braudelian panorama. Some anthropologists have drawn on the perspective known as microhistory to model multiscalar relationships from the ground up (e.g., Brooks et al. 2008; Hupperetz 2010). I find this a particularly useful way to think of household studies. Microhistorians rely on detailed case studies not merely for the objective of describing a set of events in minute detail but with the ultimate goal of demonstrating how those events can be understood within a larger historical framework. Further, their notion of the micro entails a sense of lived experience (Revel 1995).

I would emphasize that microhistory is a vantage point rather than a theoretical perspective, but it is, nonetheless, a perspective that runs throughout these chapters even if the term is not invoked. Fogle (chapter 6) and Isenbarger and Agha (chapter 8), for instance, demonstrate that the experiences and rhythms of enslaved households in the American Southeast were directly impacted by plantation owners attempting to enact new tenets of reform and management widely circulating in North America and Europe in the nineteenth century. At the same time, the daily practices of households were shaped by other, regional patterns of interaction, such as church networks. These authors could have used any one of many points of departure for how these regional and global fields converged, but by beginning with the household they are able to provide an intimate and bottom-up perspective on both the struggles and the successes of the enslaved.

Barna (chapter 5) explicitly relies on a multiscalar perspective, whereby ranch households in Hawai'i can be portrayed as occupying the juncture of a Venn model of multitiered fields. Hawai'i's growing reliance on commodity production and indigenized capitalism via sheep and cattle ranching placed it increasingly in the global economic order during the nineteenth century. This created a duality between styles of ranches, as well as among households, distinguished by ranches operated by indigenous interests versus those put into place by German transnationals.

Both global and local forms of migration played important roles in the formation of the ranch households. Along with the influx of wealthy German entrepreneurs there arrived a wide ethnic variety of immigrant workers, ranging from Mexican vaqueros to East Asians. This history of immigration was accompanied by widespread horizontal migration as ranch hands regularly moved from one range station household to another. As a result, households had a mobile and fleeting character, while comprising the practices and materiality of many cultures.

Transnational migration likewise played an important role in the constitution of Chinese households in the nineteenth-century boomtown of Aurora, Colorado (Dale, chapter 7). As both this and the Hawai'i examples demonstrate, demand for wage-labor immigrants until recent times typically focused on males. This had economic, gendered, and racialized overtones. Host nations anticipated that males would be more able to take on the arduous labor demands associated with jobs such as laying railroad track and mining ore. Further, curtailing the migration of females would ensure a low rate of reproduction of ethnic households—not a minor consideration during a century when the concept of the great chain of being held sway and racist evolutionary ideals placed immigrants on rungs below those of European descent. Further, for a variety of reasons, female emigration out of "donor" countries often was not feasible. As a result, in many places household demography was dominated by adult males bound by ties of race and class rather than kinship. Alternative corporate households of this sort—which encompass the spectrum from brothels to boardinghouses to religious communities—are commonplace over the past several centuries (Beaudry 1999: 121–122).

In Dale's study this kind of imbalance is clearly reflected in the archaeological record, in which houselots lack the kinds of objects usually associated with female and children's activities. As she points out, the fine-grained perspective of the household has allowed her to delineate hybridized patterns of consumption, where objects related to transnational movements (such as toothbrushes and opium paraphernalia) were integrated into the home along with those of North American origin (such as leather shoes).

Dale's research emphasizes the importance of consumption patterns for getting at the anthropological nuts and bolts of how households filter and mix the spectrum of inputs from larger relational fields (see also Mullins 2011). This seems to be one of the potentially richest yields of household studies, as consumption can be linked to the practices of taste and distinction as pursued by Bourdieu (1979), for example, that determine why groups make certain selections and decisions that affect the presence or absence of objects in households (see Stahl 2002). Isenbarger and Agha (chapter 8) rely explicitly on the notion of distinction and consumption (if not on Bourdieu directly) to delineate variability in consumption patterns in an enslaved household at Dean Hall Plantation in South Carolina. This theme is also picked up by Matthew Reeves (chapter 2), who uses window glass to ascertain the relative latitude in choices made by enslaved families versus sugar estate owners in Jamaica in the dictates of architectural construction.

As all of these studies show, even neighboring household assemblages could diverge greatly as a product of the articulation of local tastes and multiscalar ties. This perspective allows us to move beyond merely demonstrating the hybridized nature of household assemblages; it also allows us to set up the important question: why hybridized households? What exactly are the various activities endemic to households that differentially mesh with external fields, and which structure the materiality of the everyday? One major answer is foodways practices. Culinary etiquette in particular represents a very important way through which hybridized practices of consumption may bind and define the household. Barna postulates that the recovery of porcelain tea/sake cups from multiethnic Hawai'i ranch households may indicate the importance of fraternization among members based on Japanese customs. The localized modification and enactment of practices based on distant traditions may have been pivotal for ameliorating the internal tensions of ad hoc households that to a great degree were marriages of convenience. According to Nyman and

Kenline (chapter 4), principles of etiquette could be equally important for display purposes: the recovery of multiple teapots from George Washington's boyhood home may reflect how the communication of refinement affirmed his family's place in the social order. The economic wealth of a household allowed it to tap into the trade connections necessary to import valuable ceramic vessels; meanwhile, the use and display of the pots was a cultural broadcast back to the immediate surrounding community (especially one's peers) of the importance of this specific household.

If one views externally directed consumption as one element in the constitution of identity, as do Nyman and Kenline, this idea is balanced by the fact that identity is also enveloped in locally based patterns of consumption within the household. Colonoware, a ceramic type recovered in great volume at Dean Hall Plantation (Isenbarger and Agha, chapter 8), is widely viewed as a tangible outcome of the persistence, creativity, and identity-making of enslaved populations in eastern North America and the Caribbean (Ferguson 1992; Hauser 2008). Despite the considerable variability in colonoware that speaks to it being a product of local mores, there is ample evidence to demonstrate that the movement (voluntary and coerced) of both Native American and African/African American populations across the landscape promoted ceramic similarities among sites—a testament to the multiscalar dimension of this well-known pottery (Cobb and DePratter 2012; Ferguson 1992; Singleton and Bograd 2000).

Differential, multiscalar patterns of consumption and foodways also began to significantly distinguish Native American communities as a function of their relations with European powers. Peles (chapter 3) describes stark differences between the Upper Saratown and Fredericks sites, both occupied in the seventeenth century in what is today North Carolina. The cluster of households at Fredericks appears to have been somewhat successful at maintaining the viability of their community through actively adopting an "outward gaze" based on pursuing trade relations with the British. In contrast, the occupants of Upper Saratown, afflicted by conflict from marauding Native American groups and European diseases, appear to have adopted an inward gaze, withdrawing behind the walls of their defensive palisade. Peles hypothesizes that a pattern of restricting food consumption to varieties of plants and animals that could be easily harvested around the town lowered the chances of foraging groups being attacked.

In his seminal study *The Middle Ground*, Richard White (1991) describes a similar pattern for refugee Algonquian towns. Inhabitants pooled together in defensible locations for military security from Iroquois attacks and European encroachments. This, in turn, greatly constrained their ability to pursue foraging strategies to complement horticultural practices, and it narrowly restricted their food base. White's description of the devastating impacts of crowding and hunger on the refugee towns of the Great Lakes region parallels the descriptions of the health of the Upper Saratown residents: "The Iroquois, in effect, pushed the Algonquians onto a killing ground where smallpox and measles took a far greater toll than Iroquois muskets or scalping knives during the late seventeenth century" (White 1991: 41).

From this perspective, I would argue that situating households in multiscalar networks is an important avenue for linking structural violence with the spread of colonialism and early networks of capitalism. Typically, structural violence is construed as the development of adverse health outcomes and marginalization accruing from the institutionalization of structures of dominance. Most anthropological research tends to situate structural violence within the framework of the modern world system and the transnational networks of banks, corporations, and government entities whose activities in the name of development have far-reaching consequences in terms of obstructing households from meeting their basic needs (Farmer 2004; Scheper-Hughes 1992). However, globalization did not appear sui generis in the twentieth century. As Michel-Rolph Trouillot (2002a) observes, despite the fact that the flows we increasingly take for granted today have a clear genealogy to the 1400s C.E., one of the dominant narratives of globalization has been an exaggeration of its exceptionality through a silencing of its past. Household studies of enslaved, indigenous, lower-class, and other populations pulled into multiscalar fields prior to the twentieth century provide incredibly fertile ground for recovering the history of how families navigated a constantly shifting terrain of violence, disease, and uncertain food security—issues lurking in the background of all of the studies in this volume.

Households and Micromodernities

Modernity wears so many faces that one would be hard put to find two anthropologists who would agree on its definition. This lack of consensus is exacerbated by the fact that the study of modernity ranges across so many fields and covers so much subject matter—art, literature, politics, geography—that almost every discipline has its experts in modernity. Nonetheless, there is some common ground in the belief that modernity embodies a sense of disjuncture and discontinuity over the past five centuries or so and that this can be attributed in part to the growing centrality of Europe and North America on the world stage from the sixteenth to twentieth centuries (Cooper 2005; Thomas 2004). Of particular relevance to this discussion is Bruno Latour's (1993) argument that one of the distinguishing features of modernity was the expanded length of social networks. The multiethnic households of ranch hands in Hawai‘i, Chinese immigrants in Colorado, and Native Americans on colonial borderlands are all exemplars of the ways in which households are embedded in worldwide currents and, in turn, how global political and economic trends may destabilize established relations of domesticity within a community.

To complicate matters, postcolonial and critical theorists argue that there is a cultural dimension to the ruptures of modernity, whereby the imposition and contestation of belief systems, discourse, and ideologies must be considered alongside materialist variables. To complicate things still more, modernity does not always have to entail a sense of "bad"—although it typically takes on this connotation in anthropological discourse. Jürgen Habermas (1987) argued that modernity has a dual character that embodies notions of the avant-garde as well as of the kinds of discipline equated with oppression. And in 1907 Pope Pius X issued an encyclical, "On the Doctrine of the Modernist," summarizing the Catholic Church's views on the heresies of modernity. Ironically, these putative heresies are fundamental to much of modern anthropological thought: the importance of cultural relativity and historical contingency, and the questioning of universals of truth.

Because of its freewheeling nature, modernity is easier to discuss as an abstract notion than to analyze as a set of practices (Cooper 2005: 114). For this reason, Trouillot (2002b) criticized what he referred to as a reliance in anthropological research on "North Atlantic Universals," which included modernity, because they are more appealing to study as representations than as particulars. As he put it, terms such as *modernity* "evoke rather than define" (Trouillot 2002b: 221). One response to this shortcoming has been a movement away from modernity as generic concept and toward a focus on multiple modernities (Beardsell 2000; Eisenstadt

2000; Friedman 2002). In this formulation, modernity is not something merely imposed globally by the West in the march from the Renaissance through the Enlightenment to the postindustrial age. Instead, these historical phenomena were/are in large part a dual outgrowth of the Western interactions with the Other that accelerated so dramatically with the onset of modern colonization. Indigenous worldviews and practices (and, of course, labor and commodities) had profound impacts on European and North American intellectual and imperial projects. Moreover, this mutualism split in many directions by virtue of the different portions of the globe staked out by various Western powers. Thus, there is no singular narrative of modernity, although there are overlapping philosophies, policies, and practices.

One of the shared ideas of modernity emanating out of Europe was the importance of discipline and regulation, tenets that extended to home populations as much as they did to the colonies. Historians have argued that the emergence of the nation-state was viewed (from above, anyway) as a totalizing project, wherein moral regulation and consent were just as important as political and economic oversight (e.g., Corrigan and Sayer 1985; Pagden 1993). Geographies of management were particularly important instruments in this process, especially in the British Empire, as principles of enclosure accompanied practices of map making and cadastral surveys to facilitate administrative efficiencies and the regulation of behavior (Black 1997; Edney 1999; Johnson 1996; Trouillot 2002b)—processes that also laid the foundation for the regimentation required for the industrial revolution.

Paul Shackel's (1993) important work on Annapolis houselots has demonstrated how these ideals percolated down to the smallest levels of everyday life; he linked the upsurge in standardized objects and products to the rise of alienated labor and time discipline. Although we often turn to E. P. Thompson's (1967) work on British labor and industrialism for inspiration on these dimensions of imposed management, it must be emphasized that ideals of spatial and behavioral regulation did not flow solely or even primarily from northern Europe and Great Britain. The contributions of Spanish/Portuguese domains are often overlooked by anthropologists, although they provide an important perspective on alternative historical routes through the Renaissance, Enlightenment, and colonial practices (Trouillot 2002b: 233). Stephen Wernke's (2012, 2010) work on sixteenth-century colonial sites in the Peruvian uplands provides an important balance in this regard. For instance, he has demonstrated that households, houses, and community arrangements at the Inca settlement of Malata were reworked by Spanish administrators and clergy "to inculcate a Christian lifestyle—to interpellate Christian subjects through newly habituated rhythms of daily practice" (Wernke 2010: 80). There, the norms of Catholicism outweighed those of the emerging ideals of time and space discipline associated with mercantilism.

The idea that temporality itself was subject to manipulation and contestation in the household presents a provocative issue that is surely worthy of more research related to the materiality of modernity (see Lucas 2006: 42–45). Further, these examples from Annapolis and Peru also emphasize that different European nations may have privileged time in different ways. These are the kinds of conditions that give rise to multiple modernities, underscoring the importance of the household as a locus for exploring this kind of variation. To come full circle to my earlier discussion on microhistories, Knauft (2002) observes that modernity itself can be conceived of as a multiscalar phenomenon. He maintains that it is at the level of micromodernity that we can evaluate how the practices and ideologies of modernities are culturally constituted and inscribed. The household is a natural vantage point for developing case studies in micromodernity.

Many of the chapters here consider micromodernity through architecture and the household landscape. The studies on enslaved populations in particular highlight the ideological struggles over space between class and racial interests. Not surprisingly, on plantations the owners exercised considerable control over architectural forms. As many archaeological studies in the field of African diaspora have demonstrated, the impositions of philosophies of modernity on the slave household were countered by subterfuge and circumvention, creating a household landscape that was a blend of prescription and practice. As plantation owners rearranged architecture and community layout to enhance surveillance, enslaved groups countered with tactics to hide or disguise activities and resources (e.g., McKee 1992; Thomas 1998). Although plantation estates may represent an extreme in the disparity of power relations, one of capitalism's essential links to modernity is the alienation of property and labor. Thus, one can find analogues in the contest over the imposition of spatial regimes of order that run the gamut from plantations to coal-miner camps (e.g., Pauls 2006; Wood 2009).

As befits modernity, the household chapters in this volume exemplify how this struggle involved alienation via worldview as well as property rights. On James Madison's property the large amount of window glass recovered from slave quarters near the main house compared to the field quarters suggests that his ideals on domestic living space may have been imparted most strongly on those cabins that were within his daily viewscape (Reeves, chapter 2). In other words, the improved cabins of house slaves bore more of a semblance to appropriate living quarters than did those out of immediate range of the great house. The rediscovery of perspective and later blossoming of landscape art beginning in the seventeenth century was closely tied to modernist ideals linking the visual with order and morality (Thomas 2004: 178–179). Reeves's study suggests that images on the canvas in the parlors of Europe were not merely the subject of idle contemplation. Households may have been arranged on the landscape to facilitate the physical management of peoples, but they were also arranged to reproduce perspectives on the perceived natural order of the world.

The physical and moral regulation required to achieve this natural order was widely viewed in Europe, and later North America, as integral to the success of the emerging nation-state, imperial might, and success in colonial endeavors (Corrigan and Sayer 1985). In this context, the ruling elites believed they had to fear two sources of moral pollution and instability: colonized peoples, and the poor in their backyards. The anxiety with disorder and immorality permeated all dimensions of life. For instance, the nineteenth-century cholera epidemics in the United Kingdom were viewed by the upper classes as an import resulting from the unclean habits of South Asians, further exacerbated by the undisciplined ways of the working-class savages in the tenements of London and elsewhere (Watts 1997). The marginalized had their own suspicions that the outbreaks were related to attempts by the ruling classes to reduce the numbers and power of the poor. Not surprisingly, the household itself became a battleground over these two opposing worldviews, and it was viewed as an instrument of domestication of the colonized and the lower classes alike (Comaroff and Comaroff 1992: 265–284).

In this emerging worldview of modernity, the fabric of the house itself became the basis for a new fabric of habitus. Peter Whitridge's (2008) study of attempts to replace Inuit sod structures with European-style houses is a particularly compelling example of attempts by colonizers to restructure "bodies, characters, and souls" in the name of modernist reform. For their part, Inuit resistance to these reforms was buttressed and rationalized by their conviction of the ignorance of Europeans. Similar tensions are evident throughout the chapters in this volume. At Witherspoon Island in South Carolina, the slave quarters appear to have been built from scratch with ideals of progressive reform in place (Fogle, chapter 6). The accelerating force of these ideas is witnessed at Dean Hall Plantation, where all of the original slave quarters were demolished and replaced with duplexes during the nineteenth century in response to a new owner's concern with hygiene and sanitation (Isenbarger and Agha, chapter 8). The very robust assemblage of colonoware there is a testament to the power of households to sustain a significant degree of autonomy over production and consumption even as their physical surroundings were literally pulled out from under them.

Ironically, the vast migrations of "voluntary" labor associated with the growth of the world system led to architectural conditions somewhat similar to slavery: displaced populations with little power over where they resided. Chinese immigrants to Aurora, Colorado, moved into Western-style houses constructed before their arrival, requiring both physical and cultural accommodations to new arrangements of space (Dale, chapter 7). As these examples demonstrate, capitalism is eminently flexible with regard to the convergence of variability in labor arrangements with variability in standards of housing and living space. This flexibility is exemplified by Barna's (chapter 5) documentation of newly arrived migrants in Hawai'i moving into communal buildings that accommodated transient labor, after which they adapted to smaller group cabin households as they transitioned to more stable lifestyles that conformed to ideals of private property and privacy.

The terrain of micromodernity extended to the immediate living space around structures, as well. Fogle (chapter 6) demonstrates that the progressivist reform debates of the 1800s involved the reorganization and regimentation of yard space in the same way they did architecture. In the living space of morality, an orderly yard dovetailed with an orderly and principled family. Fogle relies on the perspective of "intimate landscapes" to describe how families produced an organic sense of place—a household *terroir*, to borrow a term from vintners—whereby the intimacy of domesticity and everyday relations extended beyond the physical remains of the house. This experiential perspective that breaks down barriers between

202 · Charles R. Cobb

scales is yet another illustration of the movement away from the false divide between public and private that at one time characterized many household studies. A similar theme is seen in Nyman and Kenline's (chapter 4) longitudinal framing of refuse dumping patterns associated with a property occupied by three subsequent generations of households. Their notion of place-making, or *landschaft*, is somewhat analogous to the idea of intimate landscapes advocated by Fogle. Both studies explicitly propose that the small particulars of household landscapes must be addressed archaeologically in fine detail, while at the same time attention must be paid to their extramural patterns of interconnectedness—an approach that is squarely in the tradition of microhistory and, I would argue, critical to the construction of micromodernities.

Conclusion

Marshall Sahlins (1993) has observed that global modernity is reproduced as local diversity. This volume demonstrates that the household is a nucleus for the production of that diversity. Further, diversity is materialized in ways that make it eminently amenable to archaeological study. At the same time, the studies here emphasize the blurry boundaries between the household and the larger fields in which it is enmeshed. Severin Fowles (2009) uses the term "villagescape" to impart the notion that one cannot easily segregate a community from its surrounding field of relations inscribed in agricultural fields, religious sites, pilgrimage routes, and of course, other villages just down the road. Likewise, the authors in this volume impel us to think about household-scapes in wide terms that include the experiential dimensions of modernity as well as its political and economic facets.

I close my thoughts with a final return to the question of scale. Thomas Pluckhahn (2010: 345) observed that few southeastern archaeologists, working in either prehistoric or historical contexts, have successfully managed to demonstrate how household relations could actually be constitutive of larger fields of relations—as opposed to being embedded within them. I think this point is generally applicable to household studies anywhere. These chapters have made great strides toward unraveling the bouillabaisse of relations accruing from multiscalar fields that are mixed in the household. For historical archaeology the continuing challenge is to return to the panoramic, to grasp somehow the way in which these smaller-scale interactions diffuse outward to create a world of cross-hatched modernities. Only in this way can we transform our notion of the household from an object of modernity into an agent of modernities.

References Cited

Anderson, David G.
1999 Examining Chiefdoms in the Southeast: An Application of a Multiscalar Analysis. In *Great Towns and Regional Polities in the Prehistoric American Southwest and Southeast*, edited by Jill E. Neitzel, pp. 215–241. University of New Mexico Press, Albuquerque.
Barile, Kerri S., and Jamie C. Brandon (editors)
2004 *Household Chores and Household Choices: Theorizing the Domestic Sphere in Historical Archaeology*. University of Alabama Press, Tuscaloosa.
Beardsell, Peter
2000 *Europe and Latin America: Returning the Gaze*. Manchester University Press, Manchester.
Beaudry, Mary C.
1999 House and Household: The Archaeology of Domestic Life in Early America. In *Old and New Worlds*, edited by Geoff Egan and Ronald L. Michael, pp. 117–126. Oxbow Books, Oxford, U.K.
Bintliff, John
1991 The Contribution of an Annaliste/Structural History Approach to Archaeology. In *The Annales School and Archaeology*, edited by John Bintliff, pp. 1–33. New York University Press, New York.
Black, Jeremy
1997 *Maps and Politics*. Reaktion Books, London.
Bourdieu, Pierre
1979 *Distinction: A Social Critique of the Judgment of Taste*. Harvard University Press, Cambridge, Massachusetts.
Brooks, James F., Christopher R. N. DeCorse, and John Walton (editors)
2008 *Small Worlds: Method, Meaning, and Narrative in Microhistory*. School for Advanced Research Press, Santa Fe, New Mexico.
Cobb, Charles R., and Charles B. DePratter
2012 Multi-sited Research on Colonowares and the Paradox of Globalization. *American Anthropologist* 114 (3): 446–461.
Comaroff, John, and Joan Comaroff
1992 *Ethnography and the Historical Imagination*. Westview Press, Boulder, Colorado.
Cooper, Frederick
2005 *Colonialism in Question: Theory, Knowledge, History*. University of California Press, Berkeley.

Corrigan, Philip, and Derek Sayer
1985 *The Great Arch: English State Formation as Cultural Revolution.* Blackwell, Oxford, U.K.

Edney, M. H.
1999 Reconsidering Enlightenment Geography and Map Making: Reconnaissance, Mapping, Archive. In *Geography and Enlightenment,* edited by David N. Livingstone and Charles W. J. Withers, pp. 165–198. University of Chicago Press, Chicago.

Eisenstadt, S. N.
2000 Multiple Modernities. *Daedalus* 129 (1): 1–29.

Farmer, Paul
2004 An Anthropology of Structural Violence. *Current Anthropology* 45 (3): 305–325.

Ferguson, Leland
1992 *Uncommon Ground: Archaeology and Early African America, 1650–1800.* Smithsonian Institution Press, Washington, D.C.

Fletcher, Roland
1992 Time Perspectivism, *Annales,* and the Potential of Archaeology. In *Archaeology, Annales, and Ethnohistory,* edited by A. Bernard Knapp, pp. 35–49. Cambridge University Press, Cambridge.

Fowles, Severin M.
2009 The Enshrined Pueblo: Villagescape and Cosmos in the Northern Rio Grande. *American Antiquity* 74 (3): 448–466.

Friedman, Jonathan
2002 Modernity and Other Traditions. In *Critically Modern: Alternatives, Alterities, Anthropologies,* edited by Bruce M. Knauft, pp. 287–313. Indiana University Press, Bloomington.

Habermas, Jürgen
1987 *The Philosophical Discourse of Modernity.* MIT Press, Cambridge, Massachusetts.

Hauser, Mark W.
2008 *An Archaeology of Black Markets: Local Ceramics and Economies in Eighteenth-Century Jamaica.* University Press of Florida, Gainesville.

Hendon, Julia
1996 Archaeological Approaches to the Organization of Domestic Labor: Household Practice and Domestic Relations. *Annual Review of Anthropology* 25: 45–61.

Herlihy, David
1984 Households in the Early Middle Ages: Symmetry and Sainthood. In *Households: Comparative and Historical Studies of the Domestic Group,* edited by Robert M. Netting, Richard W. Wilk, and Eric J. Arnould, pp. 383–406. University of California Press, Berkeley.

Hingley, Richard
1990 Domestic Organization and Gender Relations in Iron Age and Romano-British Households. In *The Social Archaeology of Houses,* edited by Ross Samson, pp. 125–147. Edinburgh University Press, Edinburgh.

Hupperetz, Wim
2010 Micro History, Archaeology and the Study of Housing Culture: Some Thoughts

on Archaeological and Historical Data from a Cesspit in 17th-Century Breda. In *Exchanging Medieval Material Culture: Studies on Archaeology and History Presented to Frans Verhaeghe*, edited by Koen De Groote, Dries Tys, and Marnix Pieters, pp. 279–284. Relicta Monografi eën 4, Archeologie, Monumenten-en Landschapsonderzoek in Vlaanderen. Onroerend Erfgoed, Brussels.

Johnson, Matthew

2006 The Tide Reversed: Prospects and Potentials for a Postcolonial Archaeology of Europe. In *Historical Archaeology*, edited by Martin Hall and Stephen W. Silliman, pp. 313–331. Blackwell, Malden, Massachusetts.

1996 *An Archaeology of Capitalism*. Blackwell, Oxford, U.K.

Jordan, Kurt A.

2009 Colonies, Colonialism, and Cultural Entanglement: The Archaeology of Postcolumbian Intercultural Relations. In *International Handbook of Historical Archaeology*, edited by Teresita Majewski and David Gaimster, pp. 31–49. Springer, New York.

King, Julia A.

2006 Household Archaeology, Identities and Biographies. In *The Cambridge Companion to Historical Archaeology*, edited by Dan Hicks and Mary C. Beaudry, pp. 293–313. Cambridge University Press, Cambridge.

Knauft, Bruce M.

2002 Critically Modern: An Introduction. In *Critically Modern: Alternatives, Alterities, Anthropologies*, edited by Bruce M. Knauft, pp. 1–54. Indiana University Press, Bloomington.

Latour, Bruno

1993 *We Have Never Been Modern*. Harvard University Press, Cambridge, Massachusetts.

Lenik, Stephan

2009 Considering Multiscalar Approaches to Creolization among Enslaved Laborers at Estate Bethlehem, St. Croix, U.S. Virgin Islands. *International Journal of Historical Archaeology* 13 (1): 12–26.

Lock, Gary, and Brian L. Molyneaux (editors)

2006 *Confronting Scale in Archaeology: Issues of Theory and Practice*. Springer, New York.

Lucas, Gavin

2006 Historical Archaeology and Time. In *The Cambridge Companion to Historical Archaeology*, edited by Dan Hicks and Mary C. Beaudry, pp. 34–47. Cambridge University Press, Cambridge.

McKee, Larry

1992 The Ideals and Realities behind the Design and Use of 19th Century Virginia Slave Cabins. In *The Art and Mystery of Historical Archaeology*, edited by Anne Elizabeth Yentsch and Mary C. Beaudry, pp. 195–213. CRC Press, Boca Raton, Florida.

Marquardt, William H.

1992 Dialectical Archaeology. In *Archaeological Method and Theory*, edited by Michael B. Schiffer, pp. 101–140. University of Arizona Press, Tucson.

Mullins, Paul

2011 The Archaeology of Consumption. *Annual Review of Anthropology* 40: 133–144.

Pagden, Anthony
1993 *European Encounters with the New World: From Renaissance to Romanticism*. Yale University Press, New Haven, Connecticut.

Pauls, Elizabeth P.
2006 The Place of Space: Architecture, Landscape, and Social Life. In *Historical Archaeology*, edited by Martin Hall and Stephen W. Silliman, pp. 65–83. Blackwell, Malden, Massachusetts.

Pluckhahn, Thomas J.
2010 Household Archaeology in the Southeastern United States: History, Trends, and Challenges. *Journal of Archaeological Research* 18 (4): 331–385.

Revel, Jacques
1995 Microanalysis and the Construction of the Social. In *Histories: French Constructions of the Past*, edited by Jacques Revel and Lynn Hunt, pp. 492–502. New Press, New York.

Sahlins, Marshall
1993 Goodbye to Tristes Tropes: Ethnography in the Context of Modern World History. *Journal of Modern History* 65 (1): 1–25.

Scheper-Hughes, Nancy
1992 *Death without Weeping: The Violence of Everyday Life in Brazil*. University of California Press, Berkeley.

Shackel, Paul A.
1993 *Personal Discipline and Material Culture: An Archaeology of Annapolis, Maryland, 1695–1870*. University of Tennessee Press, Knoxville.

Singleton, Theresa A., and Mark M. Bograd
2000 Breaking Typological Barriers: Looking for the Colono in Colonoware. In *Lines That Divide: Historical Archaeologies of Race, Class, and Gender*, edited by James A. Delle, Stephen A. Mrozowski, and Robert Paynter, pp. 3–21. University of Tennessee Press, Knoxville.

Stahl, Ann B.
2002 Colonial Entanglements and the Practices of Taste: An Alternative to Logocentric Approaches. *American Anthropologist* 104 (3): 827–845.

Therkorn, Linda
1987 The Inter-relationships of Materials and Meanings: Some Suggestions on Housing Concerns within Iron Age Noord-Holland. In *The Archaeology of Contextual Meanings*, edited by Ian Hodder, pp. 102–110. Cambridge University Press, Cambridge.

Thomas, Brian W.
1998 Power and Community: The Archaeology of Slavery at the Hermitage Plantation. *American Antiquity* 63 (4): 531–551.

Thomas, Julian
2004 *Archaeology and Modernity*. Routledge, New York.

Thomas, Nicholas
1991 *Entangled Objects: Exchange, Material Culture, and Colonialism in the Pacific*. Harvard University Press, Cambridge, Massachusetts.

Thompson, E. P.

1967 Time, Work-Discipline, and Industrial Capitalism. *Past and Present* 38: 56–97.

Trouillot, Michel-Rolph

2002a North Atlantic Universals: Analytical Fictions, 1492–1945. *South Atlantic Quarterly* 101: 839–858.

2002b The Otherwise Modern: Caribbean Lessons from the Savage Slot. In *Critically Modern: Alternatives, Alterities, Anthropologies*, edited by Bruce M. Knauft, pp. 220–237. Indiana University Press, Bloomington.

Watts, Sheldon

1997 *Epidemics and History: Disease, Power and Imperialism*. Yale University Press, New Haven, Connecticut.

Wernke, Stephen A.

2012 Andean Households in Transition: The Politics of Domestic Space at an Early Colonial Doctrina in the Peruvian Highlands. In *Decolonizing Indigenous Histories: Exploring Prehistoric/Colonial Transitions in Archaeology*, edited by Maxine Oland, Siobhan M. Hart, and Liam Frink, pp. 210–229. University of Arizona Press, Tucson.

2010 Convergences: Producing Early Colonial Hybridity at a Doctrina in Highland Peru. In *Enduring Conquests: Rethinking the Archaeology of Resistance to Spanish Colonialism in the Americas*, edited by Matthew Liebmann and Melissa S. Murphy, pp. 77–101. School for Advanced Research Press, Santa Fe, New Mexico.

White, Richard

1991 *The Middle Ground: Indians, Empires, and Republics in the Great Lakes Region, 1650–1815*. Cambridge University Press, Cambridge.

Whitridge, Peter

2008 Reimagining the Iglu: Modernity and the Challenge of the Eighteenth Century Labrador Inuit Winter House. *Archaeologies* 4 (2): 288–309.

Wilkie, Laurie A., and Paul Farnsworth

1999 Trade and the Construction of Bahamian Identity: A Multi-scalar Exploration. *International Journal of Historical Archaeology* 3 (4): 283–320.

Wong, Diana

1984 The Limits of Using the Household as a Unit of Analysis. In *Households and the World Economy*, edited by Joan K. Smith, Immanuel Wallerstein, and Hans-Dieter Evers, pp. 56–63. Sage, Beverly Hills, California.

Wood, Margaret

2009 Building the Corporate Family: Constructing Homes, Families, and the Nation. In *The Archaeology of Class War: The Colorado Coalfield Strike of 1913–1914*, edited by Karin Larkin and Randall H. McGuire, pp. 123–160. University Press of Colorado, Boulder.

Contributors

Andrew Agha is president of Archaeological Research Collective, Inc., based in Charleston, South Carolina.

Benjamin Barna is a senior archaeologist with ASM Affiliates, Inc., in Hilo, Hawai'i.

Mary C. Beaudry is professor of archaeology, anthropology, and gastronomy at Boston University.

Charles R. Cobb is Lockwood Professor of Historical Archaeology at the Florida Museum of Natural History, Gainesville.

Emily Dale is lecturer in the Department of Anthropology at Northern Arizona University, Flagstaff.

Kevin R. Fogle is principal investigator and lecturer with the Department of Anthropology at the University of South Carolina, Columbia.

Nicole Isenbarger is teaching associate in anthropology and geography at Coastal Carolina University, Conway, South Carolina.

Brooke Kenline is a senior archaeologist at TRC Environmental Corporation in Lowell, Massachusetts.

James A. Nyman is an archaeologist and researcher based in New Hampshire.

Ashley Peles is a doctoral student in the Department of Anthropology at the University of North Carolina at Chapel Hill.

Matthew Reeves is director of archaeology and landscape restoration at James Madison's Montpelier in Orange, Virginia.

Index

www.ingramcontent.com/pod-product-compliance
Lightning Source LLC
Chambersburg PA
CBHW020251290326
41930CB00039B/630